# Britain's First Photo Album

# Britain's First Photo Album

COMPANION TO
THE BBC SERIES

AS PRESENTED BY
JOHN SERGEANT

The Francis Frith Collection

First published in the United Kingdom in 2012 by The Francis Frith Collection®
Based on the television series produced by Reef Television and first broadcast on BBC Two in 2012.
Series Producer Stephen Taylor Woodrow. Executive Producer Richard Farmbrough
Executive Producer for BBC Gillian Scothern

Hardback Edition 2012 ISBN 978-1-84589-578-5

British Library Cataloguing in Publication Data

Britain's First Photo Album
Compiled, edited and designed by Sacketts (www.sacketts.co.uk)
Line illustrations from www.victorianpicturelibrary.com

The Francis Frith Collection®
Oakley Business Park, Wylye Road,
Dinton, Wiltshire SP3 5EU
Tel: +44 (0) 1722 716 376
Email: info@francisfrith.co.uk
www.francisfrith.com

Reef Television
8th Floor,
1 New Oxford Street,
London, WC1A 1NU
www.reef.tv

Front Cover: John Sergeant at Stonehenge by REEF Television
Frontispiece: Scarborough, Saint Nicholas Cliff 1890   23476ap
Contents page: Hartlepool, The Beach 1903   49993

*The colour-tinting in this book is for illustrative purposes only, and is not intended to be historically accurate*

AS WITH ANY HISTORICAL DATABASE, THE FRANCIS FRITH ARCHIVE IS CONSTANTLY BEING
CORRECTED AND IMPROVED, AND THE PUBLISHERS WOULD WELCOME INFORMATION ON OMISSIONS
OR INACCURACIES

Printed and bound in Great Britain by Butler Tanner & Dennis Ltd.
Contains material sourced from responsibly managed forests

# Contents

JOHN SERGEANT AT
HADDON HALL,
BAKEWELL,
DERBYSHIRE

# Foreword

*We met people who had no difficulty tracing their ancestors back to a group who had posed for a Frith photographer more than a century ago...*

When it was first suggested that I should present a television series based on old photographs, I have to admit that I was not overcome with excitement. How could we make pictures, taken with antique equipment from the dawn of the photographic age, live up to all the dazzling images we enjoy today? But my early doubts were soon dispelled. Once we were out filming, the old black and white images took on a life of their own. I was soon hooked on the idea of celebrating the Victorian age through the skill of the greatest pioneer photographer of the time. He and his team gave birth not only to a completely different way of looking at the world, but to an entirely new art form.

Our series, it soon became apparent, could do more than just provide marvellous examples of the skills of the old time photographers; we had a chance to make a direct contact with Victorian society, a chance to compare and contrast life today with life in Britain more than a hundred years ago. We could find out how these new-fangled pictures came to be made and how they earned a fortune for Francis Frith and his company - which before long became the largest publishing company of its kind in the world. Also, for me, there was an entirely unexpected bonus: I was provided with a brilliant modern camera, and given the opportunity to show what a rank amateur could do, trying to take on this great man at his own game.

In television there is one demand which overrides all others. You must keep up the interest of the viewers; otherwise they will understandably look elsewhere. We would have to inform, of course, and also I hoped we would be able to entertain. The pictures provided the theme for all our travels. They were centre-stage. Whenever there was a danger that we would wander off down attractive but hardly relevant byways, we would be brought back to our central task: following the trail marked out by these remarkable photographic prints.

We were greatly helped by an army of contributors, historical experts, and guides of all sorts. Some of the most gripping accounts were provided by the relatives of those who had appeared in the original pictures. It is astonishing to find how easy it can be to jump back more than a century with members of the same family. In Whitby, we met people who had no difficulty tracing their ancestors back to a group who had posed for a Frith photographer on the rocks near the harbour all those years ago. There were striking similarities; some of them still worked in the fishing business, and

WHITBY,
THE PEART CHILDREN 1891
FRITH 28866P

THE PEART FAMILY,
WHITBY HARBOUR, 2011

they seemed to share a common strength of character. For our series, my final task, once the story behind the old pictures had been told, was to take a photo of my own. This time the choice of subject was easy. We invited as many of the modern family as possible to come down to the harbour, and once again be photographed on the rocks.

On other occasions the choice was not so simple. Sometimes it was not possible to take another, similar picture; the subject of the picture could no longer be seen. A strange rock formation on the Yorkshire coast had been swept away by the tides. Military barracks at a town on the South Coast had long ago been demolished, and a cliff edge in the Isle of Wight had dramatically fallen into the sea. I would have to come up with a new composition, but at the same time try to preserve the spirit of the old photographs. It would have been easy for me to rely on the expertise of my producer and television cameraman, but I thought that would not be fair play. For good or ill, the choices of subject are mine, and apart from advice on a few technical matters I was the official photographer.

A really good modern camera gave me a totally unfair advantage in my imagined competition with Francis Frith and his team of experts. What I could manage with digital magic in less than a second would often have taken him and the others up to half a minute in exposure time. And they could have spent hours seeing that the lighting was right and the conditions were perfect. Making sure that people in the photograph did not move too much, to avoid them appearing as a blur, was another vital consideration. Printing pictures in those early days was so laborious and complicated. We had a little machine with a portable power supply, which could turn out quality prints in no time, ready to be pasted into Britain's First Photo Album.

My attempts to produce photographs which could in any way be compared with those early works greatly increased my understanding and appreciation of the efforts of the Victorian pioneers. By travelling along the same routes, to the same places,

JOHN SERGEANT AT THE TOWN
MILL, LYME REGIS

with the same object in mind, was a compelling way to relive the birth of a new age. Before then, for any record or memento of a place you visited, you would have to rely on a drawing or a painting. For those in their tens of thousands who bought the first Frith pictures, the final results must have seemed miraculous.

When we look at these pictures, printed from their glass plates, as good as new, we are looking further back in time and in more detail than ever before. Our fascination is often increased when we try to find out what attracted the photographers to their subjects. Frith was a brilliant businessman as well as an artist, and his job was to publish pictures which would sell. In learning why these images were created we can look into the minds of our predecessors in a remarkable way, discovering what excited them, what intrigued them, and what made the public want to buy the finished product. Each picture we featured told a story; and only when we had worked out what that story was could we move on.

We chose four pictures for each programme. Our first task on location was to work out exactly where the camera had been set up and what the photographer was trying to convey. Sometimes it was a familiar tourist site, such as London's Tower Bridge. But often it was almost impossible to ascertain at first glance what the attraction was. Often it required a local historian to provide the clue; on other occasions it was necessary to make a guess, to imagine that we were back in the 19th century waiting to be impressed by this latest gadget.

In 'Britain's First Photo Album' I was given an extraordinary opportunity to take part in a fascinating journey, not just across Britain but also back in time. This book is a wonderful reminder of what we saw and what we did; and I can only hope we have managed to get across some of the pleasure and excitement we enjoyed along the way.

John Sergeant 2012

# Introduction

*By 1855, at the age of just thirty-three, he had established a wholesale grocery business that he sold for the astonishing sum of £200,000*

In the 1860s a pioneering Victorian photographer and entrepreneur embarked upon an almost incredible project: to photograph the cities, towns and villages of Britain. His name was Francis Frith, and the images that he and the Frith company photographers took between 1860 and 1970 remain as a unique and outstanding topographical record of the changing face of Britain over more than a century.

What sort of man was Francis Frith? He was born in 1822 in Chesterfield, Derbyshire, into a devout Quaker family. A complex and multi-talented man, he was philosophical by nature and pioneering in outlook. His life spanned a considerable proportion of the Victorian age, an age of great inventors, doughty explorers and energetic industrialists and businessmen. It was also an era of immense changes in British society. Frith himself had a formidable instinct for business. By 1855, at the age of just thirty-three, he had established a wholesale grocery business in Liverpool, and sold it for the astonishing sum of £200,000, which is the equivalent today of over £15 million.

Now a very rich man, he was able to indulge his passion for travel. As a child he had pored over travel books written by early explorers, and his fancy and imagination had been stirred by family holidays among the sublime mountain regions of Wales and Scotland. 'What lands of spirit-stirring and enriching scenes and places!' he wrote in his autobiography (written when he was 63). He was to return to these scenes of grandeur in later years to 'recapture the thousands of vivid and tender memories', but with a different purpose. Now, captivated by the new science of photography, Frith set out on a series of three pioneering journeys to Egypt, travelling up the Nile, and to the Near East that occupied him from 1856 until 1860.

He was one of the first Europeans, and certainly the first photographer, to venture beyond the sixth cataract of the Nile. Africa was still the mysterious 'dark continent', and Stanley and Livingstone's historic meeting was a decade into the future. Frith's fame and his early reputation as a considerable photographer were based on these pioneering expeditions.

FRANCIS FRITH
WEARING ARAB
COSTUME
FRITH 413033

EGYPT, THE ISLAND OF PHILAE,
PHARAOH'S BED c1857
FRITH 1820

FRITH'S ENCAMPMENT AT SUEZ, c1857
FRITH S625301

His far-flung journeys were packed with intrigue and adventure. In his life story, Frith tells of being held captive by bandits, and of fighting 'an awful midnight battle to the very point of surrender with a deadly pack of hungry wild dogs'. Wearing flowing Arab costume, Frith arrived at Akaba by camel sixty years before Lawrence of Arabia, where he encountered 'desert princes and rival sheikhs, blazing with jewel-hilted swords'.

The conditions for picture taking confound belief. Frith had to transport three heavy wooden cameras, one of them so large that it needed its own cart, along with his supply of bulky glass photographic plates. He laboured for hours in his darkroom, a light-proof and air-tight tent (see left), in the sweltering heat of the desert, while volatile photographic chemicals fizzed dangerously in their trays.

EGYPT, THE ISLE OF AGILKIA,
TRAJAN'S KIOSK 1997
FRITH A371002K

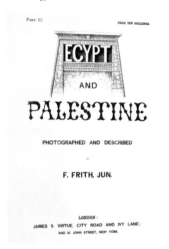

FRONTISPIECE OF ONE OF THE
PORTFOLIOS OF FRITH'S EGYPT
PHOTOGRAPHS FRITH F6010

MARY ANN ROSLING
FRITH A001155

The resulting photographs were a revelation to the Victorian public. They are still highly valued by historians and Egyptologists today as a record of the condition – and position – of historical monuments 150 years or so ago. For instance, Frith's photograph of Philae (see photograph opposite, above) shows the temple on its original island. After the Aswan dam was built in the 20th century, the island of Philae disappeared beneath the waters of the Nile, and the temple that stood on the island was moved to the island of Agilkia, which was reshaped to resemble the island of Philae (see photograph left).

Back in London Frith's work gained artistic acclaim when he exhibited his photographs at the Great Exhibition of 1861 and won a medal. He was 'rapturously cheered' by members of the Royal Society. Between 1858 and 1862 Frith published his photographs of Egypt and the Holy Land in part-work portfolios with notes by Frith and prominent Egyptologists, indicating that Frith's work had gained academic as well as popular approval. The portfolios sold for ten shillings each; it has been estimated that the total sales reached the equivalent of around £3 million today.

Francis Frith made his last visit to Egypt and the Holy Land in 1860. He recorded in his autobiography that ' … between times I had wisely fallen in love, but the girl was young; I would have one more grand spell of sunshine, and so finally brace up soul and body for the great events of life.' The girl he had fallen in love with was Mary Ann Rosling, and they married after his return from Egypt in 1860. Mary Ann was the daughter of a prominent Quaker family in Reigate in Surrey, and Frith decided to settle there. It was at this point that he conceived his ground-breaking idea of making a photographic record of Britain. This was eventually to result in one of the first and most important photographic publishing companies in the world.

With his reputation as an outstanding photographer firmly established, Frith realized that his project to photograph Britain was an opportunity for creating a new business as a specialist publisher of photographs. With typical acumen, Frith foresaw that a new market for his work was growing: excursionists and holidaymakers. For most people in the early part of Victoria's reign work was exhausting and the hours long, and they had precious little free time to enjoy themselves. However, by the 1870s the

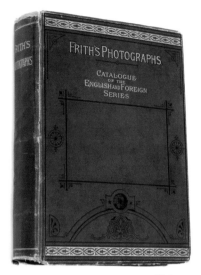

THE FRITH CATALOGUE OF 1886
FRITH F6012

A TYPICAL FRITH RETAIL SHOP
DISPLAY   FRITH 38628XP

railways had threaded their way across the country, and Bank Holidays and half-day Saturdays had been made obligatory by Act of Parliament. All of a sudden the working man and his family were able to enjoy days out and see a little more of the world. These new tourists wanted souvenirs to commemorate their days out, and photographic prints filled the bill.

Frith's studio was soon supplying retail shops all over the country. To meet the demand he gathered together a team of photographers, and he also published the work of independent artist-photographers of the calibre of Roger Fenton, Frank Meadow Sutcliffe and Francis Bedford. In order to gain some understanding of the scale of Frith's business one only has to look at the catalogue issued by Frith & Co in 1886: it runs to some 670 pages, listing not only many thousands of views of the British Isles, but also photographs of most European countries, China, Japan, the USA and Canada. By 1890 Frith had created the greatest specialist photographic publishing company in the world, with over 2,000 sales outlets. Francis Frith died in 1898 at his villa in Cannes, but his monumental project continued to grow. By 1970 the Frith archive contained over a third of a million pictures showing 7,000 British towns and villages.

The fascinating stories on the following pages are inspired by the intriguing pictures taken by Francis Frith and his team of photographers. The BBC series 'Britain's First Photo Album' follows John Sergeant on his own photographic journey through time as he travels around the country in the footsteps of Frith. The historical photographs from the Frith archive come back to life as John Sergeant meets the people living and working in the same places today who can tell the stories of the photographs and explain how they are working to keep Britain's heritage alive.

The pictures from the Frith archive offer us a unique vision of the people and places of Britain over the course of the last 150 years. Through them we can see how our past is linked with our present perhaps more closely than we realise. 'Britain's First Photo Album' is a fitting tribute to the work and vision of a remarkable man – Francis Frith.

# Frith's Battle with the Early Photographic Processes

The period during which Francis Frith was building his reputation was marked by regular developments in photographic techniques, and he shrewdly adopted and exploited those that suited him. The collodion wet plate process was invented in 1851: a solution of guncotton dissolved in ether and alcohol formed a stable bond between light-sensitive chemicals and a glass plate. This produced sharp negative images, a huge advance on the earlier somewhat fuzzy images produced by the calotype process (paper negatives). From these glass negatives Frith could produce albumen prints (the albumen in egg white bound the chemicals to paper to produce photographic prints). However, the collodion process was fraught with difficulties. Frith had to haul around a heavy and cumbersome store of glass sheets and chemicals as well as his large wooden camera. The glass plates had to be coated immediately before the photograph was exposed, and then developed straight away before the collodion coating had dried. Fortunately, by the 1870s the gelatin dry plate had been invented. This could be pre-coated in a laboratory and taken on photographic expeditions without the need of chemicals. Always keen to innovate and refine his operation, Frith took advantage of these developments as they happened.

A COLLECTION OF FRITH'S PHOTOGRAPHS, PORTFOLIOS AND CATALOGUES FROM HIS EGPYT JOURNEYS FRITH

LONDON, CHELSEA PENSIONERS ON OAK APPLE DAY c1898    FRITH L130320

# A Lasting Symbol of Duty and Courage

*John Sergeant looks at his first photograph from the Francis Frith archive:
'We are in London, Britain's capital city, a patchwork of old and new. The
fascinating Frith photograph on the previous pages shows one of London's
most loved national treasures, an institution which is never criticized. This is
the Royal Hospital, Chelsea, and a few of its inmates, the Chelsea Pensioners. I
was to find out that the pensioners today are not just spirited, but cheeky, too!'*

THE ROYAL
HOSPITAL, CHELSEA

The Royal Hospital, Chelsea, is a symbol of
Britain's military conflicts and the brave
men and women who fought in them.
The Frith photograph on pages 20 and 21 shows
some Victorian Chelsea Pensioners honouring
Oak Apple Day, 29 May, the birthday of the Royal
Hospital's founder, King Charles II and also the
day he was restored to his throne, with a parade.
The king's statue is adorned – indeed, hidden!
– with oak leaves; this commemorates his escape
after the Battle of Worcester in 1651, when he hid
from the Parliamentarian forces in the Boscobel
Oak, near Boscobel House in Shropshire.

The statue of King Charles II stands in the central court of the Hospital
(see photograph opposite). Designed by Grinling Gibbons in 1676 and cast
in copper, it originally stood near Whitehall Palace. The statue was moved
here in 1692; in 2002, it was re-gilded to celebrate the Queen's Golden Jubilee,
and shines out today in truly royal splendour.

The Royal Hospital is a retirement home for British soldiers unfit for
further duty owing to injury or old age. It was founded by King Charles II in
1681, traditionally at the behest of his mistress Nell Gwynn after she met an
old wounded soldier reduced to begging for charity. The king also set up a
system to provide pensions for those who had been injured in service or who
had served for more than 20 years, and so the residents of the Hospital are

THE STATUE OF KING CHARLES II

popularly known as 'Chelsea Pensioners', although in fact they surrender their army pensions in return for board, lodging, uniform and medical care. (The Royal Hospital was responsible for distributing army pensions until 1955.)

The architect chosen for the Hospital was Sir Christopher Wren, who based his grand design on the Hôpital des Invalides in Paris. By 1685, the year of the king's death, the main hall and chapel had been built, and in 1692 the hospital was finished, complete with two additional quadrangles, ready to house 476 former soldiers. Ever since then, the beautiful buildings have been one of the sights of London, and the pensioners themselves in their cheerful uniform are famous and popular personalities the world over.

BELOW LEFT: CHELSEA PENSIONERS c1898  FRITH L130319V
BELOW RIGHT: CHELSEA PENSIONERS c1898  FRITH L130319X

# Oak Apple Day: Branches and Garlands

Oak Apple Day is celebrated on 29 May to commemorate the restoration of the English monarchy in 1660. In that year, Parliament declared 29 May a public holiday 'to be for ever kept as a day of thanksgiving for our redemption from tyranny and the king's return to his Government, he entering London that day'.

People used to wear oak galls or sprigs of oak leaves in their hats or buttonholes in remembrance of the oak tree in which the future Charles II hid from the Parliamentarians after the Battle of Worcester. Anyone who did not wear a sprig of oak could be thrashed with nettles! 'The Book of Days', an anthology of anniversaries and customs published in 1869, recalls how 'lopping a few branches off the large oaks was never considered to do them any harm', for they were needed for garlands: 'Beautiful did these old towns and villages look, with their long lines of green boughs projecting from every house, while huge gaudy garlands hung suspended across the middle of the streets. Then there were flags hung out here and there – red, blue, yellow, purple and white blending harmoniously with the green of the branches and their gilded oak-apples'.

Like so many festivals, these celebrations might have their origin in ancient pagan beliefs and nature worship. For instance, the Garland King rides through the streets of Castleton in Derbyshire on 29 May, completely hidden by a huge garland of flowers. Oak Apple Day was officially abolished as a public holiday in 1859, but it is still celebrated in some places, including the Royal Hospital, Chelsea, and in some Oxford and Cambridge colleges a toast is drunk.

> ❝ *Beautiful did these old towns and villages look, with their long lines of green boughs projecting from every house …* ❞

# John tours the Hospital and meets the Pensioners

JOHN WITH
PADDY FOX

JOHN WITH
DOROTHY HUGHES

Paddy Fox is one of around 300 inhabitants of the Royal Hospital, and he's proud of its great reputation. I asked him if he'd ever heard a word against this place. 'No', he said, 'it's loved everywhere. I've travelled all over the world, and it's famous wherever I've been. The gratitude people show! They all shake hands with me – some of them think that I fought in the First World War, but I'm not quite that old! And of course our traditional uniform always attracts attention.'

I asked Paddy why the Royal Hospital was founded. He pointed up at the inscription above our heads: 'In subsidium et levamen emeritorum senio belloque fractorum condidit Carolus Secundus. That means that Charles II founded this place for the succour and relief of veterans broken by age and war. We veterans have been living here for 316 years!'

We looked at the Frith photograph, and Paddy told me that the Chelsea Pensioners still celebrate Oak Apple Day. 'The statue is still covered with oak leaves – maybe not quite as thickly as in the photograph. We still parade in full uniform wearing our tricorn hats. Nothing has changed.'

But surely, I thought, something must have changed over the years. 'In the ten years I've lived here', said Paddy, 'the biggest change has been the arrival of the women. They served in the armed forces, they did their bit, and they won their medals. Now that we've got some en suite rooms they're welcome to come here. At first some people did say: "What do these few women want to come and live with 300 old men for?" But the women served, so they're entitled to be here.'

It was in 2009 that the decision was made to open up Membership of the Royal Hospital to women. This was a significant moment in the Royal Hospital's history, and one which reflects the growing number of women who have joined the armed forces since the Second World War.

DOROTHY HUGHES
DURING THE WAR

Dorothy Hughes was the first woman to move here, and today she's one of only four female Chelsea Pensioners. I asked her if she thought that letting women come here was long overdue. 'Definitely', she said. 'I felt that I was a pioneer. I wanted to open the doors for younger women to come in. I think they'll arrive in hordes in about 10 years' time.'

I asked her what the atmosphere was like here. 'It's like a very large family', she said. 'Obviously sometimes there are squabbles, just as there are in any family. I know that some people say: "It's a place where you come to die." Well, we're all going to die some time, but here you don't feel alone. You're among people who are in the same position as you. We don't think about death; we live from day to day. You wake up in the morning, and you say: "Good! I've got another day!" Before I came here I'd been living on my own for 18 years, and I never liked knitting, or playing whist or bridge. I wanted an adventure – and I got one!'

# 'Pretty, witty Nell' – Charles II's Favourite Mistress

'Pretty, witty Nell', as the diarist Samuel Pepys called Nell Gwynn, born to a humble parents in 1650, rose from precarious circumstances to be a favourite mistress of King Charles II. It is said that it was she who persuaded the king to build the Royal Hospital, Chelsea.

She was making a living selling oranges in theatres when her beauty and liveliness caught the eye of the actor Charles Hart, who helped her set herself up as an actress. An excellent singer and dancer, she was at her best in comic parts, and had many successes at the Theatre Royal, Drury Lane. Charles Hart was her first protector. She then became the mistress of Charles Sackville, Lord Buckhurst, whom she nicknamed 'Charles the Second'. When she fell in love with King Charles II, he became 'Charles the Third'!

The king had many mistresses, but the affection between him and Nell appears to have been strong and long-lasting. He gave her a house near Pall Mall, and a large pension. In 1669 she bore the king a son, whom she named Charles, and the king made him Duke of St Albans.

As the king lay dying in 1685, he is reputed to have said: 'Let not poor Nelly starve!' After his death, Nell did not quite starve, but she had so many debts that she was in danger of being sent to a debtors' prison. She appealed to Charles II's successor, James II, and he repaid her debts and settled a pension on her. Nell died only two years later, in 1687, still in her 30s. Her Cinderella story has ensured her immortality as a popular folk heroine.

FAR LEFT: THE GREAT HALL

Here there is a magnificent mural of Charles II, painted by Antonio Verrio, dating back to 1690.

LEFT: THE CHAPEL

The Chapel is a superb example of Wren's work with original wainscoting, pews and plasterwork.

## JOHN'S PHOTOGRAPH AT CHELSEA

THE CHELSEA PENSIONERS, 2011

*I lined up the pensioners, Dorothy in the middle. Then I called them to order. 'Troop! Atten – shun!' They all snapped upright. 'Stand at – ease!' As one they stood feet apart, hands behind backs. This would be a piece of cake, I thought. I was about to press the button when somebody – I won't say who – shouted out: 'Knickers!' Sheer insubordination! But I thought I'd carry on as if it hadn't happened. So who was it who spoilt it all by calling out: 'Get them off!'? It surely couldn't have been Dorothy, could it? Like British fighting forces throughout history, the pensioners were disciplined, of course, but they also had the capacity to fool around. Spirited and good humoured: that sums up the Chelsea Pensioners.*

# Drama, Spectacle – and a Seething Slum

*'The photograph on the opposite page shows the heart of Victorian London. Everything hereabouts has radically changed since Frith's time. If it hadn't been for a helpful cab driver, I would never have found the spot where the picture was taken. Using his cab driver's 'knowledge', he was able to navigate by the spire of St Mary le Strand Church (in the background of the photograph opposite) to bring me to Drury Lane in London's theatreland. Curtain up!'*

VICTORIAN ENGRAVING OF THE SECOND DRURY LANE THEATRE

On first sight the main photograph on the opposite page seems rather uneventful and even gloomy: an almost unpeopled street is lined with ramshackle houses. Why did the photographer consider this scene worth recording? And why is one of the busiest streets in Britain's capital city so empty?

When we look closely at the photograph, we can see that the shop windows are boarded up. Few people live here any more. The reason is that the street was soon to be demolished to make way for the developments of Kingsway and Aldwych; it was earmarked for clearance, which finally took place in 1898. This photograph is an important historical record of a London that was about to vanish for ever.

Drury Lane has a long history. Back in the 16th century this part of London was relatively rural; the road was originally the lane that led up to Drury House, the home of the Elizabethan soldier and politician Sir William Drury, a grand house with a long drive and large gardens. After Sir William's time the house belonged to the Earl of Craven, and then became a public house, the Queen of Bohemia.

It is said that the first case of the Great Plague of 1665 occurred in Drury Lane. A Victorian commentator compared the street then to the way it was in his time, and found little difference: 'Without care for drainage or paving, it is not to be wondered at that the pestilence carried off so many that it was difficult to find room for the dead in the parish grave-yard; but it is a matter of surprise that, after two hundred years have gone by, during which knowledge has been constantly increasing, we should find, exactly on the spot which had such a notorious character in the past, the existence of precisely similar evils in the present.'

But Drury Lane cannot have been all bad, for Nell Gwynn was living at

VICTORIAN
ENGRAVING OF
THE INTERIOR OF
THE THIRD
DRURY LANE
THEATRE IN 1804

this time in the fashionable part of Drury Lane, the Strand or Covent Garden end; Drury Lane in the days of Charles II was inhabited by a very different class of people from those who later occupied it. The Theatre Royal, Drury Lane (where Nell Gwynn acted) was built in 1663, the first of four theatres on the site. The third theatre, built in 1794, was owned by the playwright Richard Brinsley Sheridan. It burnt down in a disastrous fire in 1809; a passer-by was astonished to see Sheridan drinking a glass of wine in the street while watching the fire, and Sheridan is famously reported to have said: 'A man may surely be allowed to take a glass of wine by his own fireside.'

In the 18th century Drury Lane was notorious, dominated by prostitution and gin palaces. The poet John Gay, author of 'The Beggars' Opera', wrote of 'Drury's mazy courts and dark abodes', and Pope described it only too truly as peopled by 'drabs of the lowest character', and by authors 'lulled by soft zephyrs' that blew through the broken panes of a garret window.

By the Victorian era, Drury Lane was a seething slum. Not long before the photograph on page 28 was taken, George Godwin described the street in 'Another Blow for Life' (1864): 'There was no air stirring; the footways were full of women and children sitting and standing about the entrance to the various courts behind: there was nothing bright but the gin-shops, which were ablaze with gas, and were driving a roaring trade. The condition of the atmosphere was disagreeable everywhere; but on passing a narrow turning called Ashlin's Place, the effluvium was sickening; and when led by the nose we passed down it, this became worse and worse.' It is hardly surprising that Drury Lane was marked down for clearance and redevelopment.

# Melodrama and Spectacle at Drury Lane

The Drury Lane Theatre was famous from its early days for staging lavish pantomimes and spectacular melodramas. It continued the tradition into the 20th century, and the photographs here show productions that would have thrilled their audiences.

ABOVE: SCENE FROM 'THE WHIP'

'The Whip' was first performed at Drury Lane in 1909. It featured intricate scenery and stunning stage effects, including a dramatic train crash.

LEFT: SCENE FROM AN EARLY 20TH CENTURY PRODUCTION OF 'THE HOPE'

RIGHT: SCENE FROM 'THE SHIPWRECK'

'The Shipwreck' was written by the dramatist Samuel James Arnold (1774-1852) and was first performed at the Drury Lane theatre in 1796.

PHOTOGRAPHS COURTESY OF THE GEORGE HOARE THEATRE COLLECTION

# John tours the theatre and treads the boards

JOHN TOURS THE THEATRE WITH HISTORIAN MARK FOX

## *The theatre was famous for spectacular melodramas*

THE INTERIOR OF THE THEATRE ROYAL TODAY

Most of what we see in the photograph of London's Drury Lane on page 28 has been swept away, but one landmark has endured: the Theatre Royal. I went there to meet theatre historian Mark Fox, who knows all about the rich history of this theatre. We went through backstage corridors to emerge in the vast, glamorous auditorium.

I had heard that this was actually the fourth theatre on this site. 'It is', said Mark. 'The first Theatre Royal was built in 1663 under a Royal Patent from Charles II, hence its name. This building opened in 1812.' I wondered if the auditorium looked the same as when the Frith archive picture of Drury Lane was taken. 'It's completely different, in fact', Mark told me. 'The Victorian auditorium was horseshoe-shaped, and there were more tiers of seating. Today we have three tiers; then there were four, and even a little galleried section above the top tier – the Victorian auditorium was higher. This one was remodelled in 1922.'

It must have been a big theatre in Victorian times, then, I thought. 'And the stage was one of the biggest in London', said Mark. 'That suited the productions, because the Drury Lane Theatre was famous for lavish pantomimes and spectacular melodramas. The Victorian theatre managers did whatever they could to fill the seats. They needed to attract people in and make them spend their hard-earned money to see the show.'

I learned that the theatre went to great lengths to entice audiences. Beneath the stage was complex hydraulic machinery to create special effects and spectacular scenery, such as mountains, cliffs and tall buildings, and even shipwrecks and train crashes. 'The men who worked the stage machinery had a special way of communicating', said Mark. 'A lot of the stage crew had been dock hands or sailors, so most of their cue system was done by whistling. That's why today there's the superstition that it's unlucky to whistle in a theatre. If you whistled in those days, you could have unwittingly given a cue and caused a real disaster on stage. Someone could even be killed if a piece of scenery was flown in at the wrong time.'

JOHN ON STAGE DECLAIMING LINES FROM 'ALADDIN'

I've always considered myself a bit of a thesp, so I couldn't wait to have a go at 'Aladdin', a version of which was first performed here in Frith's time. Mark and I got up on stage with our old scripts. We declaimed our parts with as much spirit as we could muster – but I have to say that the rhyming script was pretty good doggerel, and the performances were dire. I awarded Mark and myself the slow handclap we deserved!

# Drury Lane Theatre Ghosts

Drury Lane seems to be the most haunted theatre in the world. It is said that if one of its many ghosts appears, it means good luck, to the person who saw it or to the production on at the theatre at the time.

CHARLES MACKLIN

The theatre's most famous ghost is the Man in Grey, an 18th-century aristocrat with powdered hair, who wears a cloak, riding boots and a tricorne hat, and carries a sword. He is supposed to be the ghost of a murdered man whose body was hidden by walling it up; his skeleton was found in the theatre in 1848.

The actor Charles Macklin haunts a backstage corridor, the place where he killed another actor, Thomas Hallam, in 1735. The two were having a violent argument about a trivial subject – a wig. 'God damn you for a blackguard, scrub, rascal!' shouted Macklin, and thrust a cane into Hallam's face. It pierced his eye, and the unfortunate man died.

Joseph Grimaldi (1778-1837), perhaps the most famous English clown and the first 'whiteface' clown, appears on the actual stage. He is a helpful ghost, prompting nervous actors and guiding them through their parts. Another king of comedy, Dan Leno (1860-1904), master of Cockney humour and a famous pantomime dame, has been seen in one of Drury Lane's dressing rooms.

# Watching Plays at Galleried Inns

GEORGE INN, SOUTHWARK c1875
FRITH L130130

In the days before formal theatres, plays were performed in inn courtyards with the audience watching from the galleries. The Frith archive has several fascinating photographs of these inns, most of which have now disappeared.

London's only surviving galleried inn is the George Inn at Southwark. The inn was built round three sides of a courtyard, and from its balconies the inn's guests could watch plays performed by travelling troupes of actors. Shakespeare himself, who lived at Southwark, may well have come here to see his own plays performed. The old inn burned down in 1676, but it was immediately rebuilt in the same style, and remained unchanged until the 19th century. Today the beautifully restored building still functions as an inn, and is now in the care of the National Trust.

## JOHN'S PHOTOGRAPH AT DRURY LANE

THE STAGE DOOR, THE THEATRE ROYAL, DRURY LANE, 2011

*My performance on the Theatre Royal's stage may not have my greatest, but I hoped I would make up for it with my picture. This stage door is a perfect reminder of Victorian glamour and a symbol of the excitement that still pervades London's theatreland to this day. The door was here when the Frith archive photograph on page 28 was taken, and we can imagine the Victorian stage door Johnnies waiting here, hoping for a glimpse of their favourite actress.*

# The Hard Lives of Covent Garden's Flower Sellers

ELENA ELISSEEVA, DREAMSTIME.COM

*'The group of flower sellers in the Frith photograph on the previous page symbolises the many flower sellers who have worked at London's Covent Garden over the centuries; and for anyone who's seen 'My Fair Lady' or Shaw's 'Pygmalion', these girls are a reminder of the real Eliza Dolittles. I was looking forward to meeting some modern flower sellers in New Covent Garden Market.'*

The name of the Aldwych area of London derives from 'ealdwic', the 'old market' of the old Anglo-Saxon trading settlement of Lundenwic that was established in the early 7th century. Over hundreds of years this remained an important market trading centre. In the 17th century Inigo Jones designed a magnificent square with classical arcades in the Covent Garden area, north-west of Aldwych; it was here that London's most important fruit, vegetable and flower markets used to be located. It was described in a Victorian guidebook: 'All night long the rumble of heavy wagons seldom ceases, and before daylight the market is crowded. The very loading of these wagons is a wonder, and the wall-like regularity with which cabbages, cauliflowers and turnips are built up to a height of some twelve feet is nothing short of a miracle.' The market porters carried goods to and from the waiting carts in tower blocks of circular baskets on their heads, and took pride in the number they could carry.

The main Frith photograph overleaf on page 35 shows three Eliza Dolittles of the 1870s with their posies and flower baskets. They try to smile for the photographer, but in fact they probably had little to smile about, for their life

LONDON, COVENT GARDEN PORTERS 1885  FRITH L130216

was hard. Many of the young flower girls were orphans, living in boarding rooms crowded with other street traders. It was a girl like one of these who spoke to Henry Mayhew ('London Labour and the London Poor', 1851):

'I sell flowers, sir; we live almost on flowers when they are to be got. I sell, and so does my sister, all kinds, but it's very little use offering any that's not sweet. I think it's the sweetness as sells them. I sell primroses, and violets, and wall-flowers, and stocks, and roses of different sorts, and pinks, and carnations, and lilies of the valley, and green lavender, and mignonette (but that I do very seldom), and violets again at this time of the year, for we get them both in spring and winter. [Violets were forced in hot-houses for winter sale.] The best sale of all is, I think, moss-roses, young moss-roses. We do best of all on them. Primroses are good, for people say: "Well, here's spring again to a certainty." Gentlemen are our best customers. I've heard that they buy flowers to give to the ladies. Ladies have sometimes said: "A penny, my poor girl, here's three-halfpence for the bunch." Or they've given me the price of two bunches for one; so have gentlemen.'

The flower market was held outside in the open, and the cries of flower-

VICTORIAN
ENGRAVING
SHOWING THE
ENTRANCE TO
COVENT GARDEN
MARKET

*The pavement was aglow with colour of flower and leaf*

sellers echoed through the expansive square. A contemporary guidebook tells how in spring the dealers sold bedding plants, and 'the pavement was aglow with colour of flower and leaf, and in the early summer hundreds of women and girls are busily occupied in shelling peas.'

The colour and spectacle disguised the market's darker side, which Dickens described: 'One of the worst night-sights I know of in London is to be found in the children who prowl about this place; who sleep in the baskets, fight for the offal, dart at any objects they think they can lay their thieving hands on, dive under the carts and barrows, dodge the constables, and are perpetually making a blunt pattering on the pavement of the Piazza with the rain of their naked feet.'

Dickens is here uncharacteristically insensitive to the plight of London's poor and dispossessed. Henry Mayhew offers a very different and more sympathetic account, and tells of the plight of some of the market's younger traders. He spoke to a tiny and pathetic watercress girl, who walked the streets in all weathers in a thin cotton gown, with a threadbare shawl wrapped round her shoulders. 'When she walked she shuffled along, for fear that the large carpet slippers that served her for shoes should slip off her feet.' She was just eight years old. In winter she could barely buy enough cress from Covent Garden to sell, and when she did offer bunches to customers in the streets, she said, 'They're so cold, people won't buy 'em; for when I goes up to them, they say, "They'll freeze our bellies".' And in summer there was so much cress about that it was sold 'cheap as dirt'. There were occasional good days: 'One day I took 1s 6d, and the cresses cost 6d; but it isn't often I get such luck as that. I oftener makes 3d or 4d.'

Such waifs grew up quickly and became dab hands at bargaining with other traders at the market, who were not beyond cheating a young child. 'They can't take me in. If the woman tries to give me a small handful of cresses, I says, "I ain't agoin' to have that for a ha'porth", and I go to the next basket, and so on, all round ... For 3d I has a lap full, enough to earn about a shilling.'

Life for the London poor was never easy.

# John visits the old and new Covent Garden

JOHN TRACKS DOWN
THE PLACE WHERE
THE FRITH ARCHIVE
PHOTOGRAPH WAS
TAKEN

THE NEW COVENT
GARDEN MARKET AT
NINE ELMS

I found it hard to work out where the Frith archive photograph on page 35 had been taken. It had to be near St Paul's Church, I thought, so I enlisted the help of the Rev Simon Grigg, Rector of St Paul's.

'Yes, I think I know where they were', he said. 'Obviously the picture shows the flower market, which was at the east end of the church. If we come out into the Piazza, we see the famous portico of St Paul's, the Actors' Church, where George Bernard Shaw set the opening scene of 'Pygmalion', which inspired 'My Fair Lady'. The stonework to the left in the photograph is the right-hand pillar of the portico, and the railings would then have closed the portico off. Behind is the door visible in the photograph.' I was very grateful to Simon, and pleased to see that although the lamppost has gone, otherwise the scene is very much the same.

I wanted to see what it's like selling flowers today, so I went south of the River Thames to New Covent Garden Market. This vast modern covered market is a dramatic change. The old boisterous bustle has gone, but it's all so efficient now. Where else could you ask for 10,000 red roses and be told: 'Yes, sir, would tomorrow be all right?'

This purpose-built market is now the largest wholesale fruit, vegetable and flower market in the UK, and home to about 200 companies. Here I met John Hardcastle. His family have been in the flower selling business for many years, and he has fond memories of the old Covent Garden. 'It was fantastic', he told me. 'I was born and bred in the old market. It was always noisy, and always busy. The streets round about were often congested in those days because of the fog – real London pea-soupers. I used to have to find my way through the fog to

get to school. Now our business is very different. The world has got so small. You can order flowers from all over the world, and they'll be here in 24 hours. In the past, we'd rely on British growers.'

I couldn't help feeling that it was a bit sad. 'Well,' said John philosophically, 'you have to accept that the market's changed because the world's changed.' I wondered if when he looked back he thought those really were the days. 'I'm pleased I was there to experience them', John said.

JOHN TALKS TO FLOWER SELLER JOHN HARDCASTLE

# Street Entertainments at Covent Garden

The produce distribution market has now moved to the New Covent Garden Market a few miles away at Nine Elms, and Covent Garden Piazza is now buzzing with shops, cafés and tourists. It is also famous for its street entertainers. The competition to be given a permit here is fierce: would-be entertainers have to audition, and if they are successful they are then given timetabled slots.

There is nothing new about street entertainment at Covent Garden. The first recorded Punch and Judy show in Britain took place in the square here in May 1662, during the reign of Charles II; the marionette show, which featured an early version of the Mr Punch character, was performed by an Italian puppet showman called Pietro Gimonde, also known as 'Signor Bologna'. The show was watched by Samuel Pepys, who described it in his famous diary as 'an Italian puppet play, that is within the rails there, which is very pretty'. A plaque at Covent Garden now commemorates the event.

THE PIAZZA AT COVENT GARDEN TODAY

LEFT: POWELL'S PUPPET THEATRE FROM A VICTORIAN ENGRAVING

Powell's puppet theatre performed in a Covent Garden inn in the 18th century, satirising politicians and personalities of the day.

LONDON, COVENT GARDEN 1900  FRITH L130025

*❝All night long the rumble of heavy wagons seldom ceases, and before daylight the market is crowded. The very loading of these wagons is a wonder, and the wall-like regularity with which cabbages, cauliflowers and turnips are built up to a height of some twelve feet is nothing short of a miracle.❞*

FROM A VICTORIAN GUIDEBOOK

## JOHN'S PHOTOGRAPH AT NEW COVENT GARDEN

### TRADERS OF THE NEW MARKET, 2011

*With the help of some of the men and women who work here in New Covent Garden Market, I wanted to recreate an up-to-date version of the Frith picture on page 35. Here they are posing against the background of a modern flower stall. This is flower selling in the 21st century.*

LONDON, TOWER BRIDGE UNDER CONSTRUCTION 1890   FRITH L130050

# An Iconic *Tour de Force* of Victorian Engineering

*'Tower Bridge, spanning the magnificent River Thames, is one of London's most iconic landmarks. The fascinating photograph on the previous pages shows the bridge under construction. I was to see her inner workings, and little did I suspect that I would be allowed to undertake a supremely responsible task!'*

So many villages, towns and cities owe their existence to a stream or a river. Water for people and farm animals to drink, water to drive a rural mill or industrial machinery, water that enables travel and trade – communities rely on water. London is no exception. For centuries the River Thames has been the life-blood of a great city.

It's hard to believe, then, that until 1750 there was only one bridge in London. But by Frith's time in the 19th century the ever-changing skyline of London was undergoing major transformation. The Houses of Parliament, that landmark that seems to have been there for ever, was only actually completed as late as 1870. London had so quickly become so densely populated that,

LONDON, THE RIVER THAMES AND THE HOUSES OF PARLIAMENT 1897
FRITH L130327

along with the need for bridges for the rapidly expanding railway system, the building of a new bridge in the late 19th century for road traffic was not something new or surprising for Londoners to see. Albert Bridge, Battersea Bridge, and Cannon Street railway bridge had all been built in the last 20 years. Londoners probably never guessed that Tower Bridge would become a globally recognised landmark. The main photograph on the previous pages shows the bridge in a skeletal state in 1890, a full four years before its metal framework was clad in stone.

For much of the 19th century it had been recognised that a new bridge was needed – London Bridge was seriously congested (see photograph opposite, above). There was much discussion about how to finance the project, and many designs were put forward attempting to address the problems posed

by London's river. The Thames is tidal, with a difference of about 24 feet between low and high tide, so the new bridge had to be designed to allow ships to go under it at all times of day. Another problem is the river bed, which is unstable gravel and clay; the bridge's foundations needed to be deep if the bridge was to be stable.

At last in the 1880s the City Architect, Horace Jones, helped by the engineer John Wolfe Barry, came up with a viable design: a combination of a suspension bridge at each end, a girder bridge for pedestrian walkways, and a bascule bridge to let ships through in the centre ('bascule' is French for seesaw, and a bascule bridge has sections that rise as a counterpoise sinks). The first stone was laid in 1886 by the Prince of Wales. Jones died suddenly in 1887, and Barry took over the whole project, helped by Henry Marc Brunel, son of Isambard. The bridge was opened by

*In 1952
a double-
decker bus
was being
driven over
the bridge just
as the bascules
began to rise*

the Prince of Wales in 1894 (see the photograph of the celebrations below), who with other members of the royal family processed in carriages across and back again. Then he opened the bascules, accompanied by a trumpet fanfare and screeching whistles from twelve steamboats which passed through while a band played. During the first year of operation the bascules were raised more than 6,000 times.

The bascules of the bridge carrying the roadway can be fully raised to allow tall-masted ships and sailing barges to pass through, giving a clearance of 140 feet and a width of 200 feet. Driven by steam, the hydraulic machinery hoisted the heavy 1,000 ton bascules to their raised positions in two minutes. The bridge spans continued to be raised hydraulically from their completion in 1894 until 1976, when they were converted to electricity.

On 28 December 1952 a double-decker bus was being driven over the bridge just as the bascules began to rise. The driver managed to 'leap' the bus across a three-foot wide gap to land it safely on the bascule on the other side, and it continued on its journey!

The raised footway at the top of the towers of the bridge, 140 feet above the level of the river, was closed in 1909 after a spate of suicides. The upper deck was intended as a pedestrian route, but nowadays it is a spectacular function room. From it you can watch the sunset over the Thames, and remember the glory days of London as a great port.

# John takes command and raises the bascules

JOHN WITH
CHARLIE HARRISON,
BRIDGE OPERATOR

JOHN IN THE HUGE
COUNTERWEIGHT
CHAMBER

The opening of Tower Bridge is a magnificent sight. It's the responsibility of Charlie Harrison, the bridge operator, to make sure that the daily bridge routine runs smoothly. We met inside a small room overlooking the bridge equipped with a control panel with myriad buttons and a lever, a computer screen, and CCTV screens.

This had to be the control room. 'It's one of two, yes,' said Charlie. I asked him how often he opened the bridge. 'About 950 times a year, mainly from April to October – it's a summer thing, really.' But how often was it opened in Frith's time? 'Tower Bridge used to be raised about 6,000 times a year', said Charlie. 'This was an extremely busy waterway. It was the prize part of the Pool of London; ships wanted to get to the upper part of the Pool, nearer the centre of the city. They could unload and load up again more quickly there. A quicker turnaround meant a bigger profit. But it's different now. All the commercial traffic has gone, and it's all pleasure craft.'

Charlie led me below the bridge so that I could get an understanding of how it works. We went down a narrow ladder to a space chock full of gleaming machinery painted in bright colours – blue, yellow, purple and green. It looked really complicated to me. 'This machinery drives an axle,' said Charlie, 'and the axle pushes the back ends of the bridge down, which makes the front ends rise up, allowing ships to go through the gap. It's like a giant seesaw.'

There was still more to see. We climbed a ladder to find ourselves beside a huge, tall metal cylinder. 'This is the accumulator', Charlie told me. 'It's amazingly impressive!' I exclaimed. 'When you're up above you never realise all this is here.' Charlie led me on into a vast cathedral-like space where a stepped surface rose up in a semicircle. The cavernous chamber dwarfed us both. 'This is the most important part of the whole structure', said Charlie. 'Without this, nothing can happen. The counterweight comes down here into this space to lift the bridge up in the seesaw motion I told you about.' 'So,' I said, 'if we're standing here, and the weight comes down, what do we do?' 'Panic!' said Charlie. 'No, actually we could get to the safety area, and stand on a plinth with our backs to the wall, and the weight would stop just in front of us.' Very, very frightening, I thought.

JOHN OPENING THE BRIDGE

Then I just had to ask one last favour. 'Charlie', I said, 'would you let me open the bridge?' 'Well,' he said, 'I've shown you all the parts of the structure, how they work, and what they do; it'll be my honour to let you raise Tower Bridge.' 'Honour!' I said. 'It'll be an honour for me!'

This had to be one of the most unusual things I've ever done in my life, and it's something I imagine very few people get to do. We went back to the control room. Charlie told me that the first thing was to warn the bridge crew that I was about to make a start. I pressed one of the many buttons and spoke into a microphone: 'Stand by, bridge crew, about to stop road traffic.' 'Now,' said Charlie, 'press the traffic light button to initiate the closure.' 'Done'. 'Press those two buttons to shut the entrance gates.' 'Done.' 'Next, we start to unlock the bridge. Press the pause button.' 'Done.'

'There', said Charlie, 'you can see it on the computer screen – it's a diagram of the four massive hydraulic jacks below us. Now – pull that lever back, and hold it back.' 'She's opening!' I cried. 'She's going up! And how graceful she is!'

# London's Busy St Katharine Docks

Some of the thousands of ships that sailed under Tower Bridge would have passed St Katharine Docks. They came into being in 1828 during a period when the capital's trade was rapidly expanding and docks and warehouses for trading vessels were badly needed. The docks were named after the hospital of St Katharine by the Tower, which was built in the 12th century and stood on the 23-acre site. Here also were narrow streets crammed with closely-packed, insanitary slums, mostly inhabited by port workers; to make room for the docks, about 1,250 houses were demolished, and over 11,000 people lost their homes.

The innovative design of the new docks was by the great engineer Thomas Telford. He provided two linked basins, so as to give maximum quayside space, and he sited the warehouses beside the water so that goods could be loaded and unloaded easily and quickly. Ships entered the docks from the tidal Thames through a lock gate; the water was kept at a constant four feet above river level by steam engines.

They were lively: 'There were draymen and their horses, dock-labourers, sailors, empty puncheons, and a miscellaneous spectacle of life', says Nathaniel Hawthorne in his 'English Notebooks' (1870). He goes on to enumerate 'organ-grinders, men roasting chestnuts over small ovens on the sidewalk, boys and women with boards or wheelbarrows of apples, oyster-stands, besides pedlars of small wares and dirty children at play'.

THE BARGE 'GLADYS' PASSING UNDER THE
BRIDGE

'She goes up about one degree per second', said Charlie. I thought that every time he does this he must feel so powerful. 'Well, that's about 2,200 tons of structure there you've got on the move', he said.

Well, I've done some extraordinary things in my life, but never anything quite like this. I'm very grateful. 'That's normally as far as we need to go', said Charlie. 'Just a little bit more – and now release the lever.' The thrill wasn't quite over, for the boat that came through was a beautiful Thames barge, the 'Gladys', with all her crew on deck waving to us. Perfect! A Victorian boat was sailing under this most treasured of Victorian feats of engineering.

## JOHN'S PHOTOGRAPH OF TOWER BRIDGE

MY TOWER BRIDGE, 2011

*My photograph had to be of Tower Bridge, my bridge, which I've opened. Here she is in all her glory. I wonder if anyone knew when she was built what a well-loved landmark of London she would one day become.*

GRAVESEND, CLIFTON MARINE PARADE c1898    FRITH 49042

# Busy port and pleasure resort

*'The Frith photograph of Gravesend on the previous pages shows a Thameside scene with a sailing barge and its very proud owner.'*

*At the time of the Frith photograph Gravesend was the world's busiest port*

Gravesend is a busy industrial town on the River Thames. It has a long history of seafaring; fleets were assembled here in Tudor times. At Gravesend Reach the river narrows to become London's river – London Bridge is 26 miles upstream. Gravesend's situation, opposite the Essex port of Tilbury, led to its becoming the pilot station for the Port of London, where the coastal pilots handed over to the river men; at the time of the Frith photographs it was the world's busiest port.

The involvement between the town of Gravesend and the River Thames started with the building of London Docks in 1802. The Royal Dock Group began operations in 1880, and every one of their large cargo ships had to pass Gravesend. 1886 saw the opening of Tilbury Docks, initially to cater for large passenger liners serving the East India and Orient trades, which were too cumbersome to travel further up-river. The uninterrupted views of the ships of all nationalities passing on the river were a source of immense interest for visitors when Gravesend became a popular resort during the Victorian era.

CLACTON, THAMES BARGES ON WEST BEACH 1912
FRITH 64254

GRAVESEND, THE RIVER 1898 FRITH 49046

The Thames barges, of which the restored 'Cambria' is an example (see photograph below and information on page 54), were kept busy loading, unloading and ferrying cargoes to and from the big ships. These flat-bottomed barges were ideal for negotiating the shallow waters of the coast and estuaries hereabouts. Whilst some were capable of undertaking coastal trade, others were confined to the Thames and its navigable tributaries; being smaller, they could only carry a cargo of under 100 tons. The coastal barges were over 80 feet in length with a beam of 19 feet and draught when laden of between six and seven feet. They could accommodate between 120 and 300 tons of cargo and were crewed by a skipper and two men. These spritsail barges carried over 2000 square feet of canvas; the small mizzen sail was sheeted to the rudder to assist tiller steering. In the late 1890s there were over 2000 Thames barges in service.

The photograph of Clacton (opposite, below left) shows how the Thames barges could unload their cargoes (mainly bricks, sand, cement, slate, and timber to build houses for an expanding population) on a beach – this saved the barge owner from paying harbour dues. The cargo was unloaded between high tides. While straightforward in mild weather, it could be a bit tricky if the weather turned rough. Horse-drawn carts transported the cargo away when it had been unloaded.

ST OSYTH,
BARGE ON THE
CREEK 1912
FRITH 64261

THE RESTORED
THAMES BARGE
'CAMBRIA'

# Restoring the Thames Sailing Barge 'Cambria'

Thames barges reached their peak at the turn of the 19th century, when about 2,000 were in service. Thereafter, with the invention of the internal combustion engine and the growing use of lorries for the transport of goods, their usefulness as working vessels lessened, and after the First World War they went into a decline.

JOHN WITH TIM GOLDSACK

Gravesend is honoured to be the home of the 'Cambria', a Thames sailing barge built at Greenhithe, Kent in 1906. She is the last British-registered vessel to have carried a commercial cargo under sail alone (she was working up to 1970), so she is an important reminder of our industrial and maritime heritage.

Tim Goldsack was one of the skilled team who worked on the restoration of the 'Cambria'. He explains what a hard task this was: 'We almost had to re-build her – there was only about three or four per cent of the original vessel left in good condition, along with some parts of her original machinery. The project took three-and-a half-years to complete, and cost £1.4 million. I feel immense pride to have completed the project and to see the Cambria sailing again.'

Today the 'Cambria' is sailing in Thames barge races, and getting ready for a new role in sail training and other educational activities.

‘*We almost had to re-build her – there was only about three or four per cent of the original vessel left* ’

THE 'CAMBRIA' DURING RESTORATION

# John learns about Gravesend's history as a resort

JOHN WITH
SANDRA SODER

GRAVESEND,
NEW THAMES CLUB
1902
FRITH 49041

Gravesend was not only an important port; I've found out that in the Victorian era it became a resort, a popular place for Londoners to come for a day out. In the background of the main photograph (pages 50-51) we can see a paddle steamer arriving – and is that a train on the pier? Sandra Soder, the Honorary Secretary of the Gravesend Historical Society, explained to me that Gravesend's role as a resort began as long ago as 1797: 'Those towers in the background of the main Frith photograph that look like Turkish minarets were the Clifton Baths (you can see them again in the centre of the photograph below). In the late 18th century an entrepreneur bought some second-hand bathing machines from Margate, and encouraged the well-to do to come and take to the water in Gravesend.'

So was there a beach here?  'Yes', Sandra told me, 'at the time it was said that the river was so clear that you could see the beach beneath the water.

People came to Gravesend because the water had just the right amount of salt to do you good.' Looking at the river bank today, I found it hard to believe that this could ever have been a holiday destination, but Sandra assured me that it was, and a fashionable one too.

'The great attraction was Rosherville. The main Frith photograph shows visitors about to land at Rosherville Pier to enjoy a day out at the largest and most popular Victorian pleasure gardens ever. Rosherville Gardens opened in 1837, and was built by the Kent Zoological and Botanical Gardens Company as an upper class holiday destination. There were all sorts of attractions, including a flower garden and conservatory, archery, dancing, a theatre, a maze, a museum, animals and a bear pit, fireworks, tightrope walkers, gypsy fortune tellers and a balloon ascent.'

ARCHERY IN
A VICTORIAN
PLEASURE GARDEN

But Gravesend's glory days were numbered. In 1878 the 'Princess Alice', a passenger-carrying paddle steamer, collided with a coal ship at Woolwich. She was split in two and sank in four minutes – 650 people died. Up until now the paddle steamers were the most popular way for the well-to-do to travel to Gravesend, but the disaster, the worst in the history of the Thames, ended their trade.

Sandra told me about another thing that stopped visitors coming here. 'It was the Great Stink! For hundreds of years people had been treating the Thames as a rubbish bin and a sewer. In 1858 the smell of the river as it flowed past the Houses of Parliament was so horrible that the MPs were appalled, and Londoners called their river the Great Stink, but it took some time for anything to be done about it. Meanwhile sewage was flowing down the Thames past Gravesend. The smell and the pollution discouraged people from coming here.'

Another factor that contributed to the eventual decline of Gravesend as a fashionable resort was

RIGHT:
A PLEASURE PARK
IN THE LATE
19TH CENTURY

the rapid expansion of the railways from the mid 19th century, which meant that better-off people started to go further afield for their holidays. 'The rich stopped coming', said Sandra, 'and the lower classes started to come here instead. They were noisy, they got drunk – Gravesend lost its appeal to more refined people.'

It's sad that where Rosherville once was is now a bleak, disused industrial site, with only a small brass plaque to remind us of the site of the former pleasure garden.

RIGHT: THE GRAVESEND WATERFRONT TODAY

## JOHN'S PHOTOGRAPH AT GRAVESEND

THE CREW OF THE 'CAMBRIA' AND ME, 2011

*What struck me most about my visit to Gravesend was the pride of the Thames barge sailors, so I wanted to capture that with the help of the crew of the restored 'Cambria'.*

FAVERSHAM, THE RECREATION GROUND 1892 FRITH 31474

# Green spaces for all

*'The photograph of Faversham on the previous pages shows the Recreation Ground. Just about every town in Britain today has a public park similar to this one, and it is the Victorians that we mainly have to thank for this legacy.'*

F aversham's park was created in the 19th century, as so many parks were. Local historian Arthur Percival explains that it is a big park, about 20 acres, and that the view in the Frith photograph has hardly changed today. The building in the background was the Park Keeper's cottage, and the footpath is an ancient one, here long before the Recreation Ground opened, and still in the same place.

JOHN WITH ARTHUR
PERCIVAL

Parks and gardens provide a welcome relief from the congested streets and small houses that surround them – they form lungs, as Arthur Percival puts it, to help people breathe clean air. Some towns have long had their historical open spaces (the Stray in Harrogate is an example), but most parks are a Victorian innovation, provided as an additional attraction for visitors or as a philanthropic gesture to promote the health and welfare of the town's workers and their families. Today, just about every town in Britain has a park where children can play and adults can stroll, and the standard of horticulture and landscape design is often high.

Victorian town and city councils created public parks and gardens to boost the local economy by making their communities desirable places in which to work and live. Parks also promoted civic pride. Rich industrialists, landowners and philanthropists recognised that a healthy, happy community was a hard-working community; relaxation, exercise and fresh air made workers more productive and society more cohesive.

BLACKBURN,
CORPORATION
PARK 1895
FRITH 35729

As early as 1840 the medical journal 'The Lancet' was calling for a public park in Tower Hamlets, London. 'These poor people, closely crowded in confined districts, have no open spaces in the vicinity of their humble dwellings for air, exercise, or healthful recreation – circumstances which produce the most painful effects on their physical and moral condition … Fever is constantly prevailing in these places … Nor is it less revolting to contemplate the moral pestilence, which is partly produced and greatly aggravated by the want of open space. Unable to breathe the pure air of Heaven with their families, multitudes are driven into habits of intemperance, bringing in their train demoralisation, disease, and death.'

Parks were conceived as genuinely public spaces where entry was free and all classes could mix – Arthur Percival points out that in the main Frith photograph (see pages 58-59) the boys on the right are probably working class, while the girls look middle class. Parks supported Victorian family values; weekend outings to the park were popular, and many parks offered special attractions such as bandstands, conservatories, boating ponds, playgrounds, tearooms and sports facilities so as to appeal to all ages and classes.

At Faversham Recreation Ground people still enjoy themselves in all sorts of ways, especially on the bowling greens. Our Victorian forebears would be glad to see that the parks they provided still bring relaxation and recreation to our communities, and continue to be highly valued by all who use them.

BOWLING AT BOSCOMBE 1913 FRITH 66137X

JOHN AT THE FAVERSHAM BOWLING CLUB

GUILDFORD, CASTLE GARDENS 1906 FRITH 55368

# Shepherd Neame – Britain's oldest brewery

The Faversham area became the centre of England's main fruit producing region when extensive orchards of apples, pears and cherries were planted between the two world wars of the 20th century to make the country independent of foreign supplies, and the town is still surrounded by orchards of fruit trees and also by Kent's famous hop fields. Indeed, Faversham is the home of Britain's oldest brewery, the Shepherd Neame brewery established in 1698, makers of such traditional cask ales as Canterbury Jack, Spitfire Premium Kentish Ale and Bishop's Finger Kentish Strong Ale – note their sign to the left in the Frith photograph below.

The brewery stands very near to the centre of Faversham, and it has always been possible to smell the brewing processes in the surrounding streets. In Victorian times, horse-drawn drays transported Shepherd Neame's products throughout Kent. The brewery had its own wharf at Faversham Creek where barges brought malts in and carried the beer out to London. From the 1850s onwards, steamboats and then the railway were the main means of transport.

The Guildhall (Town Hall) was originally built in 1574 as a market hall; it was rebuilt in 1814, except for the splendid timber arches on which it rests, to form a shelter for the stall holders and their customers. It stands in Abbey Street, a conservation area of the town, where the 16th-, 17th- and 18th-century houses have been imaginatively restored. This part of Faversham once had the oldest gunpowder works in the county, supplying the Navy from 1558 to 1934.

FAVERSHAM,
THE GUILDHALL
c1960
FRITH F13022

# John learns about Victorian dress and fashion

A FASHIONABLE VICTORIAN DRESS WITH A LACE COLLAR

VICTORIAN FASHION PLATE

One thing that really stands out in the Frith photograph of Faversham on pages 58-59 is how different clothes were in the Victorian era. I wouldn't have liked to be buttoned up in those thick, heavy clothes on a sunny day. So I decided to have a closer look at the clothes worn by our Victorian ancestors with the costume curator at Faversham's Heritage Centre, Jennifer Shipman.

The first outfit she showed me was a woman's elegant dress (see left). 'You can tell this is a well-off person's dress by the fabric', said Jennifer. 'It's silk, and the pretty collar is lace. This dress is telling everybody that she's somebody! It's the perfect Sunday best for a walk in the park'.

I was surprised when Jennifer told me that a dark blue dress was a wedding dress. A wedding dress in a dark colour? 'In the Victorian era your wedding dress was simply your best dress', she said. 'You would want your best dress

JOHN WITH
JENNIFER
SHIPMAN

to last, and a dark colour would last far longer than a light one. In those days you couldn't wash and iron complex dresses like these made from so much fabric, only brush and sponge them, and a light dress would look stained in no time. It's true that Queen Victoria wore a white dress for her wedding, but she was rich enough to afford a dress that wouldn't last long. It's only comparatively recently that white has become the norm for weddings.'

The last dress Jennifer showed me was really thick and stiff. 'Yes, this is made of a substantial fabric that will wear well', she said, 'and it's a smart dress. People used to go to the park to see and be seen, to promenade, so they would dress up for the occasion. You wanted people to see you, your children and your husband looking prosperous and dignified.'

*People used to go to the park to see and be seen, and to promenade, so they would dress up for the occasion*

ABOVE:
SCARBOROUGH, A COUPLE
PROMENADING 1890
FRITH 23452X

LEFT:
SCARBOROUGH, TOP HATS
AND A BOWLER ON SAINT
NICHOLAS CLIFF 1890
FRITH 23476A

And what about men? 'Hats announce your status,' said Jennifer as she put a bowler hat on my head. 'In this hat, you're probably middle management – quite an important person, certainly more important than a man in a flat cap.' Couldn't I wear a top hat? 'Top hats for top people! If you're wearing a top hat, you're probably the man who gave the Recreation Ground to Faversham!'

JOHN TRIES ON A BOWLER HAT

## JOHN'S PHOTOGRAPH AT FAVERSHAM

FAVERSHAM RECREATION GROUND, 2011

*Faversham Recreation Ground has hardly changed since the Frith photograph was taken 120 or so years ago. I wanted my photograph to show how it is still being enjoyed by the entire community, so I recruited some passers-by to act as my models. Standing on exactly the same path are modern young families, and these children are having a great time on their scooters. The big difference between my photograph and the Frith one is the clothes – informal, and so much cooler and more comfortable today.*

# A Popular Seaside Resort and its Devoted Fan Charles Dickens

BROADSTAIRS, THE HARBOUR 1887    FRITH 19707

*'Broadstairs is a charming seaside town that is very proud of its 19th-century past. The Frith photograph above shows Viking Bay, the biggest beach; today on a sunny day it gets crowded with holidaymakers. This trend actually started in Victorian times, when little fishing ports were transformed into seaside resorts by the coming of the railways.'*

Broadstairs was originally a fishing village known as Bradstow. It was noted for the cliff-top shrine of Our Lady of Bradstow, so venerated by sailors that they would dip their sails in salute as they passed. Bradstow is an Old English form of the words 'broad stairs', which allude to the stairs that in the 14th century were cut into the cliffs leading from the beach to the shrine, and later provided the name of the town.

For centuries Broadstairs remained a little town devoted to fishing and boat building. Then in the 19th century it became a seaside resort. The reason was Kent's 126 miles of coastline, with its advantages of good communications

BROADSTAIRS,
THE HARBOUR c1960
FRITH B220056

to the large centres of population around London, and generally warm, dry summers. The development of the railways in the mid 19th century changed the whole county; the lines reached out from London to the nearest stretches of coast, and in 1851 four of the ten largest seaside resorts in Britain were located in Kent – Margate, Ramsgate, Dover and Gravesend. In the next few decades the resorts of Broadstairs, Folkestone, Herne Bay and Deal also grew up as popular holiday destinations. Thus tourism became as important to Kent as the county's oast houses, orchards, castles, agriculture, and historic cathedrals.

Probably the most devoted fan of Broadstairs in the Victorian era was Charles Dickens. He first came here (with his wife Catherine and their baby Charley) in 1837 while he was writing 'The Pickwick Papers'; they took lodgings in the High Street.

Thereafter Dickens came here every summer, except for two, until 1851.

CHARLES DICKENS'S
'PICKWICK PAPERS',
PUBLISHED 1836-37

He stayed in various locations, including Albion Street (where he wrote 'The Old Curiosity Shop' and 'Barnaby Rudge') and Chandos Street, where he was disturbed by the noise: 'Unless it pours of rain I cannot write half-an-hour without the most excrutiating [sic] organs, fiddles, bells or glee-singers. There is a violin of the most torturing kind under the window now (time, ten in the morning) and an Italian box of music on the steps – both in full blast.'

It was in 1850 that he took Fort House, the prominent house to the centre left of

BROADSTAIRS, THE BEACH 1907  FRITH 58327T

BROADSTAIRS, A THAMES BARGE AND THE BEACH 1897    FRITH 39591

*Here, in a room looking out over the sea, Dickens completed 'David Copperfield'*

the photographs on pages 66 and 67, now re-named Bleak House in his honour; here, in a room looking out over the sea, he completed 'David Copperfield'. Betsey Trotwood's house, in the novel transposed to Dover, had its origin in Nuckell's Place (now Victoria Parade) in Broadstairs, and just as in the novel, its owner (a Miss Strong) had a strong dislike for the donkeys. Charles Dickens's son Charley, who first came here as a baby, wrote in 1894: 'Never shall I forget being carried by a wilful donkey, who evidently enjoyed the fun, across the sacred ground, and seeing my old friend making vigorously hostile demonstrations at me with the hearth-broom.'

Dickens paid a last visit to Broadstairs in 1859. He was not feeling very well, and like so many of his fellow Victorians, believed that 'nothing but sea-air and sea water will set me right.'

# Charles Dickens on Broadstairs

Written at Fort House (Bleak House), and published in 'Household Words', one of Dickens's magazines, published weekly from 1850 to 1859.

6 *Sky, sea, beach and village lie as still before as if they were sitting for a picture. It is dead low water. A ripple plays upon the ripening corn upon the cliff, as if it were faintly trying from recollection to imitate the sea … But the ocean lies winking in the sunlight like a drowsy lion—its glassy waters scarcely curve upon the shore—the fishing boats in the tiny harbour are all stranded in the mud—our two colliers (our watering place has a maritime trade employing that amount of shipping) have not an inch of water within a quarter of a mile of them, and turn, exhausted, on their sides … We have a pier – a queer old wooden pier, fortunately without the slightest pretensions to architecture, and very picturesque in consequence. Boats are hauled up upon it, ropes are coiled over it; lobster pots, nets, masts, oars, spare sails, ballast and rickety capstans make a perfect labyrinth of it … You would hardly guess which is the main street of our watering-place, but you may know it by its being always stopped up with donkey-chaises. Whenever you come here, and see harnessed donkeys eating clover out of barrows drawn completely across a narrow thoroughfare, you may be quite sure you are in our High Street.* 9

BROADSTAIRS, THE PROMENADE 1902 FRITH 48842

# John learns about Victorian holiday fun

JOHN TALKING TO LOCAL HISTORIAN
BARRIE WOOTTON

A VICTORIAN BATHING MACHINE

BLACKPOOL, FROM THE CENTRAL PIER 1896 FRITH 38845

I asked local historian Barrie Wootton what sort of resort Broadstairs was in Victorian times.

'It was middle class, very respectable. For instance, you could bathe up until lunchtime, but people of good standing didn't bathe after lunch. It was one of those things that you just didn't do. The Victorians took social etiquette very seriously, even on the beach.'

Barrie showed me his own album of Frith photographs, including the Frith photograph on page 68. 'You can see that it was still a port in Frith's day – there's a barge, and there were fishing boats here, too.' There's also a row of bathing machines. Did people use them to undress and put on their bathing costumes? 'Not at first', said Barrie. 'People used to bathe naked.' Indeed, the Victorians were not as prudish as we think – Dickens wrote to a friend about the nude bathers: 'I have seen ladies and gentlemen walking upon the earth in slippers of buff, and pickling themselves in the sea in complete suits of the same'. Barrie explained to me that costumes came later: 'Knitted ones', he said. 'And in those days people believed that just setting foot in the sea was good for you. Holidaymakers spent most of their time next to the water.'

Thanks to the railways, in Victorian times the working classes could manage to get away for their holidays. The seaside was the favourite place to go, and the most successful seaside resort of all was Blackpool (left), a magnet for workers from all over the industrial north.

Lancashire mill owners used to close their factories for a week every year to service the machinery; these weeks became known as Wakes Weeks. Each town would close its factories for a different week, so that a steady stream of visitors came to Blackpool throughout the summer to enjoy the amusements. Other seaside resorts also grew in popularity at this time, and beach entertainers like minstrels and pierrots were popular features – such as those seen on the beach at Weymouth in Dorset in the photograph below.

I wondered what amusements there were at Broadstairs. 'Plenty of entertainments on the beach', said Barrie. 'There were people doing magic tricks, there was singing and dancing – and in the 1890s they even managed to get a grand piano down on to the sands.'

Barrie pointed out the house above the bay where Dickens used to stay, Fort House in his time, re-named Bleak House in his honour. 'Dickens was virtually anonymous when he first came here', Barrie told me. 'He'd sit in the Tartar Frigate Inn (right) and listen to what people said and watch what they did – it was all material for his writing.

'But when the railways brought so many hundreds of people here, rather than the select few, it got too busy and noisy for him.'

Dickens's last visit to Broadstairs was in 1859, but Broadstairs will always keep his memory green.

BLACKPOOL, BATHING MACHINES 1890
FRITH 22883X

BROADSTAIRS, THE TARTAR FRIGATE
TODAY

WEYMOUTH, A BEACH SHOW 1899   FRITH 43853X

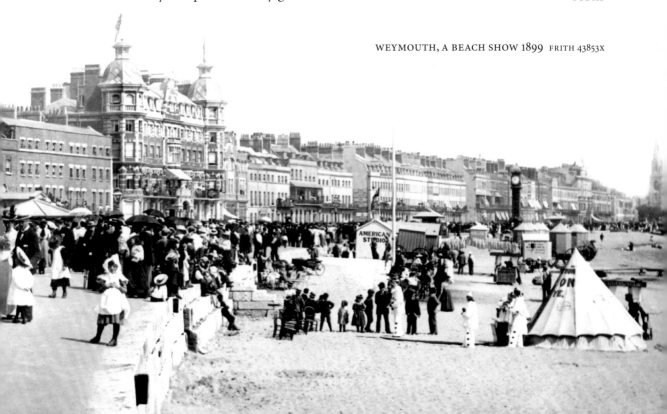

# Charles Dickens at Fort House

Bleak House at Broadstairs was called Fort House in Dickens's time; he discovered the house by chance when he was out walking, and he often made it his summer home. Re-named Bleak House in his honour, it was built for the captain of the fort in 1816, during the Napoleonic Wars, but the crenellations date from 1901, when the house was extended.

The house has been lovingly restored by Richard and Jackie Hilton, who run it as a small hotel. Richard has always been a Dickens fan, and is delighted that his work continues to reach people today through films and television. He and Jackie are proud and pleased that some of Dickens's furniture and effects are still in the house; they have set up a Dickens Museum here, and they have kept Dickens's study just as it was in his time.

RICHARD AND JACKIE, BLEAK HOUSE, 2011

Dickens's desk stands where it always did, in the window so that he had a wonderful view of the sea. Richard points out that the desk and chair are set on a platform: 'Dickens wasn't very tall, only about 5 foot 8 inches, and he really wanted to see the view.' It was at this desk that he completed 'David Copperfield'. 'Visitors always exclaim: "I can't believe I'm sitting in the chair where Dickens wrote"'.

On Dickens's desk is a copy of what he wrote here: 'I am in a favourite house of mine, perched by itself on the top of a cliff with the green corn growing all about it and the lark singing invisible all day long. The freshness of the sea and the associations of the place have set me to work with great vigour.'

## JOHN'S PHOTOGRAPH

*Broadstairs is now linked with Charles Dickens for ever, so I wanted my photograph to show the two people who are preserving his legacy.*

# A Guiding Light for Mariners

BROADSTAIRS, NORTH FORELAND LIGHTHOUSE 1894 FRITH 34192

*'The North Foreland Lighthouse stands at the most easterly point in Kent. Some of the scenes in the Frith photographs look very different from the way they look today, but the view in this Frith photograph of the lighthouse looks almost exactly the same.'*

*⁶The first idea of a lighthouse is the candle in the cottage window, guiding the husband across the water.⁹*

MICHAEL FARADAY, 1791-1867

For centuries it was beacon fires on a headland or hilltop that warned shipping of a dangerous stretch of coast. Lambarde, a Kent historian writing in the 16th century, says of the lights shown along the coast that 'before the time of Edward III, they were made of great stacks of wood; but about the eleventh yeare of his raigne it was ordained that in our shyre [Kent] they should be high standards with their pitchpots'. Since raising the height of the fire made it more easily seen, a torch on the end of a long pole, as Lambarde says, or a fire on a platform led to the idea of a permanent lighthouse.

The earliest lighthouses in this country were built by the Romans, and in Kent you can see what remains of a Roman lighthouse at Dover Castle (below right). Another early lighthouse is Smeaton's

GODREVY ISLAND, THE LIGHT-
HOUSE 1890  FRITH 24195

DOVER, ST MARY IN CASTRO CHURCH AND PHAROS c1874  FRITH 7081

Tower (below), the first stone lighthouse (after Roman times), built in 1759 on the Eddystone reef off the south Devon coast and since moved to the Hoe in Plymouth. Its light consisted of just 24 candles; a lighthouse today will have a light equivalent to several million!

Many of the lighthouses round our coasts were skilfully constructed by Victorian engineers, but the history of the North Foreland Lighthouse goes a long way further back in time. It is said that there was some sort of permanent beacon here in 1499, and the lighthouse was first built in the 17th century.

Why was it recognised so early that this stretch of coast badly needed a lighthouse? The North Foreland is the most easterly point in Kent, a chalk headland jutting out at the point where the English Channel becomes the North Sea and where busy shipping routes meet and cross. Just six miles out from the headland lies the deadly Goodwin Sands, a treacherous sandbank ten miles long. Over the centuries it has wrecked thousands of ships and claimed the lives of thousands of people, despite the presence of the lighthouse.

In 1703, for instance, this area became the scene of one of the greatest disasters in British shipping history. On 19 November severe hurricane-force winds and tremendous storms began to batter the southern coastline of England. By 23 November the weather had calmed down, but numerous buildings had been destroyed and hundreds of ships had been wrecked or blown ashore along the coast. Many people believed the tremendous storm was over, but in fact they were now in the eye of a major hurricane. When the hurricane finally subsided, the devastation was unbelievable.

TREVOSE HEAD,
THE LIGHTHOUSE 1894
FRITH 33573A

PLYMOUTH,
THE HOE AND
SMEATON'S TOWER
1913
FRITH 65978T

The coastline was a mass of wreckage and bodies. The entrances to the harbours were completely blocked with ships floating upside down. Out of the 160 ships known to have anchored around the Goodwin Sands, only 70 were salvageable, and just 10 were in reasonable condition. A total of 1,334 mariners had been drowned.

An early Victorian writer wrote this appreciation of the North Foreland Light in 'Old Humphrey's Country Strolls' (1846): 'The different lamps which illuminate it by night have behind them large brass reflectors, lined with silver, kept beautifully bright. The reflected rays mingle together, so as to form, at a distance, one concentrated blaze of light, intense and beautiful. The erection is of squared flints, and more than sixty feet high, surmounted by the lantern, whose light may be seen at a distance of thirty miles. Who shall say how many a mariner owes his life to its friendly warnings! The vessels that are wrecked through the want of a light-house are recorded, but there is no record of the greater number which, no doubt, lighthouses have saved.' Old Humphrey was also inspired to pen the following lines:

'I love the light that streams afar to save
The storm-tossed seaman from the whelming wave;
The ocean-beacon and the river-ranger,
That lures from evil, and that warns from danger.'

## The Ghost Ship of the Goodwin Sands

One of the thousands of shipwrecks caused by the treacherous sandbank of the Goodwin Sands was that of the 'Lady Lovibond' in February 1748. According to legend, the first mate deliberately steered the ship onto the sandbank in a fit of jealous rage because the captain had brought his new bride on board, with whom he was also in love.

The 'Lady Lovibond' is said to reappear as a ghost ship near the Goodwin Sands every 50 years from the date it was wrecked. The first sighting of the phantom ship, in 1798, was reported by two separate vessels. A sighting in 1848 seemed so real that a lifeboat was sent out to look for survivors; she was seen again in 1898. She appeared punctually again in 1948, when a ship's captain described the vessel as having an eerie green glow. However, there was no reported sighting when she was next due, in 1998.

# John climbs the North Foreland lighthouse

*A light in
the darkness
guiding the
weary
seafarer
home*

JOHN WITH
GERRY DOUGLAS-
SHERWOOD

We all love lighthouses. They are symbols of reassurance and safety, a light in the darkness guiding the weary seafarer home. So I was looking forward to meeting lighthouse keeper Gerry Douglas-Sherwood, who knows the North Foreland lighthouse well.

We were both struck by how little changed the lighthouse is today compared to how it was in the Frith photograph. 'But up to the 19th century the lighthouse was only as high as the first level,' Gerry told me. 'On the top was a platform where a coal fire was kept alight. We must remember that in those early days the coast was comparatively dark – there were no streetlights or any ambient light at all. So a small light from a coal fire would have been visible from far away.'

I wondered if the lighthouse was still working today. 'Yes, 24 hours a day', said Jerry. 'It's an old building, but a modern light – wonderful continuity. It was the last lighthouse to be automated, the very last in the country, and after that there were no keepers left in Britain – it was the end of an era.'

That must have had quite an effect on Gerry, I thought. 'It did, because I was here for three years as Principal Keeper. I loved it! Imagine how it felt coming here – it was like a palace. This was one of my favourite stations, no doubt about it.'

A BIRD'S-EYE VIEW OF THE LIGHTHOUSE LOOKING DOWN TO THE GROUND FLOOR

GERRY DOUGLAS-SHERWOOD SHOWS JOHN THE LIGHTHOUSE LANTERN

When we went inside the lighthouse, we could see where the top of the first lighthouse came up to. 'The platform was about 40 feet from the ground', said Gerry, 'and the keeper hauled the coal up to a large brazier which he kept charged continuously. Imagine all the dust and ash coming through the windows. He probably had his wife and family living here with him, and they wouldn't have liked that.'

We looked at the GPS monitoring system that has replaced the keeper. Gerry told me that this wasn't the first sophisticated technology to be housed here: 'During the Second World War the light was usually extinguished, unless a large convoy was passing. But there was important equipment working here, a radar jamming facility to stop the Germans finding out what we were up to.'

When we went up to the top of the lighthouse to look at the lantern, I was amazed to find out that the lens was the same one that had been here at the time of the Frith photograph. 'The lens dates from the 1860s', said Gerry, 'and it's been adapted since over the years. In Frith's day the light would have been a multi-wick oil burner.' We could see lots of ships. 'It's always busy here. The North Foreland light is an important marker for the turning point for vessels coming in and out of the Thames, through the Dover straits going up to north Europe, and sailing up the northeast coast to Scandinavia.'

Why are we Britons so fascinated by lighthouses? 'Well,' said Gerry, 'we're a maritime nation. And even today, when we've got GPS navigation accurate to a few feet, there's still a need for visual navigation aids. A lighthouse is iconic, designed to be highly visible.'

## Dickens, Wilkie Collins and their play 'The Lighthouse'

Wilkie Collins, the writer of un-put-downable mystery novels, first met the author Charles Dickens in 1851, when he was an untried journalist and Dickens was already established as a major novelist. Dickens was passionate about amateur theatricals, and a mutual friend recruited Collins to Dickens's theatre company for a play to be performed before the Queen. This was the beginning of a friendship and working relationship that lasted until Dickens's death in 1870. They went on holiday together, Collins contributed stories and novels to Dickens's magazines, and they wrote, acted in and produced plays together.

In 1855 Collins sent 'The Lighthouse', a melodrama, to Dickens, who enthusiastically took over the production. Dickens played the head lightkeeper, and other parts were taken by Collins, friends and family members. Later, in 1857, it ran for three months in a professional production, and it was also put on in New York.

The play was set in the Eddystone Lighthouse off the south Devon coast, but could Dickens's enthusiasm for 'The Lighthouse' have been caused by a visit to the North Foreland lighthouse made during one of his many holidays on the Kent coast? It's not impossible!

## John's photograph of the North Foreland Lighthouse

THE OLD LIGHTHOUSE, 2011

*I wanted to capture the essence of how the North Foreland Lighthouse looks today;*
*my aim was an exciting, dramatic picture of the last lighthouse to be automated.*
*The keepers' cottages are now used as holiday lets, the rear windows blocked.*

# Francis Frith: Pioneer Photographer and Devoted Family Man

REIGATE, FRANCIS FRITH AT BRIGHTLANDS c1885 FRITH R20311

'This photograph would have been very personal to Francis Frith, because the great man himself is in it. It shows Frith relaxing in the garden of his house, Brightlands, in Reigate, Surrey, the town where he set up both his photography business and his family home.'

# 'I reckon the real substance of my life to date from my wedding day'

FRANCIS FRITH

MARY ANN FRITH c1865
FRITH A001154

Francis Frith was not only a highly successful photographer, he was also a devoted family man.

He wrote: 'A life without love, and domestic joys and cares and the discipline of child-life is sorrowfully incomplete. Marriage gives solidity, purpose and energy to life … I reckon the real substance of my life to date from my wedding day'.

In the intervals between his expeditions to Egypt and Palestine, Francis Frith had met and fallen in love with Mary Ann Rosling, the daughter of a prominent Reigate family. She was the sister of Alfred Rosling, the first treasurer of the Liverpool Photographic Society, of which Frith was a founder member; this is presumably how the couple first met. After Frith returned to England from Egypt in 1860 he and Mary Ann married, and settled in Reigate, her home town, in a large Victorian house called Brightlands.

REIGATE, HIGH STREET AND TOWN
HALL 1890 FRITH 26016

Reigate in Surrey, at the foot of the North Downs, was the ideal location for Francis Frith's new photographic enterprise, being just twenty miles south of London and with excellent rail links. Its leafy streets were surrounded by glorious countryside, and Frith and his family would have enjoyed many breezy walks across the downs. The photograph of Reigate (centre right) shows the old Town Hall, built in 1728.

REIGATE,
BRIGHTLANDS c1885
FRITH R20312

# Mary Ann's Diary and Frith Family Holidays

FRANCIS FRITH
AND FAMILY c1875
FRITH A001156

Mary Ann kept a diary, chronicling the happy times the Frith family shared. At Ilfracombe in North Devon in February 1872 she writes: 'The dear Papa is at Lynton on a photo journey and I and all my children at Northcote Villa.' Francis Frith would be climbing the steep hill between Lynmouth and Lynton, capturing the spectacular cliff scenery of Countisbury and panoramas of the Bristol Channel.

Some of the holiday breaks extended into several months. Here we have Mary Ann's account of a stay at Poole in Dorset in 1874: 'We came to this charming place on the 1st Aug last year on dear little Mabel's account [Mabel suffered from delicate health] and are staying here through the winter – and now we have all our seven children together. We try to make their holidays happy and on the day after Christmas day we had a Christmas tree, and how Susie's beautiful round brown eyes opened in wonder and delight at the light! She forgot to raise her little hand and shout "hurrah" as she had been taught.'

FRANCIS FRITH
AND FAMILY c1885
FRITH F6501

*Their lives together may give the impression of constant happiness. However, illness was a constant threat in Victorian times, and the young children of a family were always particularly vulnerable.*

The weeks just prior to a family holiday at Grange-over-Sands in what is now Cumbria in 1878 must have proved a worrying time for the young mother: 'Our 4 youngest children commenced with whooping cough in May – dear Mabel was very ill with pleurisy and inflammation. She was in bed 12 days and kept upstairs 3 weeks – we were almost afraid she would not be able to take the long journey North, but a week of fine hot weather did her so much good, that all of us (except the two boys at Hitchin) with Sarah Snook, Cook & Annie Kelly, left Reigate at 8 o'clock on the morning of Friday the 28th June 1878 and were favoured to reach Grange in safety; the dear children bore the heat and fatigue of the day bravely. We were all very much struck with the beauty of Grange and its surroundings.'

Francis Frith and his wife had also suffered a terrible loss during the previous year – their beloved son Clement had died. Memories of it were still haunting Mary Ann during the Grange-over-Sands holiday. 'Sunday evening 14.7.1878 – I am sitting alone this evening, 5 of our children in bed and the dear Father in Lancaster [Francis Frith was at a meeting]. Since I last wrote in this book it has pleased God to take our youngest Darling, dearest Clement, to Himself, he left us on the 3rd April 1877.'

Even for a prosperous Victorian middle-class family, tragedy was never far away.

> ❛*Since I last wrote in this book it has pleased God to take our youngest Darling, dearest Clement, to Himself …*❜

# John visits the site of the Frith family home

Francis Frith was a local celebrity in Reigate. What sort of man was he? What drove him? To find out I talked to local historian Sean Hawkins, an expert on Frith. 'Frith was an interesting man', Sean told me, 'a Quaker, strong-minded, and very successful in business. By the time he was 33 he had made about £200,000.' That sounded like a lot of money, I thought. 'Yes', said Sean, 'he'd be a multi-millionaire today. Then his passion, photography, took him to the Holy Land and Egypt.'

JOHN WITH SEAN HAWKINS AT THE SITE OF FRITH'S HOME, BRIGHTLANDS

'So Frith's first commercial photographs were taken abroad, then?' I asked. 'The pioneering photographs he took in Egypt and Palestine established his reputation', answered Sean. 'He returned to England in 1860 to marry Mary Ann Rosling, a Reigate girl, and to start his new project here – an epic photographic record of Britain.'

I wondered what kind of photographs Frith and his team were taking. Sean showed me a Victorian album with photographs pasted inside. 'They took popular subjects, subjects that excursionists would like – excursions were the great thing in the 1860s. The railways had opened up Britain for holidaymakers, who wanted souvenir pictures of the places they visited. They would paste the pictures in an album like this one.' Then Sean showed me another album, a book ready-printed with photographs. 'Later on in the 19th century people could buy souvenir books like these, which were sold in stationers' and gift shops. They were very popular indeed.' And was Frith's company a large one? 'Initially', said Sean, 'Frith took all the photographs himself, but as success came he hired more and more people, and set about establishing a photographic business. Within a few years over 2000 shops were selling his prints all over Britain. Frith & Co became one of the largest photographic companies in the world.'

FRITH PHOTOGRAPHS IN A SHOP DISPLAY CASE
FRITH A001157

I showed Sean the main photograph of Frith's house, Brightlands (page 81). 'For a man who was responsible for so many photographs', said Sean, 'there are very few of Frith himself, which makes this one special. The house isn't there any more, but I can show you evidence of it.' We drove to Brightlands Road, named after Frith's house, where Sean led me to a 20th-century house. 'This is obviously not Frith's home', said Sean, 'it was built around 1970. But we do know that this is the site of Brightlands.'

Caroline Patterson, who lives here now, kindly showed us what remains of Frith's home. She led us out into the back garden, where there is a swimming pool – a touch of California, I thought! But Caroline told us that the pool is older than it looks. 'This pool is all that's left of Frith's house', she said. 'It was built in the foundations of the cellar, and in fact the outline of the bay windows forms the side of the pool. We always wondered why it was this unusual shape …' 'And now we know that Frith himself walked into this swimming pool!' I said.

Sean told us that Brightlands was owned by Mary Ann's parents, and that her father was very careful to make sure that it stayed that way. He showed us an old document. 'Here's the marriage settlement made between Francis Frith and Mary Ann Rosling. The document was drawn up by Mary Ann's father, and in it he settles the house on Mary Ann Frith for the term of her life only – he didn't want the house to go outside the Rosling family.'

I was very pleased to have the chance to photograph what remains of Francis Frith's house as it is today, and I recruited Caroline to help me.

## JOHN'S PHOTOGRAPH AT BRIGHTLANDS

AT HOME IN REIGATE, 2011

*My photograph captures the modern house in the spot where Brightlands once stood, and the swimming pool which reveals the original outline of Frith's home. Caroline Patterson lives here now, and with her help I've tried to make my photograph as close to Frith's as I possibly can.*

# From Windmill to Place of Worship

REIGATE, HEATH MILL 1894    FRITH 34164

*'This Frith photograph shows the Reigate Heath Windmill in Surrey. I was curious to find out why the Frith team had taken it – it's beautiful, but a windmill was still a relatively common sight in Victorian times. And as I wanted to take my own photograph of it, I needed to find out how to take one just as effective as the Frith one is.'*

Windmills are first documented in Britain around the 12th century, and by the 14th century technology had advanced sufficiently to enable powerful and reliable mills to be constructed. Millwrights were skilled craftsmen, and the windmills they built tended to vary regionally in design and constructional detail owing to the favourite ideas of local millwrights.

Reigate Heath Mill is a post mill, built around 1765. Post mills were named after the massive upright post which supported the mill's main structure, or 'body', and enabled the body to rotate so that the sails could face the direction of the wind. The post was held by large horizontal beams, or crosstrees, usually two cross bars at right angles with four quarter bars between them. In the early days of millwrighting the crosstrees rested on the ground, or were even buried, but they rotted all too easily; in later years the crosstrees were set on brick piers.

Inside the body of the mill was the milling machinery. On the shaft that held the sails (the windshaft) was a large gear wheel called a brake wheel, or a head wheel, and a spur wheel that transferred power to a gear wheel at right angles to it, the wallower. From this the stone nut, a smaller gear wheel, turned the millstones. Larger mills could accommodate more than one pair of stones, each pair driven by its own stone nut. Reigate Heath Mill originally had four common sails, which were cloth sails attached to wooden frames and manually adjusted by the miller according to the amount of wind. They were carried on a wooden windshaft. By the late 19th century, when it was last worked, the mill had four double patent sails – these were sails that could be automatically adjusted by a system of weights. The sails were carried on a cast iron windshaft, and the spur wheel and the wallower were made of cast iron too. There were two pairs of millstones.

For maximum power to turn the stones, it was necessary for the sails to point into the wind. On early mills, such as Reigate Heath Mill, this was done by means of a tailpole, a long lever attached to the body of the mill. The tailpole enabled the miller to push the mill around its axis; wind direction was often indicated by a small vane, mounted high up at the rear of the mill. The problem with manual adjustment was that it interrupted work inside the mill and the serving of customers. This led to the invention of an automatic system for keeping mills pointing into the wind. A small wind wheel was mounted at right angles to the airflow high up at the rear of the mill. This detected when the mill was coming out of the wind; it started rotating, and drove the mill back into the wind by a system of spindles and gears, which were attached to wheels running near the ground.

Why did windmills decline and eventually die? Wind may be an infinite power source, but it is unreliable. To catch the wind, windmills were often built in remote inconvenient places, either in flatlands or on hilltops and ridges, so access roads could be long and steep or muddy, and only light loads could be carried by wheeled carts on primitive roads. Pack animals could carry even less. The invention of the steam engine and the advent of roller mills, which were more efficient at producing flour than millstones, led to the rapid decline of country milling after 1900. Some traditional windmills installed small roller mills to try to keep up with the new technology, but they were no match for the much bigger roller mills in towns and ports.

# John discovers the unique windmill chapel

JOHN MEETS
THE REVEREND
DAVID BULL INSIDE
THE REIGATE HEATH
WINDMILL

Reigate Heath Windmill is beautifully preserved, and I was longing to find out why it had survived. I met the Reverend David Bull at the mill to find out more. When we went inside, I was amazed to see that the lovely old round interior with its massive beams had been converted into a chapel.

'It's the only windmill chapel in the country', David told me. I wanted to know why it had stopped being used as a windmill. 'By about 1870 it wasn't needed any more, and it was falling into disrepair. The last miller's son was a religious man, and he had a relative who was in the ministry, so he decided that the mill should be saved and turned into a chapel so that his relative could come and exercise his ministry here'. 'And it's still a chapel?' I asked. 'Yes indeed, we have a service here every month', David said.

I could still see the old mill mechanism, and I wanted to know more about the big timbers criss-crossing the room. 'Those are all the original beams', David told me. 'They anchor the mill to the ground, and support the upper section high above us. That would have rotated so that the sails of the windmill could be turned to the wind. This big central post takes the whole weight of the upper section of the mill.'

THE INTERIOR OF
THE REIGATE HEATH
WINDMILL

'Don't the beams make it hard for your congregation?' I asked. 'I see you've put up a 'Beware of the beams' sign.' 'They do!' said David. 'We sometimes wonder if we should hand out crash helmets! Before every hymn I warn the congregation not to hit their heads as they stand up to sing.'

I wondered when the chapel had been consecrated. 'On 14 September 1880. We still have here the original sermon that was preached on that day by the Reverend J Wilson Pickance. Here's one part of it that sounds quite contemporary: "People are now much busier than they were 300 years ago. Railways and telegraphs enable us to travel and hear news in so short a space of time that our forefathers would not have thought such results could be obtained. But our whole life seems to be spent in a hurry. Men are hurrying after business, pleasure, riches, fame, and they seek short cuts for everything, and this loss of calmness is in some sense bad for the spiritual life."' That struck me as good sound sense. My father was a vicar, and I can imagine him agreeing with it.

My meeting with David had helped me to realise why the photograph on page 86 had been taken. Frith and his team would have known that the mill had a new use as a chapel – then as now, it must have been highly unusual, and very interesting. That meant that the Frith company could sell a lot of souvenir photographs and, later, postcards of it.

THE OLD WINDMILL MECHANISM TIMBERS ARE STILL PART OF THE CHAPEL ROOF

REIGATE, THE HEATH, GOLF HOUSE AND MILL CHURCH 1906
FRITH 55370X

# Some Expert Advice on Photography

At this point in my quest to visit the places where Francis Frith and his team had taken photographs and to take photographs of my own, I felt that I needed some expert advice. I was delighted that John Gall of the Reigate Photographic Society came to the windmill to give me some tips.

JOHN TALKS TO PHOTOGRAPHER JOHN GALL

'What you're looking for', he advised, 'is something to tell a story, something of interest. From where we're standing there's a silhouette of the windmill against the sky, or we could go round to the other side and capture the evening light shining on the mill – that might make a more interesting photograph, perhaps.'

'So lighting is very important', I said. 'But what else? We need people in the picture, don't we?' 'Yes, people give interest to a photograph, but they're not essential. A person does give a human dimension, of course, but any strong point of interest can be enough.'

I showed John the Frith photograph (page 86) and asked him what we could gather from it about the skill of the photographer. 'He's leading you through from left to right', John explained, 'taking you from the bottom left-hand edge via the little girl to the key points of interest, the mill and the house. Also, he's used a composition technique that you could copy. If you mentally divide the photograph into thirds, horizontally and vertically, you can see that he's placed key elements on the intersections of the thirds – in this case, the house and the girl. The Frith photographer was telling a story. When we look at photographs, we need to try to get into the mind of the photographer, so here we need to ask ourselves what he was actually telling us, and what the important things in his story are.'

So great photography is about looking for the images that capture a real story, and that's exactly what Francis Frith and his team set out to do. I wanted to do the same. I resolved to think hard about everything that John told me, and to try to draw the viewer into some really interesting pictures of my own.

# John's photograph of Reigate Heath Mill

*We will never know who the little girl is in the Frith photograph on page 86, but David Bull has agreed to be the human interest in mine as the local curate and the man preserving the windmill's legacy. I've also tried to follow John Gall's advice; I've tried to draw the viewer in up the path, past David and on to the windmill – and he's a third of the way in from the right, and the mill's a third of the way in from the left. So here David is, standing in front of a unique place of worship.*

THE MILL CHURCH
AND CURATE, 2011

# From Redundant Port to Smugglers' Paradise

*'The wonderful Frith photograph of Rye in Sussex on the previous pages shows a two-masted sailing ship, the 'Friendship', sitting in the harbour. I think it's a perfect testament to this little town's colourful history, both as a major trading port, and in the 18th and 19th centuries as a renowned haven for smuggling.'*

RYE, THE RIVER
ROTHER AND ROMNEY
MARSHES c1955
FRITH R77102

RYE, MERMAID
STREET 1888
FRITH 21161

Looking at the fascinating photograph on the previous pages, you might well think that Rye was a seaside town with a busy harbour. In fact, the photograph shows Rye at a time when it was nearing the end of its maritime importance.

Rye, at the far eastern end of Sussex, stands on a hill at the end of the ridge between the Tillingham and Rother rivers where the county peters out into the flat sheep-grazed Romney Marshes. It was an important port and a walled town in the medieval period, when the sea surrounded the ridge on three sides; it became one of the Cinque Ports in the 1190s. The harbour lay at the foot of the town's cobbled streets (see photograph below). However, by Elizabethan times the sea had retreated as the estuaries silted up. In response, in the 18th century Rye Harbour was developed about two miles downstream on the Rother. The sea retreated further, so this harbour too became redundant. Rye's maritime trading declined all the more as the sea retreated.

It had always been difficult to get to Rye by land over the marshes, so from the 17th century onwards, as the harbour started to disappear under layers of silt, the town became more and more isolated, and its inhabitants had to look for a living other than the thriving maritime trade they had enjoyed before. The answer was smuggling, which soon took over Rye's economy. The big cargo ships could no longer reach the town, but smaller smugglers' vessels could easily sail up the river and unload their contraband virtually on the doorstep.

Thanks to the swingeing taxes imposed on imported goods such as wine, brandy, tobacco and silks, and export taxes on wool (an important commodity in Rye, for vast flocks of sheep grazed on Romney Marsh), smuggling was a vastly profitable trade. It grew to astonishing proportions all along Britain's coasts. For instance, in North Yorkshire ports like Whitby, housewives would go to market wearing loose-fitting garments, and return with buttons bursting and clothes stuffed with contraband. In Great Yarmouth, a newcomer was horrified at the goings on. 'Smuggling!' he cried, 'oh, the shame of it! Is there no magistrate to hand? Is there no clergyman? No minister?' His cries were silenced when one of the locals pointed to the vicar assisting the gang.

In Rye, one of the most popular meeting places for smugglers was the Mermaid Inn (see photograph above). Its ancient vaulted cellars were used as a store for contraband, and the Hawkhurst Gang, the most notorious smugglers in this area, regularly met here and scandalised the townsfolk by

*'Smuggling! Oh, the shame of it!'*

openly displaying their cocked pistols on the table. The gang intimidated the Rye locals by rowdily carousing and even firing their pistols at the ceiling. They were involved in one of the most famous smuggling incidents in British history, which occurred at the Custom House at Poole in Dorset in 1747 (see photograph opposite). Thirty smugglers, including members of the Hawkhurst Gang, rode all the way from Kent and Sussex to 'rescue' a cargo of tea that had been seized by the revenue men. The smugglers tied up Poole's night watchman,

ABOVE:
GOUDHURST,
THE VILLAGE
AND ST MARY'S
CHURCH 1901
FRITH 46378

BELOW: RYE,
WEST STREET 1888
FRITH 21159

broke into the Custom House, and then rode off in triumph with their cargo. The smugglers were eventually rounded up, and some were hanged for the break-in, as well as for the murders of potential witnesses at their trial.

The Hawkhurst Gang finally came to a sticky end in a fight with local militia beside the church in Goudhurst in Kent (see left). The Star and Eagle Inn in Goudhurst was a centre for the gang's smuggling trade, and was connected to the village church by a secret underground passage. Eventually the village had enough of the gang's activities, and under the leadership of Colonel Sturt the Goudhurst Militia fought the 100-strong smuggling gang in a pitched battle in the churchyard on 20 April 1747, while the villagers sought sanctuary within the church's sandstone walls. Known as the Battle of Goudhurst, this resulted in the deaths of three of the smugglers, including one of their leaders, and brought the activities of the Hawkhurst Gang to an end.

Smuggling continued to flourish in Rye up to the first half of the 19th century. Then, along with the policy of Free Trade, came the abolition of most customs duties. This, together with the reform of the customs service in 1853 to provide a more efficient force, caused the smuggling trade to wither, and Rye again had to find a new way to make a living.

It was tourism that was to provide Rye with its continuing prosperity. The town has kept its grid-like medieval plan almost intact, and its streets lined with beautiful old buildings (see photograph left), many of them timber-framed and dating from the 15th to the 17th centuries, were a magnet for Victorian excursionists, and still attract thousands of tourists today.

# A hotbed of crime! John explores the cellars and attics used by Rye's smugglers

JOHN IS SHOWN
THE STREETS OF
RYE BY JANE
FRASER HAY

I was longing to explore this fascinating little town, so I was delighted to meet local historian and guide Jane Fraser Hay. We strolled through the beautiful cobbled streets as she told me Rye's story.

The first thing I wanted to understand was why the main Frith photograph (pages 92-93) depicted what looks like an important port. Rye today doesn't have that kind of importance. 'By the end of the 19th century, when that photograph was taken, 'Jane told me, 'things were getting quite bad for Rye as a port. Some time before, the main trading area had been moved out nearer the sea, so what you are looking at in the Frith photograph is the last days of Rye as an important trading centre.'

I wondered what had gone wrong. 'The sea giveth, and it taketh away, I'm afraid!' said Jane. 'It receded and left us with very limited harbour facilities here.' 'So', I said, 'the story of Rye is the story of the disappearing sea. How far away is it now?' 'About two-and-a half miles away. That meant that Rye had to find another way of making a living.'

THE ATTICS
WHERE RYE'S
SMUGGLERS
STORED THEIR
CONTRABAND

I guessed that now I was going to hear about smuggling. 'You're right', said Jane. 'By the end of the 1700s all sorts of valuable commodities were coming here, not just brandy and tobacco, but spices from Java and tea from China – exotic goods that had travelled vast distances.' I was intrigued to hear that dear old genteel Rye had been a hotbed of crime. I wondered how many people in the town had been involved. 'We don't know the exact numbers, obviously', said Jane, 'because it was a hugely secret trade. But I imagine that quite a number of townsfolk wouldn't have had any conscience about being involved.'

So what would they do with the smuggled goods? 'First of all they would hide them', said Jane. She pointed up at the rows of dormer windows in the picturesque tiled roofs above us. 'All those attics were a safe place, and also at that date they would not have been divided between the houses, so they

*We rolled up the rug and opened a heavy trapdoor. 'Aladdin's cave!' I exclaimed*

would make a run for people trying to escape from the Revenue men. They could go halfway round the town and come down the stairs in a completely different area. The Revenue were after the smugglers all the time, but they were very much in the minority.'

Rye's smugglers, or owlers, as they were known, would store their hoards not only in the attics, but also in the old cellars under the houses. One of these cellars survives today in the White Vine House Hotel, and its owner, Javed Khan, kindly offered to let me have a look. He led me into the dining room: 'Under here is a cellar which dates from about 1340'. I was amazed to hear how old it was, because the house doesn't look that ancient. 'Yes, it's very old', said Javed. 'We don't know if the building that used to be above it was demolished to make way for the present building, or if the French burnt it down – they were raiding often in the medieval period.'

We opened a heavy trapdoor. 'Aladdin's cave!' I exclaimed. 'It's ideal for storage', said Javed, 'or for hiding things.' Was he saying that smugglers used this cellar? 'We don't know for sure', he replied. 'Well', I said, 'let's imagine that we're smugglers going down to hide our wine.' I made Javed go first down the steep spiral stone stair. Our torches lit up a huge, spectacular stone-lined, stone-vaulted cellar, complete with cobwebs and that authentic cellar smell.

I wanted to know if there were many cellars like this in Rye. 'We think there are about 12 or 13', said Javed. 'This is one of the better ones in terms

JOHN AND JAVED
KHAN INVESTIGATE
THE WHITE VINE
HOUSE HOTEL
CELLARS

of age and condition. You can almost see smugglers making their plans here and counting their loot.' He led me through a narrow passage and showed me a long chute. 'This is bricked up now', he told me, 'but we think it would have come up in the High Street. Barrels, other goods, even contraband, maybe, could have been slid down and stored here.' It was easy to imagine all the black market booty that could once have packed out those cavernous cellars.

Having experienced subterranean Rye, I felt it was time for a bird's-eye view. At the Heritage Centre I met its curator, Peter Cosstick, who had something spectacular to show me – a beautiful, meticulously made scale model of the town. 'We're tremendously proud of this', said Peter. 'The model shows Rye as it was in Victorian times – and the town hasn't changed much today.' I asked Peter about smuggling in Rye. 'It was rife here', he told me. 'The gangs were ruthless, and they ruled the roost. There was little law and order, and there weren't enough Revenue men to stop them. But in the 19th century Victorian values – and

JOHN WITH PETER
COSSTICK AND THE
RYE MODEL TOWN

the stopping of taxes on luxury goods – put the smugglers out of business.'

As I looked at the town model, I was struck by how many of the buildings still exist, and how attractive they were and still are. I showed Peter the main Frith photograph (pages 92-93). 'The two prominent buildings in the photograph still exist', he told me. 'The one to the top left of the picture is the Hope and Anchor pub, and the ship would have been on the river, just here on the model.' Peter had really helped me to see exactly where the Frith photograph had been taken. But we agreed that the picture was rather a sad one. 'It shows the end of an era', said Peter. 'The days of maritime trading were nearly over.'

## JOHN'S PHOTOGRAPH OF RYE

### A SAILING BOAT AT RYE HARBOUR, 2011

*Peter from Rye Heritage Centre helped me to pinpoint the exact spot from which the Frith photograph was taken, but when I got there, there were no ships in sight, so I've taken my photograph a little way away, where I found some boats. Here it is: my boat bathed in colour as the sun sets over Rye. I think the Frith picture and mine tell the same story, of a harbour on a tidal river a long way from the sea. They both have a rather sad air, perhaps. The Frith photograph shows a ship at the end of the trading era, and my boat is just a pleasure boat – Rye is no longer the important port it once was.*

# A Stalwart Defence of the Realm against Invasion by Napoleon

HYTHE, THE SCHOOL OF MUSKETRY 1890   FRITH 25890

*'This photograph shows the School of Musketry at Hythe in Kent. But when I arrived in Hythe, I was very disappointed to find that there is no trace of the school left – the site is now a supermarket car park! I hoped to find out more about the buildings, and what had happened to them. I also wanted to find out what sort of training the soldiers had here.'*

> ❝ *I want only for a favourable wind to plant the Imperial Eagle on the Tower of London* ❞

NAPOLEON BONAPARTE

JOHN MEETS
LOCAL HISTORIAN
MICHAEL GEORGE

Hythe means 'haven on the estuary'. In 1050 it was one of the original five Cinque Ports defending England from the French. Hythe flourished during the Cinque Ports era, despite raids by the French in the early 14th century. Then, like Rye's, its harbour silted up – in 1450 the harbour was abandoned. The tidal scour had increased, and shingle was being carried eastwards, to mass at Hythe and smother the entrance to the original Hythe Haven. By the time of the Spanish Armada in 1588, Hythe could no longer meet its obligations to the Cinque Ports.

Then, in the early 19th century, Hythe was to confront the French again. Local historian Michael George explains that the buildings of the School of Musketry were originally military barracks, built 200 years ago at the time of the Napoleonic Wars to house a defence force against a Napoleonic invasion. 'All my thoughts are directed towards England. I want only for a favourable wind to plant the Imperial Eagle on the Tower of London.' So said Napoleon, who had amassed a force of 200,000 troops just across the English Channel. They were waiting for the right weather conditions to sail over to the natural anchorage of Hythe Bay, the perfect place from which to land on the beaches of southern England. But the invasion never happened. Napoleon turned his attention to his campaigns in Egypt and Austria, and any plans to invade Britain were shelved for good in 1805.

Michael George describes how at the end of the Napoleonic Wars the barracks fell into disuse until 1853. At that time, the rifle had been introduced, a much more accurate weapon. Its barrel, unlike that of the musket, has spiral grooves along its inner surface which cause the projectile to spin, which increases the accuracy of the weapon. The old weapon's name, though, was retained for the training school. The troops had

ENGRAVING OF A TIRED SENTRY WITH A MUSKET FROM
THE NAPOLEONIC PERIOD

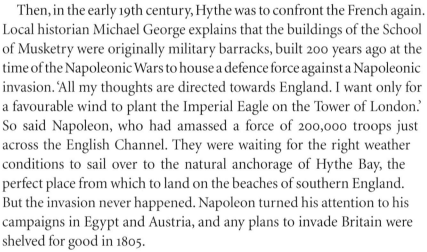

VICTORIAN
ENGRAVING SHOWING
INFANTRYMEN
DRILLING

to be instructed in how to use the new weapon. It was decided that a school was needed to train groups of soldiers, who would then go back to their regiments as instructors to train the rest of the men there.

During the Victorian period anything military was extremely popular with the general public. Michael George tells how crowds came to Hythe specifically to see the troops, to watch them on parade and being trained; it was a form of entertainment. This must be the reason why the Frith team decided to capture the school in their photograph – it would have made a popular souvenir.

In the 20th century the School of Musketry served as a training base through both world wars. In 1929 it was renamed the Small Arms School Corps, and in 1968 it was relocated from Hythe to Warminster in Wiltshire, where today it is still training the soldiers of the British Army. The original buildings in Hythe were demolished, and a supermarket car park occupies the site. All that remains of the Hythe School of Musketry today is a small plaque in the supermarket wall. It says that 88,000 soldiers were trained here between 1853 and 1968.

HYTHE,
THE SCHOOL OF
MUSKETRY 1903
FRITH 50380

HYTHE,
THE ROYAL MILITARY
CANAL 1899
FRITH 44787

*1,500 navvies and soldiers laboured with picks and shovels on the Royal Military Canal which was completed in 1809*

Another defence against the expected Napoleonic invasion was the Royal Military Canal (see photograph above), which was dug across Romney Marsh from Seabrook, near Hythe. It divides the newer part of the town from the old town with its narrow, twisting streets leading up to the medieval church. The excavated soil formed a parapet on the northern bank so that soldiers could march and be positioned without being seen by an invader from the sea. Bends in the canal allowed firing along its length. The first sod was dug in 1804.

Soon 1,500 navvies and soldiers were labouring with picks and shovels, but it was not until 1809 that the project was finally completed. By this time, having been defeated at Trafalgar, Napoleon had withdrawn his troops from the French coast, and the army had a white elephant on their hands.

To recoup what they had spent the government opened the canal for commercial and public use so that they could collect tolls. However, the coming of the railways killed most of the canal's trade, and from the 1860s the canal was sold off – Hythe bought its stretch as an amenity.

The canal briefly regained its military glory in the Second World War when it was lined with pillboxes as a defence against Hitler, but again the enemy never invaded. Today the Royal Military Canal is an SSSI (Site of Special Scientific Interest) and a Scheduled Ancient Monument; its tree-lined banks are the perfect place to wander, walk, fish or watch wildlife. Every two years Hythe stages its waterborne Venetian Fair on the Royal Military Canal, a summer carnival visited by tourists from far and wide.

# A Defence against the Might of Napoleon

The threat of invasion during the Napoleonic Wars led to the building of a chain of 103 circular forts called Martello towers along the southeast coast between 1805 and 1810. You can see a line of them along the coast in the background of the photograph of Hythe below. Named after a formidable fortification on Mortella Point, Corsica, these brick and masonry towers were massively strong. Most of them were constructed under the direction of Captain Ford and General William Twiss. Twiss also helped with the construction of the Royal Military Canal, and he is commemorated by Twiss Road, Twiss Avenue and Twiss Grove in Hythe.

Each tower contained a powder magazine, storerooms, and living accommodation – each tower was manned by one officer and 24 men. On the roof was a 24-pounder cannon with a range of 1000 yards, mounted on a pivot so that it could rotate through 360 degrees. A drainage system from the roof fed a cistern with rainwater.

HYTHE, THE PARADE, WITH A LINE OF MARTELLO TOWERS IN THE DISTANCE 1899  FRITH 44783

FOLKESTONE, MARTELLO TOWER NO 3  2004  FRITH F35709K

ALDEBURGH, MARTELLO TOWER c1950 FRITH A28021

As Napoleon never invaded, we will never know how effective the Martello towers could have been; however, they were a help to the Revenue men in hindering smuggling. A few were demolished for their masonry, and four were destroyed by the army to test their artillery. Much later, some towers were used as observation and firing platforms in the Second World War. Three of Hythe's towers were demolished in the 19th century to make room for the promenade, but one still stands on Western Parade, converted to a private house, and a handful of derelict towers stand on Hythe Ranges.

ABOV: DYMCHURCH, MARTELLO TOWER c1955  FRITH D74006

RIGHT: HASTINGS, MARTELLO TOWER RUINS c1880  FRITH H36302

# John shows his skills at firing a musket

JOHN AND HIS
INSTRUCTOR
IAN 'BULLY' BULL

*'Everyone
says, "Don't
stand next
to Bully!"'*

I think it's a little sad that the School of Musketry has been replaced by a supermarket car park, but the military tradition still continues here in Hythe. Today the town is home to firing ranges used by the Ministry of Defence, so I went to see if I could discover how the troops were and are trained. Andy Rixon, Chairman of Lydd Rifle Club, met me on the ranges. He gave me a rigorous safety briefing, and then introduced me to Ian 'Bully' Bull, who had kindly offered to give me a taste of what the cadets would have experienced at the School of Musketry.

Bully is a born teacher – and a born joker! There was a lot of banter and teasing as he equipped me with earmuffs and tinted protective goggles. I had heard that there was a long tradition of soldiering in his family. 'Yes, five generations of soldiers', said Bully. 'My son's in the army now, I was in the army, and so were my father, my grandfather, and my great-grandfather.' It's possible, then, that his great-grandfather could have been trained at the School of Musketry back in Victorian times. I felt that soldiering certainly seemed to be embedded in Bully's genes.

'We were an unlucky family, really', Bully told me. 'My great-grandfather was killed in the Boer War, my grandfather was shot up on the first day of the Somme – two wounds, one in the leg, one in the foot – and my father was taken prisoner at Singapore, so everyone says: "Don't stand next to Bully!"' 'No, you'll be all right with me, Bully', I joked. 'I'll look after you!'

PUTTING POWDER
INTO A MUSKET

The first thing Bully taught me was how to use a musket. When Napoleon's armies were preparing to attack, our soldiers were ready to defend our shores with muskets just like the one Bully handed to me. Muskets were hard to aim and not very accurate, so rather than picking out specific targets, the idea was that a large number of infantry firing at once would deliver a hail of musket balls into the enemy lines. First Bully put a ball in the muzzle of the gun and rammed it in with a wooden rod. Then he put black powder in the pan, and blew off the surplus powder. Then he told me to fire standing up. I shot the musket a number of times, and hoped I'd hit the target.

Next I was shown how to fire a more contemporary weapon. It was a civilian version of the sniper rifle used by the British Army today.

JOHN TAKES AIM AS HE FIRES
A MODERN SNIPER RIFLE

To fire it I had to lie down, set the rifle to my shoulder, and squint down telescopic sights. 'Squeeze the trigger very gently',  I was told. There was quite a recoil. After I'd shot several times, it was time to see if I was any good as a sniper. We walked up to the targets to check.

I was delighted to see that the paper target was holed in several places. 'That's very good', Bully told me. 'This big hole up at the top – you can put your finger through it. That was the Brown Bess. To have hit the target at all with a musket is quite a feat. And these hits in the black, near the centre – those are all the sniper rifle. You've done very well for a first time ever, and using a 'scope, too.'

'Will I get a medal?' I asked. 'No, a sore shoulder!' said Bully.

## JOHN'S PHOTOGRAPH AT HYTHE

MY BEST SHOT, HYTHE RANGES, 2011

*I'm very proud of my target, and I want everybody to appreciate it! So here we are – a testament to the skills of Infantryman Sergeant. I think I did rather well. The bit of this picture I like best is the big hole at the top, because that was made with a ball fired by a gun which could have been fired at the Battle of Waterloo. If the hole had been in the centre of the target, who knows? It might have got Napoleon.*

# The Victorian Theme Park that Dropped into the Sea

BLACKGANG CHINE c1883  FRITH 16445

*'This is an unusual photograph, because at a first glance it doesn't look very interesting. Here's a group of rather nondescript buildings by the seashore; it's not clear what their purpose is, and it's not clear where the path is going. But this was a major Victorian tourist attraction, and it still is a big attraction today, owned by the same family that first created it. We are on the Isle of Wight, and this is Blackgang Chine.'*

## The population soared, and towns enjoyed a building boom

QUEEN VICTORIA
c1890  FRITH F6505

The expansion of the railways, the advent of regular holidays and Bank Holidays for the workers, increased prosperity – all of these things contributed to the rise of the seaside holiday and the seaside resort in Victorian times, especially after the medical profession decreed that sea bathing and sea air were beneficial to health. Promenades, piers, amusement parks, boating ponds, bandstands – the Victorian tripper lapped them up and asked for more, and happily sent photographs of local scenes to their friends to prove what a good time they were having. As the 19th century wore on the Frith company took more and more photographs to satisfy the holidaymakers' hunger for souvenirs.

The Isle of Wight, with its cliffs, beaches and glorious scenery, and only half a day away from the smog and grime of London, was a favourite destination, and especially popular because Queen Victoria was often in residence here at Osborne House. As heir to the throne the Princess Alexandrina Victoria had spent holidays on the island, playing on the seashore at East Cowes, and gathering seaweeds and shells in much the same way as any other little girl at the seaside. She never forgot the experience. After her marriage to Prince Albert she bought Osborne House, using it as her favoured winter retreat until the very end of her life, dying there in January 1901.

The consequences of this royal patronage changed the way of life on the island for ever. Fishing villages became resorts. The population soared, and towns enjoyed a building boom as houses and hotels were built to cater for the increased demand for homes and holiday accommodation. The locals, who might otherwise have found employment in farming and fishing, found themselves instead the pioneer workers of a burgeoning tourist industry.

An early tourist attraction was the dramatic scenery of Blackgang Chine. Through millions of years, soft sands and clays slipped over the underlying gault clay to form the green and abundant world of the Undercliff. It is a haven for wild plant and animal life, and much of the island's

BLACKGANG CHINE c1883 FRITH 16443

southern coastline can be seen from the clifftop. The Chine is a great cleft in the bright yellow sandstone and blue clays of the cliff that plunges 400 feet, and was popular with smugglers in the past. The massive gorge of Blackgang Chine was a magnet to Victorian visitors with its spectacular paths, dramatic waterfall and eroded colourful cliffs. Entry to the chasm was relatively inexpensive in Victorian times. One guidebook writer noted that the 'entrance to the Chine is through a bazaar, where one must either make a purchase or pay sixpence before he descends to this great chasm, echoing with the ocean waves that break on the beach below'.

THE UPPER CHINE c1883 FRITH 16444

This wonderfully melodramatic poem is a testament to the enthusiasm with which the Victorian excursionist embraced the experience of visiting dramatic scenery:

# Black Gang Chine

*Path of darkness! Road of night!*
*Black Gang Chine!*
*Way of gloom for cataract bright*
*Unto the brine!*
*Thine the dizzy height, the edge*
*Of wondrous line,*
*Whirling on its mammoth ledge,*
*Black Gang Chine!*
*Thine the black rock; thine the chasm;*
*Thine the vast spine,*

*High, wide, and growthless; born of spasm!*
*Monster divine!*
*Thine dark beauty, wooing tender,*
*Like Moorish lips!*
*Thine dark grandeur; thine the splendour*
*Of an eclipse!*
*Thine the path of grand dark spirit,*
*Lost to the divine,*
*Fallen from that it did inherit—*
*Black Gang Chine!*

FROM 'THE RETURN OF THE SWALLOW: AND OTHER POEMS' BY GOODWYN BARMBY, 1864

# The Tragic Wreck of the Clarendon

6The most disastrous wreck that has occurred on our shores for the last 20 years, was that of the Clarendon, on the 11th of October, 1836, exactly opposite the cavern of Blackmails Chine [Blackgang Chine]. She was of 350 tons burthen, laden with sugar and rum, from the West Indies. The crew were 17 men; and the passengers ten – four of them female. At five o'clock on the fatal morning, the weather dark and tempestuous, land was discovered at but a short distance to leeward; there was no pilot on board, and in vain were the most strenuous efforts made by the astonished crew to ward the vessel off! In a short time the passengers were assembled on deck, – their horrid destiny was apparent: for the ship, rapidly driven by the raging elements, was soon a-ground, engulphed between the mountain waves that incessantly broke over her, and the steep descent of the beach against which she struck. In this horrible state the vessel remained for about five minutes, during which the convulsive screams of the unhappy sufferers might be heard, and many of them distinctly seen in all the agony of despair, clinging to whatever could afford them a hold. But short, alas! was their distracting suspense; for ere any measure could be taken for their escape, the ship was stove in by one tremendous surge bursting over her with such inconceivable force, as to wrench the hull asunder into a thousand pieces!

We shudder at the recollection of the scene which followed: the shattered hull, broken masts, yards, sails, and rigging; the ponderous goods which chiefly composed the cargo; and (most appalling to behold) the lacerated bodies of the lifeless crew and passengers, tossed about in the foaming breakers, or hurled in dire confusion on the stony beach. Only three escaped! – the mate and two seamen, who were washed overboard previous to the fatal stroke. 9

FROM 'THE PLEASURE VISITOR'S COMPANION IN MAKING THE TOUR OF THE ISLE OF WIGHT', G BRANNON, 1842

*The ship, rapidly driven by the raging elements, was soon a-ground, engulphed between the mountain waves that incessantly broke over her*

# John stands at the edge of a precipice

JOHN WITH SIMON
DABELL INSIDE THE
WHALE SKELETON

Today Blackgang Chine is one of the Isle of Wight's biggest and oldest attractions, and its owners conjure up images of smuggling and pirates here. They've been running it for 160 years. I met the current owner, Simon Dabell, at the entrance.

'My ancestor started the business in 1843,' Simon told me. 'He created a very early theme park, and that's what Blackgang Chine still is today. My great-great-grandfather was a shopkeeper by trade, and he felt that he'd make most money here by opening a shop, with the added bonus of its being in a scenic location. Then he felt that he needed a museum. Just by luck, in 1844, the year after he'd opened the shop and the entrance to the chine, a whale was found floating in the Solent. The Admiralty towed it ashore and were about to blow it up. My ancestor stepped in and bought it. He sold the blubber at auction, had the bones bleached, brought them here by horse and cart, and reassembled the skeleton.'

The whale was originally housed in a tin shed, the building that's end-on in the centre of the Frith photograph on page 108. The shed is long gone, but the whale's skeleton still survives – all 13 tons of it. Simon led me to the building that houses the whale today, and we walked through the huge tunnel formed by its ribs. I realised that the Victorians must have been thrilled to get so close to a whale. 'Yes, indeed,' said Simon, 'in Victorian times there was a wishing chair – you could sit and make a wish inside the belly of a whale. And they had a shop and a tearoom so that you could eat and drink with the bones around you. You couldn't get closer!'

THE CLIFFS HAVE FALLEN AWAY WHERE THE BUILDINGS ONCE WERE

SNOWDON, WOMEN
ON THE SADDLE 1895
FRITH 36556X

VISITORS SITTING
ON THE LOVERS SEAT
BY THE LANDSLIP AT
BONCHURCH, ISLE OF
WIGHT 1913
FRITH 66186A

I'd heard that royalty had visited Blackgang Chine. 'Queen Victoria visited', said Simon, 'and so did Queen Mary. She would often come through the Chine building to look at the view. On one occasion her hat was knocked off by a projecting bit of whalebone. The story goes that within a few minutes a workman rushed up and sawed the offending piece of bone off.' Simon showed me the place where the bone had been sawn off, and the place on the other side of the skeleton where the corresponding bone was still in place. 'So a great chunk was cut off!' I said. 'You have to do what royalty might want you to do!'

Simon took me outside and we walked down a coast path. 'As well as the shop and the skeleton', said Simon, 'it was the walks down the gorge to the sea that were just as important to the Victorian visitor. In the Victorian age, resorts and spectacular scenery were being discovered for the first time by the general public. Here, it's the sea that drew them – they were so close to it on the Island with its fresh air and glorious vistas. It was the perfect contrast to the smoke and fog of crowded cities.'

The Victorians' urge to explore didn't stop at the seaside. Frith and his team of photographers were taking souvenir pictures all over the country, and even ventured to the top of Mount Snowdon. There, the only thing that's changed since Frith's day is the clothing.

Back on the clifftop, I showed Simon the Frith photograph (page 108) and asked him where the buildings were. 'Well, they're in midair', he said. 'The cliff edge is falling away every year, and those buildings were about 40 metres away from the present cliff edge.' In the time since the Frith photograph was taken in 1883, Simon's family have lost over 200 metres of land – it's simply fallen into the sea, victim of the harsh south-westerlies blowing off the Atlantic. It means that the very top of the gorge path is all that's left of the original spectacular Blackgang Chine.

'So every year you've got to be conscious of the fact that your land is getting smaller', I said. 'How do you cope?' 'A bit like a crab', said Simon. 'We move sideways and backwards. We have to take down attractions and move them when the cliff gets too close. We call it managed retreat!' I thought that retreat was always supposed to be the hardest manoeuvre to accomplish. 'Well, we've been doing it for a while now,' said Simon, 'so we know what we're doing.'

EROSION OF THE CLIFF AT BLACKGANG CHINE TODAY

## JOHN'S PHOTOGRAPH AT BLACKGANG CHINE

THE LOST CHILDHOOD, 2011

*I've given my photograph a melodramatic title, but that's what the Victorians would have done – they liked a bit of melodrama. They also loved the seaside, and here they loved it so much that they built a theme park on land destined for destruction – each generation of Simon Dabell's family has had to deal with a different coastline. I wanted to record a fleeting moment in time along this ever-changing clifftop. I wonder how many other people will capture this scene before it's lost for ever?*

# Ventnor! All Aboard the Invalids' Express!

VENTNOR, ROYAL NATIONAL HOSPITAL FOR CONSUMPTIVES 1899   FRITH 43141

*'This photograph is all about good health. It was taken on the Isle of Wight, and this incredible building, almost 500 yards long, was Ventnor's Royal Hospital, an institution that treated tuberculosis. It opened in the late 1860s with Queen Victoria as its patron, and became renowned throughout Europe for successfully treating chest diseases.'*

Ventnor, on the south coast of the Isle of Wight, transformed itself from an obscure fishing hamlet to a fashionable watering place during the last half of the 19th century. A sheltered location and mild climate have brought generations of holidaymakers here. The town lies at the foot of an 800ft hill with gradients in some streets of 1 in 4; this shelter aids the growth of luxuriant vegetation in the steep gardens. Ventnor never compared to Sandown or Shanklin as a centre for sea bathing, although bathing machines for ladies and gentlemen flourished in the 19th century. Bowling greens, tennis courts, concert shows and walks were provided for those too nervous to dip a toe into the cool waters of the English Channel.

Ventnor is said to have the most equitable climate in the country; indeed, the eminent 19th-century physician Sir James Clark made the resort's reputation in Victorian times by comparing its climate to that of Madeira. Victorian Ventnor became a refuge for consumptives, the kind climate aiding their condition. In a few short years four large homes for sufferers from tuberculosis were established in the resort. The good weather, fresh air, and regime of long bracing walks probably did a great deal to alleviate their condition.

During the 1800s tuberculosis, or consumption, as it was then known, was a huge problem, being an extremely infectious disease. Arthur Hill Hassall, a member of the Royal College of Physicians, had come to the Island in 1866 to recuperate from a chest illness. He was

ABOVE: VENTNOR, THE BEACH 1899  FRITH 43138
BELOW: VENTNOR, THE BEACH 1899  FRITH 43133

so impressed by the beauty and 'highly favourable locality', as he put it, around Ventnor that in 1867 he conceived the idea of founding a specialist chest hospital here.

Dr Hassall's conception was to build a hospital divided into houses or 'cottages', providing a separate bedroom for each patient, a unique and innovative design at that time. The architect was Thomas Hellyer, and the builders were Ingrams – who are still in business in Ventnor today. The Royal National Hospital for Diseases of the Chest, also known as the Royal National Hospital for Consumptive Diseases, with Queen Victoria as its patron, opened in 1869. The railway had arrived three years before, so patients could travel to Ventnor on the 'Invalids' Express'.

The British Medical Association visited the hospital in 1881, and its report stated: 'The Ventnor hospital

VENTNOR AS IT IS
TODAY

*The railway had arrived … so patients could travel to Ventnor on the 'Invalids' Express'*

VENTNOR,
ROYAL NATIONAL
HOSPITAL FOR
CONSUMPTIVES 1892
FRITH 30063

is universally admired, indeed no other in Europe can compare with the completeness with which the 'cottage system' is carried out, and for the combination of comfort and scientific purpose'. The hospital was famous far and wide for its successful treatment of those with chest diseases.

By the 1960s the hospital was no longer needed, largely thanks to the discovery of antibiotics, and it was mostly demolished. However, a few of the original buildings remain. To the east the lodge still stands (bearing the initials NCH, standing for National Chest Hospital), and the Burgoyne Library (where the patients used to enjoy whist drives, spelling bees, and film shows) is now the Harold Lanfear Library and the administrative offices of Ventnor Botanic Garden, which occupies the site of the hospital grounds. The present potting shed was once chalets where patients could sit or lie, sometimes all night, to get maximum fresh air.

The grounds were always an important part of the hospital. Their purpose was not only recreational: the Annual Report of 1873 states that they should be used to supply pure milk, fresh eggs, vegetables and fruit to the patients and staff. Walking around Ventnor Botanic Garden today, it's good to remember the energy and pioneering philanthropy of our Victorian forebears.

# John tours the gardens of the old hospital

The hospital building is long gone, but its grounds where medicinal plants once grew are now Ventnor's Botanic Garden, where I met garden volunteer and historian Jonyth Hill. As we strolled round she told me that she had a personal connection with the garden. 'My father actually convalesced in the hospital in the 1960s when it was used just for convalescents and not for tuberculosis any more. I've got a deep affection for this place, and that's why I'm delighted to work here now.'

I asked Jonyth what the reaction had been when it was announced that the hospital would close. 'By that time, tuberculosis was curable. Hospitals like this one weren't needed any more, thanks to antibiotics. They could be treated at home.' 'People still get TB now, don't they?' I said. 'There are better ways of treating it today', said Jonyth. 'Although this was a very good hospital and an amazing building, look at what we have here now!' From where we were standing, we had a wonderful view of plants and trees thriving in the beautiful garden.

JOHN WITH GARDEN
VOLUNTEER JONYTH
HILL

When the Frith team were here in the late 1800s, the hospital was at the height of its success and fame, and its treatment methods were highly innovative. 'Each patient had a separate room,' Jonyth told me, 'and the rooms all faced south to get the most of the lovely climate and fresh air.' I wondered if the treatment actually worked. 'On the whole it did seem to', said Jonyth. 'To get away from the smoke and dirt of the big cities and come here to the fresh air obviously benefited the patients greatly. They would probably stay here quite a long time, from three to six months, and would go home cured, or at least considerably better.'

It was a pity that we couldn't see the amazing hospital, but Jonyth told me there was a remnant of it left. She showed me a wooden chalet-like building. 'This was one of the wards. The standard treatment for tuberculosis was that the patients should get as much fresh air as possible, so during the day they'd be here with the ward wide open to the air. Sometimes they'd spend

THE POTTING SHED
THAT WAS
ORIGINALLY
A WARD

BELOW LEFT:
JOHN WITH HEAD
GARDENER
CHRIS KIDD

BELOW RIGHT:
JOHN TOUCHES THE
TRUNK OF A PALM
PLANTED IN QUEEN
VICTORIA'S REIGN

the night here too – it's hardly ever too cold for that in Ventnor.'

I'd noticed lots of flower pots stacked outside. 'And now it's a potting shed!' I exclaimed. 'Yes, it's funny to think that it was once a ward', said Jonyth. This was probably a men's ward; the men and women were kept separate, the women at the east end of the hospital, and the men this end. Even in the garden, the men walked this end and the women the other.'

Jonyth led me into the glasshouses, where there were lots of beautiful plants in pots. 'In the old days,' she told me, 'they grew sweet smelling pot plants like lavenders, and lots of cut flowers too – they would arrange them in the hospital so that the patients could enjoy their lovely smell and feel more cheerful.'

There's one part of the Botanic Garden that's been preserved just as it was at the time of the Frith photograph. Today, it's looked after by Chris Kidd, the Head Gardener, and he led me to a grove of tall palm trees. 'Were these palms here when the hospital was here?' I asked him. 'They were donated to the Isle of Wight', said Chris, 'and given to Queen Victoria, who recommended that this was where the palms should go. She was a patron of the hospital, and visited several times.' I put my hand on the trunk of one of the palms. 'So I'm touching a plant that was alive when Queen Victoria was alive!' 'Yes,' said Chris, 'and she might even have planted it.'

# Loose Lacing of Stays, Deep Inspirations …

'The hygienic management of consumptive patients is of extreme importance. Attention to the state of the digestive organs, moderate and frequent exercise in the open air, either active (riding and walking,) or passive (carriage, swinging, or yachting,) the cold, tepid or warm bath, with friction of the skin, the use of flannel next the skin, loose lacing of the stays in females, exercise of the respiratory muscles and lungs by deep inspirations, reading aloud, and movements of the arms, are all of essential service. Exchange of profession or trade, from the sedentary and laborious to the more active and those but slightly taxing the intellect, is advisable.

MIDHURST, KING EDWARD SANATORIUM 1907
FRITH 58337

KNIGHTWICK, THE SANATORIUM 1906
FRITH 54298X

Change of climate, when it can be accomplished, is unquestionably, in the early period of the disease, of fundamental service … In the selection of a climate for any particular case, the dry or moist character of the attending bronchitis … is the best guide: in the former case, the climates of Madeira, Teneriffe, the Azores, Rome, Pisa, Torquay, Penzance, Ventnor, and the Undercliff generally; in the latter, those of Egypt, Cadiz, Algiers, Genoa, Nice, Clifton, and Bournemouth, are the most advisable for winter residence.'

FROM 'A PRACTICAL TREATISE ON THE DISEASES OF THE LUNGS', WALTER HAYLE WALSHE, 1851

OCKLEY, THE SANATORIUM 1914  FRITH 67029

Patients suffering from consumption were encouraged to spend time outside. They worked in the sanatorium gardens planting, hoeing and weeding, and played gentle games such as croquet, while the sunshine and fresh air helped their recovery. Perhaps the patients at Ventnor were encouraged to work in the gardens around their sanatorium.

Not all sufferers played along, though: at Ockley, when the sanatorium was dismantled and removed, the building contractors discovered considerable numbers of broken clay pipes near the surface. In spite of their life-threatening illness, many patients were clearly unable or unwilling to abandon their devotion to tobacco!

# John's photograph at Ventnor

QUEEN VICTORIA'S PALM TREE, BOTANIC GARDENS, ISLE OF WIGHT, 2011

*At first I wondered if I should take my photograph from the same place that the Frith photograph on page 116 had been taken. Although some features in the Frith photograph are still there, like the cricket pavilion, I decided that I could take a more interesting picture in the garden. So here it is – an image linking the present day with the founding of the TB hospital. I wonder what Queen Victoria would think of it. She donated this palm, it was still growing in the next century, and it's still growing in the century after that. It's a direct link with Queen Victoria.*

ROMSEY, THE PALMERSTON MONUMENT 1898   FRITH 42103

# Feeling Tipsy? You must have been to Romsey

*'The beautifully composed image on the previous pages shows the Market Place in Romsey, Hampshire. The star of the show is Lord Palmerston, twice Prime Minister in the 1850s and 60s, the local hero. But if you look at the photograph closely, you will see clues to one of Romsey's traditional industries, and I was very much looking forward to finding out more about it.'*

*'You're in the Strong Country'*

A VICTORIAN
ENGRAVING
SHOWING THE
LORD
PALMERSTON
STATUE

Romsey, a pleasant small market town in Hampshire, stands on the River Test, and it is the river that has determined how the town made its living. From medieval times, the river was essential to the woollen industry that was important here. When competition from the north of England killed the woollen trade in the 18th century, the river was essential to the new industries of papermaking, sack making, and above all brewing.

Romsey prospered with the improved turnpike roads of the 18th and 19th centuries. The roads from Salisbury to Southampton and from Winchester to the west crossed the river here, and the coaching trade brought much business to the town's pubs and inns. There were a great many public houses in Romsey at one time, and Romsey had a reputation for alcoholic over-indulgence.

The brewers Strong & Co of Romsey were founded in the mid 19th century and endured until the 21st. At their peak they employed 600 people, and their bitter was served in pubs all over the south of England. Many people will remember those iconic advertisements showing an archetypal country scene and proclaiming 'You're in the Strong Country', and many people have smiled in anticipation as the train pulled out of Waterloo passing the huge poster telling them that 'You're going to the Strong Country'. Today a new brewery, the Flack Manor Brewery, flourishes here.

But why does Lord Palmerston stand on his plinth watching over the town? The third Lord Palmerston, Conservative Prime Minister during Queen Victoria's reign, lived just outside Romsey at the magnificent Palladian mansion of Broadlands, built by his father, where he was born in 1784. A great national figure, he nevertheless showed a keen interest in his native town's affairs, writing in his own hand to the mayor on very basic matters; for instance, he suggested that the Corporation should take steps to improve sanitation in the town if they were to avoid outbreaks of typhoid.

ABOVE LEFT:
ROMSEY, ONE OF THE
TOWN'S MANY PUBLIC
HOUSES 1911
FRITH 63780X

ABOVE RIGHT:
COURAGE BREWERY
SIGN IN ONE OF
ROMSEY'S PUBLIC
HOUSE DOORWAYS

ROMSEY,
MARKET PLACE 1904
FRITH 51431T

Again, the 'Farmer's Magazine' of 1861 reports on a meeting held at Romsey 'for the purpose of taking into consideration the best means of improving the dwellings of the labouring classes. Lord Palmerston took the chair'. The Right Honourable W Cowper, MP and Chief Commissioner of Public Works, spoke eloquently on how bad housing led to the demon drink: 'The living-room becomes untenantable to the father and children, and they desire to get out of it as often and as soon as they can. In my opinion, that is the cause by which one of the greatest curses of our country, viz., drunkenness, is promoted and encouraged. It is the discomfort of a man's home which induces him to withdraw from it whenever he can, and resort to the public-house for comfort which he cannot get in his own house. He is led into a habit of drinking, which he would probably have abstained from, if he had had a more comfortable home.'

Lord Palmerston and Mr Cowper were obviously aware of Romsey's reputation when it came to pubs!

# John checks the sparge and smells the fuggles

JOHN WITH LOCAL
HISTORIAN
PHOEBE MERRICK

ONE OF ROMSEY'S PUBLIC
HOUSES TODAY

A TYPICAL SMALL
PUBLIC HOUSE 1892
FRITH C221302

Looking around the modern town, there was no getting away from the fact that Romsey seems to enjoy its beer – there are still a great many pubs here. I met local historian Phoebe Merrick beside Lord Palmerston's statue, and I asked her about Romsey's reputation for strong drink. We looked at the Frith photograph (pages 124-125), in which there's an off-licence to the left of the statue and a pub to its right. So was Romsey famous for its pubs?

'Very much so', said Phoebe. When we were researching the history of pubs in Romsey, we found that there had been 84 pubs here in a town with a population of 5,000.' 'That's a pub for every family, almost!' I said. 'Mind you,' said Phoebe, 'many of them would have been no more than ale houses. They'd sell beer and cider, but they didn't have wine and spirits licences, and often the business would simply be in the front room of a house, run by the housewife as an additional source of income. It wouldn't have been like a pub is now, when to run it is a full-time job.'

I wondered why Romsey needed so many pubs. 'We're on the main road from Winchester to the west of England, and on the road between Salisbury and Southampton. All those travellers needed refreshment, and so did their horses, of course.' I'd heard that in the old days people thought of Romsey as a place to get drunk. 'You're right!' said Phoebe. 'The old saying is: "He's so drunk he must have been to Romsey", and there's another saying, too – "It's a straight road to Romsey, and a zigzag back again".'

There was one thing about the Frith photograph that mystified us both: it doesn't show Romsey's famous abbey church. 'It's extraordinary,' said Phoebe, 'because it's such a dominant feature of the whole of the town. Almost everywhere you stand you get a glimpse of the abbey church. It would have been really hard for the Frith photographer to find a place where it couldn't be seen.'

It was now time for me to check out a new example of Romsey's most famous industry. This was the perfect

JOHN WITH FLACK
MANOR BREWERY
OWNER
NIGEL WELSH

THE FLACK BREWERY

*Brewing only takes eight hours, and in seven days' time the beer will be ready to drink*

assignment: I was off to explore a brewery. In 2008 it looked as if the grand tradition of brewing in Romsey had come to an end, but 18 months ago the arrival of Flack Manor Brewery put the smell of fermentation back in the air.

The owner of the brewery, Nigel Welsh, let me see a side to beer that was unfamiliar to me. Wearing overalls and a pair of rather natty white wellingtons, I found myself climbing a ladder up to the top of a cylindrical stainless steel tank. 'You're going to climb up to the mash tun to regulate the flow of the sparge', Nigel told me. 'Mash tun? Sparge?' I said. I opened the lid of the tank to see a spray of hot water revolving over what looked like steaming beige porridge.

'It's very important to make sure that we've got the right amount of liquor washing the goodness through', said Nigel. 'What's liquor?' I asked. 'Liquor's water – we don't use the word water in brewing, though, dirty stuff! What you can see here is hot liquor going over the malted barley, and now you're going to check the dial and make sure the regulated flow of 30 litres a minute is going through.' There was an array of dials and levers next to the tank, and I managed to see that the dial said 35.4 – too much – and then adjust the flow with a lever.

I wondered how this brewery compared with a brewery in Victorian times. 'It would have been a traditional tower brewery', said Nigel. 'A multi-storey building meant that gravity helped to move the liquid. Now we have mechanical pumps to move it, and a lot less manpower, but the process is actually very similar, despite all this modern-looking stainless steel. It's quite a simple process – it only takes eight hours, and in seven days' time the beer will be ready to drink'.

One thing I do know is that a good pint relies on two key ingredients. The first is the hops. Nigel opened a sack. 'These are fuggles.' 'Fuggles?' 'Fuggle hops. Take some in your hand, squash them a bit, and smell the aroma.' Ugh! I thought it was horrible! Time to try the second key ingredient, the malted barley. Nigel had various different samples in jars, and gave me one to try. 'This one's got a sort of Horlicksy flavour, like a rich tea biscuit', he said. We were making enough noise as we chewed to irritate a lot of people if we'd been in a cinema.

'You've done enough work now', said Nigel, 'and you deserve a drink'. He led me to the sample room and pulled me a pint. 'Mmm. Not bad. Rather good, in fact', I said. After that it would have been foolish not to try the bottle-conditioned house special. 'Mmm. Great.' Then there was the deceptively strong local porter. 'Mmm. Terrific.' 'Like another?' said Nigel. 'I'll have another of each!' I said.

# Lord Palmerston and Broadlands

Broadlands estate, south of Romsey overlooking the River Test, belonged to Romsey Abbey before the Reformation. The impressive Georgian house was built by the Palmerston family, whose most famous member was the third Lord Palmerston, the Victorian statesman, who was born here in 1784. The first Viscount Palmerston had bought the property in 1736, and since then it has never been sold again.

In 1939 the estate was inherited by Edwina Ashley, who married Lord Louis Mountbatten, Admiral of the Fleet and Earl Mountbatten of Burma (1900-1979), and they made their home at Broadlands. It remains in the care of their descendants.

The house has been a centre of hospitality over the centuries. A frequent Victorian visitor was the influential art critic and social reformer John Ruskin, who was a close friend of William Cowper, Lord Palmerston's heir, and his wife Georgiana. An early visitor to the Broadlands estate was James I in 1607, who planted two mulberry trees, which still survive; 350 years later, two more were planted by Queen Elizabeth II and Prince Philip, who spent part of their honeymoon at Broadlands, when their hosts were the Mountbattens. More than two hundred individual trees have now been planted in the grounds by famous people.

## JOHN'S PHOTOGRAPH AT ROMSEY

ROMSEY ABBEY, 2011

*Romsey Abbey was founded in the 12th century as a house for Benedictine nuns. Its church was already 600 years old when Lord Palmerston was living here. This beautiful piece of architecture is the most famous sight in Romsey, and I thought it would make the perfect focal point for my picture, especially as it can't be seen in the Frith photograph.*

# Ancient Stones Restored and Druid Ceremonies

STONEHENGE c1861  FRITH 721  Copyright Victoria and Albert Museum, London

*'These are the magnificent stones of Stonehenge in Wiltshire, one of the most famous ancient monuments in the world. This mysterious prehistoric stone circle seems changeless. Yet I found out that it's not true – the stones have been moved, and the changes to Stonehenge over the last 100 years or so have been considerable. The great value of this Frith photograph is that it records what Stonehenge looked like just before a number of alterations were made here.'*

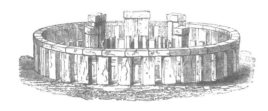

ENGRAVING SHOWING THE VICTORIANS' IDEA OF
THE ORIGINAL APPEARANCE OF STONEHENGE

*The Frith
photographs
show
Stonehenge
in a perhaps
rather
untidy and
sorry state*

VICTORIAN
ENGRAVING OF
STONEHENGE WITH
A SHEPHERD
AND HIS SHEEP

Stonehenge, the most famous prehistoric stone circle in the world, was built and adapted in three phases over a huge time span (about 15 centuries) between approximately 2,950BC and 1,600BC.

The first Stonehenge was a circular bank and ditch, probably containing timber uprights. It was during the second phase (approximately 2,900-2,400BC) that new timber settings were erected in the north-east entrance and at the centre. During these early phases, it seems that the purpose of the monument was the observation of the movements of the moon through the entrance. It may also have been linked with death and funerary rituals – deposits of burnt human bone dating from this period have been found.

In the third phase (2,550-1,600BC) the Stonehenge we see today was developed. The Hele Stone and another stone west of it were erected outside the monument pointing towards the approximate point where the midsummer sun rose. Bluestone pillars were erected – they had been brought all the way from the Preseli mountains in Wales – surrounding the Altar Stone. Then came a horseshoe-shaped setting of large trilithons. Around this were more bluestones, then a ring of sarsen stones. The Avenue was constructed, emphasising the change of observation from the moon to the sun. But Stonehenge was not just a temple; it was a place where people

met to engage in all sorts of celebrations and ceremonies, so around it are many related monuments, including a cursus (a long linear feature) and barrows (burial mounds).

The Frith photographs show Stonehenge in a perhaps rather untidy and sorry state. In 1901 the decision was taken to restore the monument. William Gowland oversaw this major restoration, which included the straightening and setting in concrete of stone number 56, which was in danger of falling. In

STONEHENGE 1887
FRITH 19800

STONEHENGE 1887
FRITH 19797T

straightening the stone he moved it about half a metre from its original position!

In 1920 William Hawley undertook another restoration; he had dug at Old Sarum nearby, and at Stonehenge he excavated the base of six stones and the outer ditch. Richard Atkinson, Stuart Pigott and John F S Stone re-excavated much of Hawley's work in the 1940s and 1950s. Atkinson's work was instrumental in furthering the understanding of the three major phases of the monument's construction.

In 1958 three of the standing sarsens were re-erected and set in concrete bases. The last restoration was carried out in 1963 after sarsen stone 23 fell over. It was re-erected, and the opportunity was taken to concrete three more stones. More recently, archaeologists have campaigned to give the public more knowledge of the various restorations, and in 2004 English Heritage included pictures of the work in progress in its book 'Stonehenge: A History in Photographs'.

# The Sacred World of the Druids

FROM 'HALF HOURS OF ENGLISH HISTORY', CHARLES KNIGHT, 1853

The account which Julius Caesar gives of the Druids of Gaul, marked as it is by his usual clearness and sagacity, may be received without hesitation as a description of the Druids of Britain: for he says, 'the system of Druidism is thought to have been formed in Britain, and from thence carried over into Gaul; and now those who wish to be more accurately versed in it for the most part go thither (ie to Britain) in order to become acquainted with it.' Nothing can be more explicit than his account of the mixed office of the Druids: 'They are the ministers of sacred things; they have the charge of sacrifices, both public and private; they give directions for the ordinances of religious worship. A great number of young men resort to them for the purpose of instruction in their system, and they are held in the highest reverence. For it is they who determine most disputes, whether of the affairs of the state or of individuals: and if any crime has been committed, if a man has been slain, if there is a contest concerning an inheritance or the boundaries of their lands, it is the Druids who settle the matter: they fix rewards and punishments …'

After noticing that a chief Druid, whose office is for life, presides over the rest, Caesar mentions a remarkable circumstance which at once accounts for the selection of such a spot as Sarum Plain, for the erection of a great national monument, a temple, and a seat of justice: 'These Druids hold a meeting at a certain time of the year in a consecrated spot … which is considered to be in the centre of all Gaul. Hither assemble all from every part who have a litigation, and submit themselves to their determination and sentence.' At Stonehenge, then, we may place the seat of such an assize. There were roads leading direct over the plain to the great British towns of Winchester and Silchester. Across the plain, at a distance not exceeding twenty miles, was the great temple and Druidical settlement of Avebury. The town and hill-fort of Sarum was close at hand. Over the dry chalky downs, intersected by a few streams easily forded, might pilgrims resort from all the surrounding country. The seat of justice which was also the seat of the highest religious solemnity, would necessarily be rendered as magnificent as a rude art could accomplish.

# John learns about the stones and bangs a drum

JOHN WITH DAVID
BATCHELOR OF
ENGLISH HERITAGE

THE VIEW IN THE
FRITH PHOTOGRAPH
ON PAGE 131 AS IT IS
TODAY

The fact that Stonehenge has been restored doesn't make it a sham. Any changes here have been part of careful and expert conservation, as David Batchelor of English Heritage explained to me. As we walked round the outside of the huge circle of stones, I asked him if Stonehenge was a great tourist attraction in Victorian times.

'It's been an attraction since the 12th century', David told me. 'Geoffrey of Monmouth put it in a medieval equivalent of a guidebook of essential places to visit. Since then architects, scientists, archeologists, and the general public have been eager to look at it, and of course it was a must for Victorian visitors.' That explained the Frith photographs of Stonehenge, I thought – Frith would have seen that this was an obvious subject for souvenir pictures that would sell well.

We studied the Frith photograph carefully, and David identified where it had been taken from. 'But it doesn't look at all the same today as in the photograph!' I exclaimed. 'No, it doesn't', said David. 'This photograph was taken before any restoration had been done. It shows the fallen stones of a trilithon that had collapsed in 1797. The large stone on the ground to the right of the picture is the trilithon's upright, with its top surface facing us, and the end of its lintel is in the foreground to the right. Those stones were re-erected relatively recently. The sloping stone behind is stone 56, part of another trilithon, which has now been straightened up.'

As we walked around Stonehenge and looked closely at the stones, I realised that prevention is indeed better than cure – we could see where some of David's archeologist predecessors had taken measures to prevent any more collapses. 'This is concrete!' I said. We were looking at the base of the upright stone to the left of the Frith photograph. 'Yes, it's not prehistoric concrete', said David. 'That

THE DRUID
FRANK SOMERS

was put in about 50 years ago to support the stone. There's no attempt to deceive here – no one has tried to make it look old. It's quite obvious which is the ancient stone and which is the restoration. Stonehenge has actually changed a lot over the years, and that's why a regular photographic record is important. This Frith photograph was taken as a souvenir, but it's also a really valuable historical document.'

However much Stonehenge may have been patched up and re-erected, the mystical aura of the great stone circle is still captivating. There's one group of people who know that better than anyone, which is why I was keen to meet Frank Somers. Frank is a druid.

He advanced solemnly into the circle, bareheaded, wearing white robes, and carrying a wooden staff twined with greenery and a drum. 'It's wonderful to be here today', he said. 'It's wonderful to meet you, to be with you in this sacred space that was chosen as a special place by the ancestors.' He closed his eyes. 'What goes through my mind is the peace, the sanctity, and the very special energy that Stonehenge has. It's a blest place.'

'Do you have to be a druid to appreciate that side of Stonehenge?' I asked. 'Of course not!' said Frank. 'We can speak on the same level, even though you're not a druid.' I wondered if Frank minded that people think of druids as fakers, or lunatics, or new age cranks, even. 'Stonehenge has attracted a lot of eccentrics,' said Frank, 'people from the fields of science, mysticism, and druidry itself. Yes, I do mind. I mind because the druid tradition is very ancient; it has a great deal to offer to the modern world, especially as we go into this transition of climate change. We as people of earth have to find a new way forward. There's nothing new age about that.'

JOHN BANGS THE
DRUID DRUM

I wanted to learn more about druid ceremonial, but I was worried that I didn't have any white robes. 'Never mind,' said Frank, 'we'll dress you as a bard. The bards were poets and artists who would travel round the country and share the news. They were journalists, in fact – the perfect part for you!'

Frank entered the circle beating his drum, and I followed in a long flowing dark green cloak carrying the staff. Frank explained what happens in a druid

*We don't behave with too much reverence. We're loud, and we have fun*

ceremony. 'We've entered a sacred place that belongs to the ancestors, so we have a moment of silence, and then we greet them.' 'Hello, ancestors!' I called. 'Is that right?' I asked Frank. 'You can say it out loud, or you can just think it', he told me. I wanted to know if I could beat the drum. 'Absolutely', said Frank. 'When we druids come to Stonehenge, we believe in what we're doing, of course, but we don't behave with too much reverence. We're loud, and we have fun.'

So while I beat the drum, Frank called out a greeting: 'Welcome to Stonehenge, everybody. We are here this day to celebrate being in the presence of the ancestors at the turning of the year at the autumn equinox.' As we left the sacred circle, I asked Frank what he did when he wasn't being a druid. 'I work full-time as an IT consultant', he told me. It's a wonderful thought that behind an everyday desk or shop counter there's possibly a druid.

## JOHN'S PHOTOGRAPH OF STONEHENGE

STONEHENGE, 2011

*David Batchelor of English Heritage told me that a regular photographic record of Stonehenge was historically important as documentation of change, so I felt that this was my cue to make my own small contribution to Stonehenge's four and a half thousand years of history. So here it is: a great immoveable monument of prehistoric Britain – but it's not quite as immoveable as you might think.*

# Dorset's Jurassic Coast: A Fossil Treasure-House

*'In the photograph on the opposite page, the Frith photographer has captured the most exciting thing about Lyme Regis for the Victorians: the fact that this is where they could find fossils. Amateur palaeontologists came here from all over the country hoping to discover a new dinosaur, or at least an ammonite or two. So I chose this picture of the Fossil Depot and its proprietor – and I was also lucky enough to find out what the mystery object displayed outside the shop is!'*

The pretty fishing and seaside town of Lyme Regis straddles the border between Dorset and Devon. It has been popular as a seaside resort since the early 19th century, thanks in part to its spectacular and dramatic coastline.

Lyme's coastal scenery has been shaped by active geology. Major earth movements have occurred here over the years. For instance, a massive slippage between Branscombe and Beer Head was recorded in the winter of 1789, and what was described as 'the subsidence of the land and elevation of the bottom of the sea' at Dowlands took place on Boxing Day in 1839 – there, a cottage was left in the picturesque isolation of a chasm three-quarters of a mile long and 400 feet wide. Nearby Whitlands slipped on 3 February 1840, and Rousdon trembled on 3 October 1901.

These earth movements and erosion produce a wondrous harvest of fossils, for this is the Jurassic Coast, a World Heritage Site, attracting fossil-hunters and geologists from far afield. Several fossil shops thrive in the town, for this has become quite an industry in Lyme since the early 19th

*The Jurassic Coast, a World Heritage Site*

LYME REGIS,
BROAD STREET
1900 FRITH 45242

LYME'S FOSSIL
HUNTER
MARY ANNING

century, when Mary Anning, perhaps the most famous fossil hunter ever, made fossicking for fossils a popular pastime. She was only twelve years old when she found a 30ft ichthyosaurus, and she and her family went on to find many fine specimens which they sold to museums all over the country. The popularity of fossil shops grew as richer holidaymakers preferred to buy their souvenirs rather than get dirty finding them for themselves.

The Victorian Fossil Depot, shown in the main Frith photograph on page 138 (and below), was first run by James Dollin. He was followed by Thomas Seager, and then Sidney Curtis, who may well be the gentleman smoking a pipe standing to the left of the doorway. The sign (between the upper windows) boasted that the shop was patronised by His Royal Highness Prince Alfred, Duke of Edinburgh (1844-1900), the second son of Queen Victoria. Then, as now, dinosaur bones and ammonites were the mainstay of Lyme's fossil trade.

LYME REGIS, BRIDGE STREET AND THE OLD FOSSIL DEPOT 1909 FRITH 61625

# Mary Anning's extraordinary discovery

*Thus was brought to light the first Ichthyosaurus, a monster some thirty feet long*

In August, 1800, little Mary Anning was taken to see some horse-riding in the Back Field. A thunderstorm came on: those in charge of her hurried her under a tree; a flash of lightning struck the party, killing two women on the spot, and making the child insensible. A warm bath restored her to consciousness, and, strangely enough, she who had been a very dull girl before, now grew up lively and intelligent. She soon got to accompany her father in his rambles. 'Fossiling', however, does not appear to have paid so well as steady carpentry, for the family went down the hill. The father died of consumption, and Mary, at ten years of age, was left very badly off. Just then a lady gave her half-a-crown for a very choice ammonite. This encouraged her to take to collecting as a regular means of life. But she soon proved something more than a mere 'fossiler'.

In 1811, she saw some bones sticking out of a cliff; and, hammer in hand, she traced the position of the whole creature, and then hired men to dig out for her the lias block in which it was embedded. Thus was brought to light the first Ichthyosaurus (fish-lizard), a monster some thirty feet long, with jaws nearly a fathom in length, and huge saucer eyes ... Mr. Henley, the lord of the manor, bought it of the enterprising young girl for twenty-three pounds. It is now in the British Museum ... She had in a high degree that sort of intuition without which it is hopeless for any one to think of becoming a good collector of fossils.

FROM AN ARTICLE IN CHARLES DICKENS'S MAGAZINE 'ALL THE YEAR ROUND', 1865

DRAWING OF THE ICHTHYOSAURUS, FROM THOMAS HAWKINS'S COLLECTION, LYME REGIS

FRITH L121307

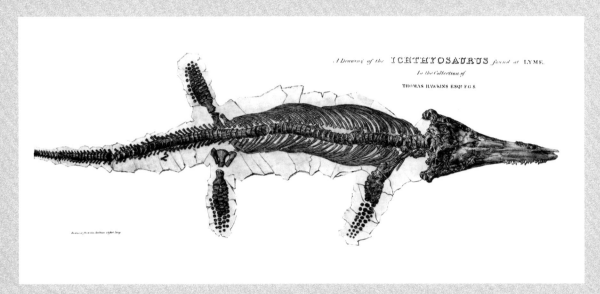

# John discovers fossils on the beach at Lyme

I was disappointed to find that the Fossil Depot seen in the Frith photographs had been demolished (the Rock Point Inn now stands on its site), so I decided to try to find some fossils on the shore. There I met Chris Andrew, a fossil expert, who runs fossil-hunting tours. The first thing I needed to know was what to look for.

*You can always find fossils at Lyme*

'It's the grey rocks you want', Chris told me. 'They're blue lias, the same rocks you can see in the cliffs. They're from the Lower Jurassic, the very start of the Jurassic period, so they're round about 200 million years old. The most common fossils you'll see are ammonites, but you might also find trace fossils, which are the marks ancient creatures made in the mud, and you could also find loose belemnites among the rocks – they're fossil mollusc shells.'

I was excited to find a rock with a great many small ammonites in it. 'Yes, that's a lot of ammonites!' said Chris. 'You can always find fossils at Lyme. But the best time to collect them is in winter. If you can come here when the storms and heavy rain have washed rocks down, that's when you're most likely to find things.'

JOHN WITH LYME
FOSSIL EXPERT
CHRIS ANDREW

We came to an area of flat rock studded with fossils, and I wondered if this place had a name. Chris told me that this area was known as the ammonite graveyard, or the ammonite pavement, and it's a great tourist attraction. 'You can see that the whole surface of the limestone is absolutely covered in ammonites, small ones, big ones – about 200 million years old. Geologically speaking that's not very old, but it's still fairly impressive!'

Chris had models of ancient creatures to show me, and the first was an ammonite, a spiral shell with a tentacled creature inside. 'People think that ammonites were a kind of snail because of their spiral shells', said Chris, 'but in fact they're much more interesting than that; they're related to squids and octopuses, like a modern nautilus. The animal had tentacles at the front for catching his prey, and we think that ammonites had well-developed eyes. Their bodies occupied about half the shell's outer coil, and all the rest of the shell was divided up into little gas-filled chambers. The animal controlled the amount of gas and

A MODEL OF AN
AMMONITE

VICTORIAN
ENGRAVING OF A
FOSSIL AMMONITE

water in each chamber so as to move up and down in the sea. When he died, he sank to the sea floor, his soft parts rotted away, and mud washed into the outer parts of the shell, but the chamber walls stopped the mud getting any further in. As the mud piled up on top, the centre collapsed, and we're left with a semi-circle with very little in the middle.'

Chris had also brought a model of an ichthyosaur, an ancient fish-like creature, and a fossil of part of an ichthyosaur's jawbone. 'You can see his nostril, his upper and lower jaw, and his sharp teeth all along his jaw. There's plenty of ichthyosaur bones to be found here at Lyme.'

I asked why so many fossils were to be found here in particular. Chris told me that this part of Dorset was once a shallow tropical sea full of sea creatures; their fossils were well-preserved because the rock formed from the mud they fell in had never been much compressed. 'Now, all along the Dorset coast, these rocks are eroding away, and so fossils are being revealed on the beach. Fossils appear in a similar way in quarries, for instance, but people don't see them – people don't go to quarries for their holidays!'

## The Fossil Depot's Mystery Object Revealed

JOHN CLIMBS THE STAIRS AT THE LYME REGIS
MUSEUM WITH KEN GOLLOP

Ken Gollop is a trustee of Lyme Regis Museum, which has stood here for nearly 100 years. The museum is strong on fossils, but it also has a lot to tell about other aspects of Lyme's history. Ken explained that the mystery object displayed in front of the Fossil Depot in the Frith photograph is the shoulder bone of a whale – and it is now on display in the museum.

It was found among the rocks by one of the Curtis family, who were fishermen; another family member, Sidney Curtis, was the last owner of the Fossil Depot, and he displayed the whale bone there. When the shop was pulled down for road widening in 1913, the family kept the bone; it was inherited by a distant relative of Ken's about 14 years ago, and he has loaned it to the museum. Ken is very proud to display this family heirloom.

# The Cobb – Lyme's Massive Stone Breakwater

Lyme's harbour is famous for its curious curved stone breakwater and quay, the Cobb; its wall provided both a breakwater to protect the town from storms and an artificial harbour. The Cobb was the location for dramatic events in Jane Austen's novel 'Persuasion' (1818), and in the film 'The French Lieutenant's Woman', based on the 1969 novel of the same name by the local writer John Fowles.

The Cobb was first erected in the reign of Edward I; the first written mention of it is in a 1328 document describing it as having been damaged by storms. The massive structure was made of oak piles driven into the seabed with boulders stacked between them. The boulders were floated into place tied between empty barrels. The Cobb was of huge economic importance to the town and the surrounding area, allowing Lyme to develop as both a major port and a shipbuilding centre from the 13th century onwards.

The Cobb was refurbished and maintained over successive reigns, and by the time of Elizabeth I the level of shipping visiting Lyme was recorded as being one-sixth of London's. A 1685 account describes the Cobb as being made of boulders simply heaped up on each other: 'An immense mass of stone, of a shape of a demi-lune, with a bar in the middle of the concave: no one stone that lies there was ever touched with a tool or bedded in any sort of cement, but all the pebbles of the sea are piled up, and held by their bearings only, and the surge plays in and out through the interstices of the stone in a wonderful manner'.

The Cobb was rebuilt in 1793 following its destruction in a storm the previous year. This is thought to be the first time that mortar was used in the Cobb's construction. The Cobb was reconstructed in 1820 using Portland stone.

ABOVE: LYME REGIS, THE COBB 1900
FRITH 45239

RIGHT: LYME REGIS, THE COBB C1910
FRITH L121301

# Jane Austen in Lyme Regis

Jane Austen was very fond of Lyme Regis, and visited it in 1803 and in 1804, when she stayed for some weeks. She immortalized Lyme and the Cobb in 'Persuasion', and lovers of the book have flocked to see the steps (left) where Louisa Musgrove fell:

'There was too much wind to make the high part of the new Cobb pleasant for the ladies, and they agreed to get down the steps to the lower, and all were contented to pass quietly and carefully down the steep flight, excepting Louisa; she must be jumped down them by Captain Wentworth. In all their walks, he had had to jump her from the stiles; the sensation was delightful to her. The hardness of the pavement for her feet, made him less willing upon the present occasion; he did it, however; she was safely down, and instantly, to shew her enjoyment, ran up the steps to be jumped down again. He advised her against it, thought the jar too great; but no, he reasoned and talked in vain; she smiled and said, "I am determined I will": he put out his hands; she was too precipitate by half a second, she fell on the pavement on the Lower Cobb, and was taken up lifeless!

There was no wound, no blood, no visible bruise; but her eyes were closed, she breathed not, her face was like death. —The horror of that moment to all who stood around!'

FROM 'PERSUASION', 1816

LYME REGIS, THE COBB 1912
FRITH 65040

## JOHN'S PHOTOGRAPH OF THE JURASSIC COAST, LYME REGIS

### ICHTHYOSAURUS SCULPTURE, 2011

*Having learnt so much about fossils, and about their importance to Lyme, I now understood why the Frith team had taken the photograph of the Fossil Depot. So I wanted to take my own fossil photograph.*

*Here's the ichthyosaurus fragment Chris showed me perched precariously on top of the stones that would have been under water when this ancient dinosaur was swimming here about 200 million years ago.*

LYME REGIS, THE LYNCH 1892 FRITH 31311

# Water Power for our Daily Bread

*'The photograph of Lyme Regis on the previous pages shows the Lynch, a raised footpath that runs between the deep main channel of the River Lim (left) and the higher-level leat, or mill stream (right), that turns the water wheel at Town Mill. I thought this a very interesting picture, because it shows the industrial area of Lyme – for hundreds of years Lyme Regis was a centre for milling.'*

*Town Mill still stands; it ground to a halt not that long ago, in 1927*

Lyme Regis is named after the River Lim, which is just over five kilometres long and falls 200 metres from its source to the sea at Lyme Bay. The river may be a small one, but it flows fast, and once provided enough power for 13 water mills which stood on its banks and ground the townspeople's flour, or ran looms that produced woollen cloth.

Local historian Martin Roundell Greene explains that the main photograph looks northwards to the Angel Inn, at this date with its thatched roof; the building, now tiled, was still a pub until very recently. It is possible to find the exact spot from which the Frith photograph was taken, for although the buildings around look superficially different with their fresh paint and new shutters, when you look closely it is possible to see that in fact little has changed here since the 1890s.

JOHN MEETS LOCAL HISTORIAN MARTIN ROUNDELL GREENE

Water-powered mills in Britain date back hundreds of years, with 6000 recorded in the Domesday Book of 1086. But why did the mills on the Lim disappear? What happened to the milling industry? Martin describes how by the end of the 19th century grain was coming here from Canada, and roller mills to grind it were being built at the ports (see the photograph of the roller mill at Par in Cornwall below).

As a result mills in small towns began to struggle. However, Lyme Regis is lucky, Martin says, in that Town Mill still stands; it ground to a halt not that long ago in 1927. Now it has been rescued from dereliction, and its waterwheel turns the millstones to grind flour again today.

TOWN MILL AS IT
IS TODAY

PAR, THE ROLLER
MILL AND
HARBOUR 1927
FRITH 79875

Town Mill used to be known as King's Mill, and royal consent was given for the construction of the leat in 1341. At Mill Green, about 150 yards upstream from Town Mill, a weir controls the flow of the Lim and channels some of its water into the leat. When the leat is full, the surplus water flows over the weir and onward to the sea. At the mill, the water from the leat is fed to the top of the waterwheel via a wooden launder, or trough. The miller can control the flow of the water,

VICTORIAN
ILLUSTRATION OF AN
OVERSHOT WATERMILL

## *The Town Mill has been lovingly restored to full working order by local volunteers*

and thus the speed of the wheel, by moving a lever which raises and lowers a penstock, or sluice gate, in the launder.

Martin tells how Town Mill has been lovingly restored to full working order by local volunteers. The process was long and arduous. Following archaeological recording surveys, which started in 1992, refurbishment of the buildings began in 1995. The initial phase of renovation included the provision of art galleries, studios, workshops and a café. During the last phase of renovation, completed in 2001, the miller's house was purchased and converted for use as the mill shop, a community room and offices. Finally a salvaged Victorian waterwheel was installed, and in 2001 the wheel and millstones turned again for the first time in 75 years.

The Lim also powers a hydro-electric plant. The fully automatic system enables the mill to use the renewable energy of the River Lim to produce 'green' electricity for the mill and for the National Grid, whilst retaining the mill's traditional function of producing stone-ground flour with water power.

## Higher Mill, Lyme – Jericho, Jordan and Baptisms

Higher Mill (in the distance on the left in the photograph) ground corn and also produced oil. The two thatched cottages standing above the waterfall were known as Jericho and Jordan; their Biblical names preserve the memory of Baptist squatters, who met here from 1653, and built a series of thatched hovels. The further cottage was Jordan, and it took its name from the point chosen for baptisms in the River Lim, which the community called the Jordan River. Across the river, towards Slopes Farm, the fields were regarded as Paradise.

LYME REGIS, HIGHER MILL 1892   FRITH 31315

# Waterwheels and the Lie of the Land

Watermills are as old as civilisation: the oldest documented wheel dates from the 3rd century BC in ancient Greece. It appears that the Greeks also invented the three main types of waterwheels, undershot, breastshot, and overshot, which are still used today.

So if you were building a watermill, what would govern your choice of waterwheel type? Basically, it would be the lie of the land. If your river was flowing through level country, your only possible choice would be the undershot wheel, where a wheel with flat paddles is simply set into the flow of the mill race. Unfortunately, this is the most inefficient kind of wheel. This is because the wheel enters the water behind the thrust of the flow that drives it and lifts out of the water ahead of the thrust, impeding its own operation. This kind of wheel needs large quantities of fast-flowing water to drive the mill.

If your river was flowing in sloping country, so that you could have a head of water above your mill of about 6ft to 8ft, you could choose a breastshot wheel. Here, the water strikes the wheel about half-way up and falls into buckets, making the wheel revolve in the opposite direction to the flow of the mill race, and falls out with the rotation of the wheel, which is more efficient. It was this kind of wheel, often immensely wide and made of metal, that ran the huge mills that powered the Industrial Revolution. The wheel at Quarry Bank Mill in Cheshire, for instance, is 22ft wide and weighs 20 tons!

But if you could build your mill beside a steep slope, with a head of water of at least 15ft, then you could choose the most efficient kind of wheel of all, an overshot wheel. The water can fall into the buckets very near the top of the wheel, which means that the weight of the water, falling further, works harder; also, this kind of wheel can be set above the channel that leads the water away, so that the water never impedes the wheel. As this wheel needs less water, a small stream could serve your purpose. This is the kind of wheel that powers the Town Mill at Lyme.

UNDERSHOT WATERWHEEL

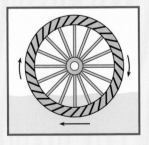

BREASTSHOT WATERWHEEL

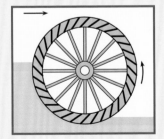

OVERSHOT WATERWHEEL

# John grinds and bags his own organic flour

I wanted to meet the miller, Steve White, to see if I could get some expert advice on how to grind flour. First of all I had to dress the part, so I put on a big white apron. How did I look?

'You look like an authentic miller!' Steve told me. He took me upstairs to the Stone Floor, which contains the millstones that grind the grain, and the grain hoppers that deliver the grain to the stones. I thought it looked rather like an engine room. 'It certainly is', said Steve. 'This is the centre of the grinding process. It's been restored to how it would have been in 1888'. 'Roughly the time of the Frith photograph, then', I said. 'Absolutely. And these wooden cogs on the wheel that turns the millstones were mostly missing when our restoration began – you can see that most of them are light-coloured. The dark cogs are the old ones that were here in 1888.'

*'How do I look?'*

*'You look like an authentic miller!'*

It was time to get started. We poured a bucketful of wheat grain into the wooden hopper ready to be ground; then we had to get the waterwheel turning. Steve opened the sluice gate that allows the water to flow in. 'Now, as you can see, there's lots of water in the troughs of the wheel, but it isn't turning. So what we need to do is to walk the wheel.' He told me to put my foot inside the wooden casing that protects the millstones. 'Put your foot in there, on the stone, and push your foot forward, time and time again. That will start to turn the water wheel.'

I could feel the force of the stone beginning to turn by itself beneath my

foot. 'That's enough – you can stop now', said Steve. 'What's happening is that the wheat is dropping into the centre of the stones. As the stones grind it finer and finer, the flour eventually comes out round the edge. The two stones don't actually touch each other. The entire weight of the top stone is supported on a shaft and a bearing that goes down to the floor below. You make an adjustment to give you the quality of flour you want.'

'You mean how fine the flour is?' I asked. 'That's right', said Steve. 'If you try to grind the flour too finely, so that the two millstones touch, then they'll bind together, and

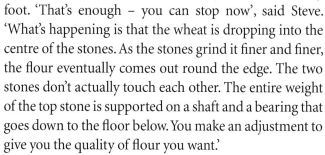

JOHN BAGS THE ORGANIC
WHOLEMEAL FLOUR HE HAS
JUST GROUND

you grind to a halt.' 'So if you get it wrong', I said, 'you – grind to a halt! That's where the phrase comes from!' 'Yes', said Steve, 'it's a term we all use, and most people don't realise that it's a milling term.'

By now the waterwheel, the cogged wheels and the millstones were all turning busily. Steve told me that when he started his career, it was as an engineer, and that's why he likes working with old machines. He took me down to the Meal Floor, where my flour was coming down a wooden chute into a sack. All I had to do now was to weigh it out and bag it up.

'You need 3lb exactly', said Steve. 'See if you can get it on the nose first time. There! That's one bag of stone-ground, wholemeal, organic, brown, plain, traditionally ground flour – which you have ground yourself.'

## John's photograph of Town Mill, Lyme Regis

### THE MILLER, 2011

*The Frith photograph was taken at a time when tourists didn't come to this part of Lyme; but now they do, to see how flour used to be ground. So my photograph shows one of the few millers left who are keeping this industry alive, Steve White. What a fantastic fellow he is, proudly posing in the beautifully restored Town Mill of Lyme Regis.*

# From Civic Splendour to Terrifying Imprisonment

EXETER, THE GUILDHALL 1896   FRITH 38003

'This lovely Frith photograph of Exeter shows an intriguing old building in a busy city street. It's an amazing survival, for Exeter was badly bombed during the Second World War and lost a quarter of its old buildings. But some very good buildings still remain, particularly this one, which I wanted to know more about. It's Exeter's Guildhall.'

The Guildhall is probably the oldest building in Exeter after the cathedral, with parts dating back to 1160 and much 13th-century work, and it has undergone various rebuilds over the centuries – the ornate frontage overhanging the High Street dates from the 1590s, during the reign of Elizabeth I. Historian Todd Gray tells how the granite columns came from Dartmoor, and that it took 40 cartloads of Beer stone to build the upper structure. It is thought that this façade was once richly coloured, for traces of blue, cream, red and gold have been found on the stonework. Todd says that the Guildhall is this country's oldest still serving civic building, and one which the city of Exeter dearly loves.

Todd explains that the Guildhall survived in a relatively unaltered state because Exeter's wealth and importance declined in the 19th century, so there was no money to 'improve' it. It therefore still looks much the same now as it has done for hundreds of years – except that today its stonework is cleaner than it was. In the old days locals called the building 'liver and bacon'; Todd says that before the grime of centuries was cleaned off the building, it was various shades of brown, taupe, mushroom and tan – just like liver and bacon cooked together.

But Exeter's history goes far further back than the building of the cathedral and the Guildhall. The area by the River Exe was settled by a Celtic tribe, the Dumnonii. In about AD 55 the Romans established a town here as a base for the Second Augustan Legion, and named it Isca Dumnoniorum, making Exeter Britain's most south-westerly Roman fortified settlement. Remains of the Roman walls can still be seen around the city, and archaeological excavations have discovered the site of one of the largest bath houses ever found in Roman Britain in the cathedral yard.

EXETER,
THE CATHEDRAL
1887 FRITH 19601

Exeter suffered several attacks by the Vikings, and it was the last town in England to hold out against William the Conqueror, who besieged the town for eighteen days in 1068 before the townspeople were forced to surrender. The pride of Exeter is its magnificent medieval cathedral, famed for its stone sculptures and its wonderful vaulted roof (the longest stretch of Gothic vaulting in the world).

EXETER, HIGH STREET
1896 FRITH 38010

The city was a major centre for the Devon woollen industry, and exported finished cloth to France, Spain and the Netherlands. Its position by the River Exe gave it a reliable supply of water to power the industry; however, the trade declined as a result of the Industrial Revolution. This meant that Exeter did not become heavily industrialised or developed in the 19th century, and much of its historic city centre remained untouched until it was destroyed in the air raids of the Second World War.

Exeter's modern prosperity owes much to the building of the railway (constructed by Isambard Kingdom Brunel) in the 19th century. It is said that when the railway came, an MP stood up in the House of Commons and said: 'This morning I was in Exeter!' He caused a sensation. His fellow MPs were amazed to realise how fast modern travel could be. Today Exeter is a bustling commercial city and Devon's county town; the city centre's striking modern architecture forms an interesting contrast to the medieval cathedral and its tranquil close.

EXETER, FORE STREET
1896 FRITH 38007

# Exeter's Historic Quay and Canal

The River Exe is tidal, and up until the late 13th century it was navigable right up to the city, thus contributing to Exeter's success as a great trading centre. But weirs built in the early 14th century forced ships to load and unload down-river at Topsham. Despite repeated pleas by the city to the king, it was not until 1550 that Edward VI granted permission to re-open the river. He was too late, however – the river had silted up.

So in 1563 the merchants of Exeter employed John Trew to build a canal to bypass the weirs, but it ran for a mere 2.8 km, and could not be entered at low tide. The canal was lengthened in 1677, and deepened and widened in 1701, and again in the 1830s, so that access for bigger ships was much improved. The canal, finally five miles long, was hugely successful until the

EXETER QUAY TODAY

19th century, when the dwindling wool trade and the rise of the railways brought about its decline.

Commercial use of the canal continued spasmodically until the early 1970s. Today the role of the quay and the canal is largely a recreational one, with cafes, shops, cyclepaths and footpaths, and mooring for pleasure craft. Some old warehouses have been redeveloped as flats, and the beautiful red brick Custom House still stands.

An authentic quayside atmosphere remains, and the quay is often used by film and television producers looking for a historic location. Perhaps the most famous television series to be filmed here was 'The Onedin Line'.

EXETER, SHIPS IN THE PORT 1896 FRITH 38036X

EXETER, THE PORT 1896 FRITH 38034

# John endures the darkness of the dungeon

JOHN SITTING IN
THE JUDGE'S CHAIR
TALKING
TO HISTORIAN
TODD GRAY

I wanted to see what was behind the ornate façade of the Guildhall, so I was really pleased that the historian Todd Gray came inside with me to tell me more of its history. He explained that the Guildhall was built as the meeting place for the medieval trading associations known as guilds. It has functioned as a prison, a police station, a place for civic functions and celebrations, a city archive store, a market hall, and the meeting place for the City Council. As we stood in the hall itself, with its lofty beamed ceiling and panelled walls, I learnt about one of its most important roles – that of a court.

We imagined the scene when Judge Jeffreys came here to subdue the West Country after the Monmouth Rebellion in the 17th century. 'Judge Jeffreys is still a hate figure today', said Todd, 'and he's remembered as "the hanging judge". He was notorious for the severity of his sentences. He had a painful kidney disease that no doubt made him extremely irritable, but his harshness was unusual even for those times.'

We sat on carved chairs on a raised platform and looked down on the hall. 'The judge would sit up here', said Todd, 'and look down on the court below

THE GUILDHALL
TODAY

him. The prisoners came in from behind this dais, and from here he would make his dreadful pronouncements.' In this impressive setting I could almost hear the judge saying: 'You will be hanged by the neck until you are dead'.

I wondered what the most trivial offence was that a person could be hanged for. 'Stealing a sheep', said Todd. 'That meant an instant death sentence, or at least transportation.' But what did the city authorities and the general public think about such severe punishments? Todd told me that it was important to remember that back then there was only very loose political control. 'There were hardly any equivalents to our modern police, so the state at that time was supportive of a structure that intimidated people into behaving well.'

THE
GUILDHALL'S
BEAMED CEILING

Exeter's Guildhall has a fascinating archive of documents dating back 800 years, which tell amazing stories of the cases that were held here. Todd turned the pages of an old book, and found a case that he thought I'd love. '"This year"', he read, '"the mayor was much troubled about the punishment of one Joan Luter, a very strumpet and harlot."' So what year was that? 'It was 1524', said Todd. 'But her supporters did not agree that she should go to jail, and so they attacked the mayor, right here in front of the Guildhall.' I was intrigued. Why didn't they think she should go to jail? Why did they feel so strongly? 'Because she was so beautiful!' Todd told me. A very good reason, I think.

*We switched off our torches, and the pitch blackness was night-marish*

Poor Joan was sent down to the dungeon all the same, and so we went down, too, to see what it would have been like. We clambered down a ladder armed with torches, and found ourselves in a dark brick-lined cellar. Todd told me that the Guildhall cellars were known as 'the pit', and served as the dungeon for prisoners. 'It was a very unpleasant place to be. You could have been confined here for months. If you were violent you were manacled to the walls; otherwise you could roam around.'

I found the place had a powerfully gloomy atmosphere, and I didn't think I'd do well in those conditions. The air was musty and damp. 'Imagine the sewerage from the streets filtering down', said Todd, 'and seeping up from the earthen floor as well.' I supposed that for most of the time the prisoners would have been in complete darkness. 'Yes', Todd told me. 'There is one tiny grating to let in a little light, but that's all.' We switched off our torches, and the pitch blackness was horribly nightmarish. The thought of being imprisoned here was too much to bear, and I wanted to escape. What a relief it was to get back to the light and the fresh air.

JOHN AND
TODD GRAY IN THE
DUNGEON

# The Baedeker Raids on Exeter

In the spring of 1942, on the explicit instructions of Adolf Hitler, several of England's most attractive and historic cities (chosen, it was said, from the Baedeker series of guidebooks) were targeted in what he called 'reprisals' for the British bombing of Lübeck.

On three successive nights at the end of April and again in May, bombs rained down on Exeter. As many as 1700 buildings, including some of the city's finest medieval and Regency houses, were destroyed. A further 14,000 were damaged, and civilian casualties were heavy. Three bays of the south choir aisle of the cathedral were also demolished.

When repairs were being carried out on Exeter cathedral, a fascinating collection of wax models was found hidden in a cavity in the stone screen by the choir. The little models were mainly of human and animal limbs, but there was also a complete figure of a woman. It is thought that these were offerings from medieval pilgrims to the tomb of Bishop Edmund Lacy, left by people who had come to pray for the recovery of either themselves, their friends and family or of their sick animals. The models are now kept in the cathedral library.

## JOHN'S PHOTOGRAPH OF EXETER

EXETER GUILDHALL, 2011

*Even after all the destruction of the Second World War, it's astonishing how much of the old city of Exeter remains. Look at my photograph, and follow the road round with your eyes – the ancient Guildhall is encouraging you to see what's at the centre of the picture. Only a bus, you may say, but it's doing an important job. My photograph is showing a real city scene: people are working and shopping, just as in the Frith photograph. And it's a handsome picture. Why? Because it's got a very handsome old building in the middle of it.*

# Horses and Haymaking: the Good Life?

BARNSTAPLE, HAYMAKING 1890 FRITH 24878X

*'This photograph was taken in the farmlands just outside Barnstaple in North Devon, and it shows a farm labourer making hay with horse-drawn equipment. I think you get the impression from this photograph that the person taking it is trying to say: "Isn't country life wonderful!" But both the farm hand and the horse look dejected and tired. I wanted to find out what country life and farming were really like in Frith's time.'*

## *By Frith's time the day of the horse was nearly over ... soon the tractor would be replacing the horse*

A VICTORIAN
ENGRAVING SHOWING
A YOUNG GIRL
TURNING HAY

CHIDEOCK,
GATHERING HAY 1922
FRITH 72803

The photographs of farming in the Frith archive seem to give a nostalgic picture of a golden age. But in Victorian times life in the country was not as idyllic as we think. Farming was a hierarchical business. At the top of the pyramid was the squire, the landowner, who took to himself nearly all the profit from his land. Below him were his tenant farmers, who claimed a reasonable share. Right at the bottom were the farm labourers, who did all the hard physical work on the farm for a pittance.

Farm labourers were among the poorest people in Britain, and their living conditions – in tumbledown cottages with leaking roofs and earth floors – were often a disgrace. Men, women and children worked outside in blazing sun or freezing rain for hours on end for little reward. Many contemporary illustrators, artists and writers portrayed farming as a happy rustic idyll, but one has only to read Thomas Hardy's description of Tess in 'Tess of the D'Urbervilles' grubbing up turnips in bitter wind and rain to realise that country life was not all harvest home and maypoles.

From the 17th century onwards, the agricultural revolution, spurred on by unprecedented population growth, enclosure, mechanisation and crop rotation, meant that farming by Frith's time was far more productive.

By the late 19th century Victorian inventiveness had produced an enormous range of agricultural machinery, not just ploughs, but grubbers, cultivators, harrows, rollers, drills, reapers, binders, rakes and much more, which could all be drawn by horses. However, by now the day of the horse was nearly over: a steam traction engine could do the work of a dozen horses – and petrol engines were soon to follow. By the 1930s, the tractor would be replacing the horse.

The main photograph on page 161 shows haymaking at Chestwood,

HOLMWOOD,
HAYMAKING 1909
FRITH 61659X

NETHERBURY,
HAYMAKING 1912
FRITH 65068T

just south of Barnstaple on the River Taw in North Devon, a sturdy town in a predominantly rural area. North Devon lies to the west of Exmoor and north of Dartmoor. These two natural barriers meant that until the railways pointed their iron fingers north-westwards relatively late in the railway age access to this area was difficult, and few people made the effort to explore its rolling countryside and spectacular coast. Thus a feeling of being cut off from the rest of the country – until Victorian times at least – created an altogether different culture and atmosphere.

Barnstaple's position in fertile country on a tidal river meant that it must always have been a thriving trading and farming centre. Its fair has been held since time immemorial. It started off as a celebratory event after the huge annual market, which lasted for a week. Horses, other livestock, and produce were traded, and farm labourers found new positions here.

# An Over-Romanticised View?

Victorian town-dwellers often viewed rural life as happy, pleasure-filled, and enjoyable. They rarely took into account the hard labour, the long hours, and the poor conditions that country people had to endure. Typical over-romanticised accounts include the following from 'The New Monthly Belle Assemblée', 1844:

> *Of all English rustic employments with which we are acquainted, haymaking is assuredly the most delightful … Can anything be more charming than a stroll through a newly-strewn field, when the sweet scent of the fresh-cut hay is perfuming the evening breeze, and rendering the whole atmosphere odoriferous? Can anything be more delightful than to mingle with the merry groups of haymakers whilst they are busily engaged in turning the fragrant crop? … No other employment seems half so healthy or exhilarating. All are brimful of mirth, that vents itself in innocent jests and hearty laughter.*

HAYMAKING 1888 FRITH H35303

HAYMAKING 1925 FRITH 77074X

Haymaking could sometimes have been pleasant, but the farmer always had a wary eye on the weather – a sudden rainstorm could ruin his crop of hay and result in hunger for the animals and financial hardship to him in the winter months. However, you would never guess it from Marianne Farningham's account in her 'Life Sketches, and Echoes from the Valley' published in 1868:

> *The machine goes up and down the field, and the haymakers sing their merry songs, and the children who are so highly favoured as to live in the fresh beautiful country go and play among it, and roll on it, and bury one another in it, and otherwise turn it into general disorder, as their manner is with everything they like, so that they may enjoy the fun generally.*
>
> *And so altogether the haymaking is a festive time, a time of pure enjoyment and general fun, a time of resting tired limbs, of regaling the senses, and of giving every power we have its utmost of innocent and healthful delight and recreation.*

When the sun shone the mood in the fields may have been 'merry', but for the farmers and their labourers the hay harvest was always a time of stress and worry.

# John learns about the realities of farming

I was looking forward to meeting Jonathan Waterer, who runs a heritage farm in North Devon. He uses heavy horses in combination with relatively modern equipment to farm the land in a way remarkably similar to the way it was in Frith's time, so I was hoping that he would be able to tell me what farming life was really like in the 1880s and 90s.

I met Jonathan and his team of beautiful horses in his farmyard. I showed him the Frith photograph (see page 161), and asked him what was going on. 'It's probably June', he said, 'and they're haymaking. The grass has been cut, and the horse is hitched up to a hay tedder. That's a machine that spreads the grass out so that it can dry in the sun. Until two or three years ago we used hay tedders like that on this farm – well, they were a bit more modern than the ones in the photo, but essentially the same.'

I thought the horse in the photograph didn't look as healthy as Jonathan's team.

JOHN MEETS FARMER
JONATHAN WATERER

'You have to remember that in Victorian times, when horses did all the work on every farm, they were like machines are to us', Jonathan told me. 'Times were hard, and farmers had to make money any way they could, so the horses didn't get as good feed as mine do now, and they certainly worked hard day in day out seven days a week. The horse in the photo actually looks quite

healthy, but you get the impression that he's certainly done a hard day's work.'

'What about the farm hand?' I asked. 'He looks poor – and exhausted.' 'I would, too, if I only got sixpence a week!' said Jonathan. 'The wages of farm workers in Victorian times weren't like wages are now. They would count themselves lucky if they had food in their bellies and a roof over their heads to house their families.'

I felt, though, that the photographer wanted to make farming life look wonderful. 'When you're in lovely country like this, townies like me think it must all be idyllic', I said. 'Well, to be fair', Jonathan answered, 'you and I have had a great time hitching the horses up, and it's a lovely day today. But when I'm on my own, and it's pouring with rain, and I've got to fork up a load of dung, it is hard. And I worry a lot about the weather, too. Maybe I'm making hay, and I'm trying to get it cut and made and in the barn before the weather breaks.'

LOADING THE CART
READY FOR
MUCKSPREADING

'So life's tough in paradise!' I said. 'Yes', said Jonathan, 'and now we've got to get on with the muckspreading. Not exactly romantic, is it? But it's got to be done all the same. And in Victorian times, after he'd made the hay, that labourer in the photo would be doing just the same as we are now, loading muck on the cart, hitching up the horses and spreading the muck on the fields to fertilise them. Even if we were using a big modern tractor, it's exactly the same process.'

So far, everything I'd seen would have been reasonably familiar to an 1890s farmer. I asked Jonathan if there was anything here that a Victorian would find surprising. 'If he came back today, he'd be amazed that the countryside was so empty. With modern machinery, it doesn't take many people to work even a big farm, and most people find jobs in the towns. This farm's just 90 acres, but there would probably have been at least three or four people working here in Frith's day.'

*'Muck-*
*spreading.*
*Not exactly*
*romantic,*
*is it?'*

It was time for us to spread the muck, and Jonathan let me have a go at sitting on the cart and driving the horses. It was great fun – but I felt it was a job best left to the professionals!

JOHN TRIES HIS
HAND AT
MUCKSPREADING

# Pannier Markets

North Devon's remoteness, and its rolling hills and valleys, meant that its roads were rough and narrow, unsuitable for big carts and wagons. Farmers' wives came to market on horseback, carrying their produce in big panniers, or baskets. Barnstaple Pannier Market was built in 1855. Its spectacular wooden vaulted roof is as impressive as a cathedral's. On the fringes of the crowd stand the stall holders – farmers' wives, country women and old men. For most, the shillings they earned here were a vital part of their survival.

BARNSTAPLE, THE PANNIER MARKET 1919  FRITH 69324

## JOHN'S PHOTOGRAPH OF NORTH DEVON

THE HERITAGE FARMER, 2011

*In a way, my picture is like the Frith picture, which is a town dweller's version of life in the country. The Frith photograph shows a town in the background where most people live, but there are still people in the countryside, and it's bathed in sunlight. However, we know that in fact life was hard on the farm. That's what I was keen to convey in my picture, that there can be a darker side to life in the country. I wanted to take an inspiring image of a happy farmer with his handsome horses, but we need to remember that the countryside isn't always paradise.*

# Miraculous Feats of Water Engineering

NEWPORT, ON THE CANAL, FOURTEEN LOCKS 1896 FRITH 38707

*'Britain's canals and their ingenious locks were a miraculous feat of engineering. Their builders were so ambitious and inventive that they managed to make water go up hills! This picture was taken near Newport in South Wales at Fourteen Locks, part of the Monmouthshire Canal. I wanted to learn why this canal had been so important, and what it's like here today.'*

## Up to 1,100 boats used the Monmouthshire Canal in its heyday

Newport, on an important shipping route on the Severn Estuary, had been a significant port throughout its history, but its vast expansion began in the late 18th century with the birth of the canals. The coal mines and iron works of South Wales, the basis of the Industrial Revolution, were opening up, and a way had to be found to bring the coal and iron ore to the ports so that they could be shipped to other parts of Britain and all over the world. In the 18th century most roads were no more than tracks. It was difficult to move goods, especially heavy goods, and the answer remains one of the glories of our landscape: the canal system. At their peak, four and a half thousand miles of canals criss-crossed the country. Here in South Wales, the Monmouthshire Canal was the stimulus for the development of Newport. It grew from a small trading town with a population of about 1,087 in 1801 to a large industrial and commercial centre with a population of 67,270 in 1901.

The Monmouthshire Canal was begun in 1792. It consisted of a main line 11 miles long from Newport to Pontnewynydd via Pontypool, and a branch to Crumlin, which left the main line at Malpas just outside Newport. The canal (serviced by a network of tramroads for horse-drawn trucks carrying coal and ore from the mines) was officially opened in 1799, although parts of the canal were already open. It allowed coal and iron to be transported to Newport much more efficiently, but it was also used for other goods including timber, lime and farm produce.

As early as 1798 almost 44,000 tons of goods were being carried by the canal. The first quarter of the 19th century was the golden age of the Monmouthshire Canal, and up to 1,100 barges were using it. The Blaenavon Ironworks alone sent 300 tons of iron a week by canal.

However, the weather affected the viability of delivery by water, and freezing conditions could bring the narrowboats to a halt. Competition from the faster, more resilient railway system began to hasten the decline of the canal from the 1860s. Canals all over Britain began to fall into disrepair; they collapsed or silted up, and parts of them were even closed, drained and used as the route for the railways. The Monmouthshire Canal lingered on, however; the last cargo was carried on the Crumlin arm in 1930, and on the Pontnewynydd in 1938. The Crumlin branch finally closed in 1949 and the eastern branch was abandoned in 1962. The Fourteen Locks Canal Heritage Centre opened in 1976, and in recent years passionate volunteers have started to return many of Britain's canals, including this one, back to their former glory, not for industry, but for pleasure, tourism and education.

One interesting sidelight on the canal is that in 1984 Mr John Evans, a farmer at Tredunnoc, some miles north of Newport and Caerleon, noticed a large boat protruding from beneath a bank of the River Usk. In 1987 the boat was excavated by the Glamorgan Gwent Archaeological Trust. The archaeologists hoped to lift it out of the river and take it to Newport for conservation and eventual display. Days before a crane was due to undertake the delicate business of lifting the boat, a flash flood in the Usk dragged the boat off the river bed. It floated a hundred yards downriver before it was smashed to pieces on the river bank.

Much of the boat was salvaged and recorded, and it proved to be a very early canal boat, some 18 metres long, double-ended and flat-bottomed. It would have been towed along from a canal or river bank, and its structure indicated that it had been built early in the 19th century. Its condition suggested that it had had a long life. The Town Dock, which gave the only access from the canal to the river, was not opened until 1842. By this time the railway was overtaking the canal, but a river trade in timber still continued between Newport and Tredunnoc. The Tredunnoc boat could have been used for this trade before being abandoned and left to provide extra protection to the banks of the River Usk. Canal boats of this date are exceedingly rare; it is hoped that one day the surviving sections of the boat will be put on public display.

NEWPORT, ALLT-YR-YN, ABOVE THE LOCK 1893 FRITH 32637

*Volunteers are now restoring the canal not for industry, but for pleasure, tourism and education*

# Gruelling, Back-breaking Work

Narrowboats were continually having to negotiate locks. Moving the heavy wooden balance beams to open the gates was gruelling work for the boatmen. At Newport they had to ascend a notoriously steep flight.

The Fourteen Locks, on the Crumlin branch of the Monmouthshire Canal near Rogerstone, is also known as the Cefn Flight. Completed in 1799, its complex of weirs, sluices, pounds and ponds control the water supply, with no gates shared between locks, making this a flight of locks rather than a staircase lock. Boats rise or descend about 160 feet, making this one of the steepest flights in Britain. In fact it was difficult to keep the long flight of locks supplied with enough water to function properly, and this was one of the reasons why competition from the railway system began to hasten the decline of the canal from the 1860s.

*Moving the heavy wooden balance beams to open the lock gates was gruelling work for the canal boatmen*

The Caen flight of 29 locks at Devizes in Wiltshire on the Kennet and Avon Canal (see photograph below) and the Bingley flight of five locks on the Leeds and Liverpool Canal in Yorkshire (see photograph, right), are both spectacular examples of canal engineering.

TOP RIGHT: WATFORD, CASSIOBURY PARK AND IRON BRIDGE LOCK 1921
FRITH 70492T

ABOVE: DEVIZES, THE CAEN FLIGHT 1898
FRITH 42320

RIGHT: BINGLEY, LOCKS ON THE LEEDS AND LIVERPOOL CANAL c1900
FRITH B98501T

We stand on a picturesque hump-backed bridge gazing dreamily down at the smooth filament of water. Brightly painted narrowboats chug gently by. The entire scene conjures up peace and contentment, with its fields and tree-fringed towpaths. However, in their heyday the canals were busy commercial arteries, carrying freight across the country, and connecting major manufacturing centres with cities and ports.

The men and women who worked on the canals had precious little time or opportunity to enjoy the scenery. Narrowboats were always on the move. The boatmen worked six- or seven-day weeks, receiving no sick pay or salary during winter freeze-ups.

A narrowboat had to deliver its cargo whatever the season or weather, and a family with children had to endure cramped conditions day in, day out. In the winter months the whole family would huddle round the smoky stove for warmth and comfort.

Keeping body and soul together was hard for a canal boat family and especially for the canal boat wife. One of the common commodities the narrowboats carried was coal, and this dirty cargo was a major obstacle to good housekeeping. There was always cooking and cleaning to do, and it was common to see lines of washing hanging from the boat and billowing in the breeze. The children were continually running up and down the towpath, opening and closing locks, and leading the horse around the canal bridges. As a consequence, canal children rarely had a proper education. By the time they were ten or eleven they worked full-time on the boat.

# A Hard Life on the Canals

VICTORIAN ENGRAVING OF A CANAL
BOAT FAMILY BY WALTER CRANE

RICKMANSWORTH, THE CANAL 1921  FRITH 70506X

The family had to cope in a tiny cabin, stooping the whole time. Yet canal families still managed to take a pride in their tiny homes. Furniture and fittings were skilfully designed to take up as little space as possible – beds folded into cupboards, for instance. Everything was polished to a shine. Brassware was always popular, and pots and pans were painted in bright colours with roses and other motifs. This pride in their way of life helped them to deal with the day to day drudgery.

# John learns about vital restoration work

JOHN TALKS TO LOCAL HISTORIAN PHIL HUGHES

❝*Water was paramount. Every time you opened a lock, you lost about 52,000 gallons*❞

THE SCENE SHOWN IN THE MAIN FRITH PHOTOGRAPH ON PAGE 168 AS IT IS TODAY

The fortunes of Fourteen Locks are now looking up, thanks to the determination and dedication of local historian Phil Hughes, the Canal Trust, and Newport Council over the last decade. Phil showed me the exact spot from which the Frith photograph (page 168) was taken.

'We're looking at the bottom of a 14-lock flight', Phil told me. 'It's a unique structure. It rises 169 feet in half a mile to take the canal boats uphill.' Looking at the Frith photograph, we could see just three locks. I wanted to know how much farther the locks stretched. 'Right up to the top of the hill', said Phil. I asked him about the people in the photograph. 'They're operating the lock gates; you can see that they were fully operational at that time. Those gates were still working up to about 1935.'

I asked Phil what was unique about the locks. 'They were designed to save water', Phil explained. 'Water was paramount. Every time you opened a lock, you lost about 52,000 gallons of water. At this flight, though, when you opened a lock the water would spill into the ponds on each side of the locks. So when you opened the top lock, by the time you got to the bottom you had only lost one lock's-worth of water.' 'But people think it never stops raining in Wales!' I exclaimed. 'Well', said Phil, 'we're always short of water here. In summer there's droughts, and in the winter the water freezes. That's the main reason why the railways meant the end for the canals.'

I realised that when the Frith team were taking these photographs in the late 19th century, canals in Britain were already in rapid decline, and that these pictures were a record of a disappearing way of life. By the start of the 20th century, only a few working canals remained. Phil told me, though, that in 2000 the monumental task of restoring Newport's Fourteen Locks got under way. He showed me the first of the locks that had been restored. 'It looks wonderful!' I said. 'How much did it cost?' 'Not far short of £1 million', Phil told me.

The future holds yet another major restoration project for the Canal Trust. A group of volunteers has rescued an old barge, and aim to return it one day to the canal. I went to have a look at the barge. When I saw her, she looked like a rectangular tube made of rusty metal, but educational consultant Tom Maloney was bursting with enthusiasm. 'That space you see now will have a nice floor on it, and we'll have benches on each side so that when we have people, particularly children, on the barge they can look out and have a magical experience. Any child who comes on board this boat is going to have a dream ride.'

ONE OF THE RESTORED
LOCKS ON THE CANAL

I asked Tom what it is about canals and canal boats that attracts people. 'Inside us all there's a love of water', said Tom, 'and I think it goes back a very long time. Canals and canal boats are part of our wonderful landscape, and we don't want them to disappear!'

I wondered what the canal folk in the Frith photograph would have thought about all these efforts to restore the waterways. It's sad that their identities are lost in time. I was very pleased, therefore, to be able to meet Mary Bailey, a real link with the past. 'My grandfather, Henry Bailey, was the lock keeper at Fourteen Locks', she told me. 'He worked here nearly all his life before retiring

HENRY BAILEY

in 1922.' Mary showed me a photograph of Henry – I thought it was a shame he wasn't in the Frith photograph. 'Never mind', said Mary, 'he would have known those men by the lock. He knew everyone. It was his job to walk up and down the canal, checking that everything was in order.'

I was thrilled to be talking to someone with a direct connection to the Frith picture. I asked her what impression she had of what life was like on the canal. 'It was a very close community', she said, 'a rural community, the kind of comradeship that perhaps we've lost today.'

VOLUNTEERS RESTORING A LOCK

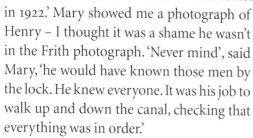

JOHN WITH EDUCATIONAL CONSULTANT TOM MALONEY
AND THE BARGE THAT IS BEING RESCUED AND RESTORED

JOHN MEETS MARY BAILEY, THE LOCK KEEPER'S
GRANDDAUGHTER

## JOHN'S PHOTOGRAPH ON THE MONMOUTHSHIRE CANAL

### THE LOCK KEEPER'S GRANDDAUGHTER, 2011

*After a hundred years of neglect the canal is at last starting to come back to life, so as a direct link between past and present, I decided to take a picture of Mary Bailey, granddaughter of one of the last of Britain's lock keepers, the man in charge of the Fourteen Locks when the Frith picture was taken. She's standing at the lock so painstakingly restored by the Newport team. How exciting for her that these locks will be as good as new – she never thought that it would ever happen. So in a way, this is a picture of the future.*

NEWPORT, A TRAM IN COMMERCIAL STREET c1899 FRITH 47896x

# Whisked along on Tramlines

*'The atmospheric photograph on the previous pages shows a mode of transport that flourished in the Victorian era – the tram. We are still in South Wales, and now in Newport itself. Commercial Street runs though the centre of the town, and the horse-drawn tram is making its way along the road with some Victorian passengers perched on top. I wanted to find out more about the growth of Newport and how its transport systems changed over the years.'*

Newport stands in the southeast corner of Wales, a border city where English and Welsh influences intermingle. The city stretches on either side of the River Usk, a few miles from where the mouth of the river joins the Severn Estuary. Newport's bridges take traffic over the Usk, the first great obstacle as the traveller goes from England into South Wales after crossing the Wye or the Severn.

By the 16th century Newport had become an important port. In the reign of Elizabeth I there are records of two ships of over 100 tons here, as well as many small ships. No other port on the Severn had any ships of over 100 tons apart from Bristol. The port grew more and more busy, and as the Industrial Revolution took off, it became a vital hub from which to transport the coal and iron ore from the South Wales valleys. By the 1850s Newport was bigger than Cardiff.

The late 19th century saw a rapid expansion, both of the town and the docks; in the 1890s Newport's South Dock was the largest masonry dock in the world, and it handled a correspondingly large global trade. Now the town sprawled on both sides of the River Usk. There were docks, factories, railways, roads, shops and houses, all reflecting the expansion of the town. The generation of power for domestic and industrial use, street lighting, and transport was vital for the smooth running of a busy trading city.

Gas supplies had been available as early as the 1820s, and were gradually extended to provide lighting across most of Newport. Newport's first electricity power station was opened in Llanarth Street in 1895. Seven years later the larger East Power Station was built in Corporation Road, bringing electricity into town to replace gas lighting, and to power the new tramway opened by the Corporation once it took over public transport in 1901. Horse tramways had come to Newport in 1875, but once the Corporation had converted to electricity with overhead electric power wires most horse tramways were replaced with electric powered cars, and the old horse-drawn trams were almost all gone by 1903.

'John's Newport Directory', a trade directory published in 1927, reported: 'The Electric Tramways consist of some 7.59 route miles, mostly double track, embracing five routes, and there are 58 cars. There are also several Motor Bus routes in operation.' By 1928 the Corporation had converted several tramcar routes to motorbus routes, and by 1936 they had decided to scrap the remaining trams. The last tram service was withdrawn in September 1937, and a large enthusiastic crowd gathered in the town to see the last tramcar depart for the depot (see photograph overleaf). Souvenir hunters then got busy removing anything they could as a memento. One tram car seat resurfaced some years ago, and was presented to Newport Museum. Today, in Newport and all over Britain the more versatile motor bus has replaced the tram.

NEWPORT, TRAMS IN
THE HIGH STREET
1903 FRITH 49481X

# John learns about Newport's love affair with trams

Local tram enthusiast and historian David Thomas has a collection of tram photographs, and he kindly brought a few along to show me. The first showed a tram packed with passengers and surrounded by a large crowd.

JOHN MEETS TRAM ENTHUSIAST
DAVID THOMAS

'This marks the end of an era', said Dave. 'It shows an electric tram, the last tram to operate in Newport leaving Westgate Centre at 11pm on 6 September 1937. This was its final journey. Packed with passengers, it proceeded along Corporation Road to the depot.' 'Well', I said, 'if it's 1937, it's just before the war. That makes the picture rather sad – although the people in the photograph are smiling and happy, in a couple of years their world will have changed.'

Dave told me that there was a great deal of affection in Newport for the trams. 'You can see that from the big crowd who have gathered to say goodbye. All the trams ended up at a breaker's yard on the river bank, and they were quickly scrapped.' His next photograph showed tram carcases piled on top of each other in an undignified heap. 'So this is the graveyard of the trams', I said. 'Yes', said Dave, 'hardly anything of them remains today. I managed to retrieve an inside door from one of the trams, and I keep it in my garage.'

BELOW LEFT:
NEWPORT'S LAST
TRAM, 1937

BELOW CENTRE:
TRAM CARCASES IN
THE BREAKER'S YARD

BELOW RIGHT:
TRAM MODELS IN THE
CITY MUSEUM

The trams have gone, but our love affair with them lingers on, as I saw when I visited Newport's City Museum. In this bright modern building there are plenty of echoes of the past, including some beautiful scale models of trams built by a local enthusiast. The museum also has an old book of regulations for the tram conductors. I particularly liked this strict instruction: 'Keep cars tidy. Conductors must keep cars clear of paper and used tickets; this should be done when cars are stationary at the terminus.' Very sensible!

NEWPORT, COMMERCIAL STREET c1899 FRITH 47896T

NEWPORT, THE TRANSPORTER BRIDGE 1906 FRITH 54935A

# Over the Usk by Gondola

Newport's trams have the fascination of nostalgia for us now, but they were hardly an unusual form of transport. However, Newport is proud to be the site of a very rare form of transport (there are believed to be only eight working examples in the entire world): a transporter bridge.

One could explain this kind of bridge by saying that it is a section of road that travels across the water. From a tall framework a platform, or gondola (you can see it just to the left of the right-hand tower in the photograph above), is suspended by cables from a carriage (known as a traveller) which is driven by cables from an engine and moves along a high-level girder supported by towers on either bank. It is used where a conventional bridge or a ferry would impede shipping.

The idea was first envisioned by Charles Smith, manager of an engine works in Hartlepool, in 1873, but it was the French engineer Ferdinand Arnodin who patented the concept in 1887. He helped Alberto Palacio to build the world's first transporter bridge, Vizcaya Bridge in Spain.

In Newport, the expansion of the town and its industries was putting increasing pressure on the Town Bridge. A new bridge was needed close to the docks on the west of the river and to the new Orb Steelworks on the east of the river. With the problems of the tide here, a ferry was not considered a suitable option. A conventional bridge or a swing bridge was also ruled out because the Usk is very broad and its banks very low at this point, and it would have been hard to build a normal bridge high enough to allow ships to pass beneath it.

The Borough Engineer, Robert Haynes, eventually came up with a solution. He had seen a transporter bridge designed by Arnodin at Rouen, so he commissioned him to design a similar bridge for Newport. It took four years to complete, and the estimated cost for the work was £98,000. Despite the complicated technology used during the building of the bridge not a single life was lost. The bridge opened in 1906, and is still in use today.

The vital statistics of Newport's transporter bridge are impressive. The height of the towers is 242ft. The distance between the towers is 645ft, and the transporter platform, or gondola, travelling at 10ft per second, can carry 6 cars and 20 foot passengers. It takes about one and a half minutes to cross the river once the gondola is moving.

NEWPORT, THE TRANSPORTER BRIDGE 2004 FRITH N25714K

NEWPORT, HIGH STREET 1910 FRITH 62509X

## JOHN'S PHOTOGRAPH OF NEWPORT

COMMERCIAL STREET, NEWPORT, 2011

*I've taken my picture in the same place that the Frith photograph was taken, looking down the main street. This is modern Newport. The road looks more cluttered than in Frith's day – there are cars now, and more street signs and street furniture – and it's sad to see a few too many 'To Let' signs outside empty shops. The horse-drawn tram has gone for ever from the British high street. There's certainly much replacing it – but have our streets got as much character now? I'll leave you to decide.*

COLEFORD, THE SPEECH HOUSE 1893   FRITH 32450

# From Royal Hunts to Ochre Mining

*'The scene today looks almost exactly the same as it appears in the Frith photograph on the previous pages. We're near Coleford in the Forest of Dean, Gloucestershire. In the picture you can see a coach and horses arriving at a hotel. It still is a hotel, but it's not just any hotel. This is the Speech House; inside is one of the oldest and strangest courts in Britain, and its job is to administer one of Britain's oldest and finest forests.'*

AN OAK TREE IN THE FOREST OF DEAN

The Forest of Dean stretches over 100 square kilometres; it is mixed woodland, a good example of Britain's surviving ancient woodland, tucked between the Severn and Wye rivers in Gloucestershire, and it offers some of the finest scenery in the country. It is a place with a wealth of history and a sense of independence that is tangible in its traditional customs, lore and laws.

As well as forestry and charcoal production, mining and iron working have long been at the heart of the Forest's economy. There is evidence that people have lived and worked here since the Mesolithic era, and the Romans established various mining industries and built a road from near Ross-on-Wye to the Severn to enable trade. As well as being an industrial centre, the area was a hunting forest for the Anglo-Saxon and then the Norman kings.

A VICTORIAN ENGRAVING OF A MEDIEVAL HUNTING SCENE

It was the Normans who formulated many of the laws and customs that remain in place today in the Forest of Dean. They appointed verderers to act for the king and protect his rights, and at the same time local people were given common rights. The rights of the freeminers originate from the siege of Berwick-on-Tweed in 1296: miners from the Forest of Dean were used by Edward I to undermine the defences, and as a reward the king granted them and their descendants free mining rights. They were regulated by the Court of Mine Law.

The Forest continued to be used as a royal hunting ground by the Tudors and Stuarts, and mining and charcoal production remained important industries for centuries, along with timber production for ship building. It was not until the 1960s that these industries went into decline on a commercial scale. Even today, though, freeminers exercise their rights to dig coal, iron ore and ochre from private pits, as they have done for generations beyond recall. Despite its industrial heritage, the Forest of Dean remains an area of mixed woodland roamed by wild deer and common land used for pasturing livestock.

CHARCOAL BURNING c1955
FRITH L123013

*Even today, freeminers exercise their rights to dig coal, iron ore and ochre from private pits, as they have done for generations*

SHEEP GRAZING IN THE FOREST OF DEAN

JOHN IN THE FOREST
WITH VERDERERS BOB
JENKINS AND MAURICE
BENT

LORD
NELSON

Bob Jenkins and Maurice Bent are verderers, elected judges of the historic Forest court, and they still actively govern the business of the Forest of Dean. They explain that today they do not have quite the powers that their predecessors did. For instance, in the past if someone stole a sheep, they would have had the power to sentence him to be hanged. Now their role is to help the Forest in every possible way – that is their duty as verderers. They tell how Nelson, another person who had a strong sense of duty, came here to look at the Forest, for its oaks were reputed to be the best for ship building. Nelson was shocked to find that most of the trees had been felled, mainly to fuel the smelting of iron ore. He made it his business to see that an Act of Parliament was passed to renew the Forest, so thousands of oak saplings were planted for future generations.

Overlooking the Cannop Valley, the Speech House was built in 1682 to house the Court of Mine Law and the Court of Speech. At these courts the verderers and the miners managed, and still manage, the trees, the game and the mineral resources of the Forest of Dean. By 1858, it was also an inn catering for those attending the courts; it was extended and enlarged in the latter part of the 19th century, and is a hotel today. Speech House Pudding (you can find the recipe on page 190) was a traditional speciality served here. It is said that it was first served to Charles II when he stayed at the Speech House, which was then his hunting lodge.

Today, the mining customs and laws are overseen by the Deputy Gaveller, whose office is in the Forestry Commission offices in Coleford. Although the Verderers' Court of the Speech House is now used as the hotel's magnificent oak-beamed restaurant, adorned with 19 pairs of antlers, it still continues in its original function as the courtroom and meeting place of the Foresters of Dean, who are concerned with the administration of Forest law and managing and protecting the 'vert and venison' of the Forest – the local deer and their habitat.

THE VERDERERS'
COURTROOM

# John digs deep in the Forest's ochre mines

Jonathan Wright is a freeminer, whose family have for generations been granted permission to mine ochre from the caves that lie deep beneath the forest. He kindly agreed to teach me all about ochre mining. 'First, I'll

OCHRE POWDER

JOHN DEEP INSIDE
THE MINE WITH
JONATHAN WRIGHT

show you what we produce', he said. Beside a mortar and pestle stood a big bowl full of a deep purplish-red powder and some lidded jars. 'We get lots of different colours, red, yellow, purple, brown – they're ground into powder to make paints.'

I wondered how far back in time ochre mining went. 'I'm at the end of four and a half thousand years at least of mining here – it's good to be continuing in an ancient tradition', Jonathan said. I was astonished. 'So ancient prehistoric cave paintings ...' 'Yes,' Jonathan said, 'chances are, they'll be ochre.'

We put on overalls and helmets with torches, and Jonathan led me into the mine. We walked through a vaulted brick-lined passage into a vast, spectacular complex of huge caves in the rock, lit by the occasional electric light and with a railway line for trucks at our feet. Jonathan told me that freemining was a tradition in his family. 'What are the

qualifications?' I asked. 'You have to be male, over 21, and you have to have worked for a year and a day in a mine in the Forest of Dean – and you have to be born here. Once you become a freeminer, you're allowed to mine anywhere under the Forest of Dean except under churchyards.' I wondered if the miners ever got together. 'We meet every year', said Jonathan, 'at the Speech House, just as we have done for over 300 years.'

I was marvelling at the magnificent lofty caves. 'These are natural caves', Jonathan told me, 'made by water. Long ago there was an underground river

JONATHAN WRIGHT DEMONSTRATING
THE NELLY

running here. You can imagine it rushing through – it must have been spectacular. There are hundreds of caves like this, and they extend for about 600 acres.'

We were going deeper and deeper into the mine, and we arrived at a rock face where trucks were waiting to be filled. I wondered what the reality of life was for miners in the past. 'It would have been much darker, for a start', Jonathan said. 'Here's what they used for light – it's known as a nelly. It's a ball of clay with a stick in the side and a candle stuck in the clay. The miner held the stick sideways in his mouth like a pipe as he worked.' We lit the candle and Jonathan demonstrated the nelly.

# Speech House Pudding

115g/4oz butter, softened to room temperature
50g/2oz caster sugar
4 eggs, separated
115g/4oz plain flour

2 large tablespoonfuls raspberry jam
1 teaspoonful bicarbonate of soda
2 tablespoonfuls milk
Extra raspberry jam to make a sauce

Grease a 1.2 litre (2 pint) pudding basin with a little of the butter. In another basin, cream together the butter and sugar until light and fluffy. Beat in the beaten egg yolks, a little at a time, alternating with a spoonful of the flour, beating well after each addition. Beat in any remaining flour. Mix in the two tablespoonfuls of jam and combine well.

In a separate bowl, whisk the egg whites until they are stiff and stand in peaks. Mix the bicarbonate of soda into the milk and stir it into the flour mixture. Use a large metal spoon to quickly, very gently, and thoroughly fold the beaten egg whites into the mixture. Pour the mixture into the prepared pudding basin (it should only be about three-quarters full). Cover the basin with its lid, or make a lid out of a piece of pleated greaseproof paper and then a piece of kitchen foil (pleated to allow room for expansion during cooking), and tie it down securely with kitchen string. Place the pudding basin in a large pan of boiling water, cover the pan with its lid and steam over boiling water for 2½ - 3 hours, replenishing the pan with more boiling water when necessary to ensure that the pan does not boil dry. When the pudding is cooked, turn it out by inverting the basin over a large warmed plate and tipping it out. Heat up more raspberry jam to make a sauce and serve the pudding with the jam sauce poured over the top, and also a little cream if required.

Then Jonathan told me we'd arrived at a good seam of ochre, and he showed me how to actually mine. With a small pointed pickaxe I hacked ochre from the seam and scraped it with my hands down on to a tray on the ground. 'It's satisfying work', Jonathan said, 'because you often find yourself working next to pickaxe marks that are hundreds of years old. See these marks? They're Victorian.'

'When would a miner in past times have known when it was time to stop?' I asked. 'By the number of candles he burnt', said Jonathan. 'Each candle would last about an hour, so he'd bring down ten candles, and when he'd burnt half, it was lunchtime, and when he got to the last candle it was time to go home.'

I thought we'd achieved enough for the day. 'I think we've done our ten!' I said.

A VICTORIAN ENGRAVING
SHOWING MINERS WORKING
WITH PICKAXES AT A SEAM

## JOHN'S PHOTOGRAPH OF THE FOREST OF DEAN

THE FOREST OF DEAN FREEMINER, 2011

*Jonathan's solitary working life deep underground is probably not for me, but meeting him has inspired my photograph. Freeminers don't appear in the Frith picture, but they do meet at the Speech House, so although my photograph is very different from the Frith one, I hope that like it this picture encapsulates some of the traditions still alive in the Forest of Dean.*

# Suffer Little Children

*'In the Frith photograph on the previous pages we are in the beautiful cathedral city of Gloucester, so when I looked at it, I wasn't quite sure why the Frith team had decided to take it. An old cottage, a pub – why did they deserve to have their photograph taken? I was hoping that my visit here would shed some light on the importance of this picture.'*

Poverty was a common problem in Gloucester in the 18th century. The city council used every means they could to get the poor off the streets. Many people had to live in degrading conditions in the workhouse. If a woman gave birth to an illegitimate child, she was given detention for three years. Whilst in the workhouse mothers of bastard children were treated badly, only having leftover food to eat. To keep out of the workhouse and to earn a few pennies for food, young children worked long hours in factories and workshops, and ran riot in what little free time they had.

GLOUCESTER, SOUTHGATE STREET, RAIKES HOUSE 1891 FRITH 29006

In 1780 a Gloucester man, Robert Raikes (1736-1811), embarked on his philanthropic mission, and his extraordinary legacy has shaped the lives of millions of children world-wide ever since. He was the founder of the Sunday school movement, and his first Sunday school was in the cottage on the left of the Frith photograph on the previous pages. Through his schools Raikes offered free education to any child, and so his Sunday school movement is widely regarded as the forerunner of the state school system. Because so many of Britain's children were going to Sunday school at the time when state education was being set up, it was an easier transition to make.

Robert Raikes was born at Ladybellegate House, and educated at the nearby Crypt School until he transferred to the Kings School at the age of 14. His father was the highly respected publisher and printer of the Gloucester Journal. On his father's death in 1757, Raikes's mother took over the running of the business until Robert reached his

BUST OF ROBERT
RAIKES ON THE
'GLOUCESTER
JOURNAL AND THE
CITIZEN' BUILDING

GLOUCESTER,
SOUTHGATE STREET
1904
FRITH 51987T

25th birthday, when he became editor of the newspaper. The company moved from Blackfriars to a 16th-century house in Southgate Street opposite St Mary le Crypt church. Here Robert made some major changes to the layout of the Gloucester Journal, and his first philanthropic act was to use the paper to tell its readers of the appalling conditions in Gloucester prison.

In 1767 Robert Raikes married Anne Trigg in London, and then returned home to Gloucester to bring up a family of six daughters and two sons. Raikes was quite a dandy, wearing fashionable clothes complete with brown wig and a three-cornered hat. He was nicknamed 'Bobby Wildgoose' because he was so forward and tended to speak so much, but all conceded that he was witty and good-natured.

He happened to be in St Catherine Street one day seeking the services of a gardener. There he saw poor ragged children playing in the street. This was one of the most impoverished areas of Gloucester, and he was disturbed at what he saw, especially when he learnt from the gardener's wife that it was worse on a Sunday. Then, he was told, many more children played here, cursing and swearing, letting off steam from working in the city's local pin factories six days a week (see page 197). Robert Raikes and the Reverend Thomas Stock, of St John the Baptist church, concerned about the behaviour of the children, decided to open several Sunday schools around the city.

VICTORIAN
ENGRAVING OF A BOY
AT A RAGGED SCHOOL

GLOUCESTER,
ROBERT RAIKES
STATUE 1931
FRITH 83833

The first was in the home of Mrs King of St Catherine Street, the house on the left in the main Frith photograph on pages 192-193. Children aged from five to fourteen were admitted, no matter what the state of their clothes – hence the nickname for the schools, 'Raikes's Ragged Schools'. The building has since been demolished, and the modern building of St Catherine's Knapp, at the junction of St Catherine Street and Park Street, now stands on the site. The Coach and Horses pub on the right of the photograph is still there.

The children were rough and rowdy. Fights in class were frequent, and Raikes told of 'turrible chaps' and 'wild animals'. However, he encouraged parental responsibility and involvement, and children had to attend with clean hands, combed hair and clean faces. Raikes's original schedule for the schools was this: 'The children were to come after ten in the morning, and stay till twelve; they were then to go home and return at one; and after reading a lesson, they were to be conducted to Church. After Church, they were to be employed in repeating the catechism till after five, and then dismissed, with an injunction to go home without noise.' In the early years, Raikes bore the cost of the schools himself, but as their fame spread, donations flooded in.

Raikes reported on the progress of his schools in the Gloucester Journal, and other newspapers took up the story. Soon news of these Sunday schools spread far and wide, and the evangelist John Wesley remarked: 'I find these schools springing up wherever I go'. (Indeed, by 1831 Sunday schools were teaching 1,250,000 children every week, about a quarter of the population.)

Robert Raikes retired in 1802; he sold the Gloucester Journal, and went to live in a house in Bell Lane. He died suddenly, aged 74, on 5 April 1811, and was buried in a vault in St Mary le Crypt church, Southgate Street. At his funeral, children from his Sunday schools followed the cortège, and in accordance with Raikes's wishes, each child received one shilling and a piece of plum cake.

Wherever you go in the city centre today, you can find references to Robert Raikes. Addison's Folly in Greyfriars was built in 1864 by Thomas Fenn Addison as a memorial to Robert Raikes. There is a statue of him in Gloucester Park. Numerous blue plaques around the city mention him, and in St John's Lane, home of the 'Gloucester Journal and the Citizen', there is a bust of him on their building (see photograph on page 195).

# Pin Making for a Pittance

Pin making was one of Gloucester's largest industries by the 18th and early 19th centuries, and it employed mainly women and children working for very small wages. It all began in the early 17th century with John Tilsley, a local man, who had started his career as a wire-drawer, and then become a pin maker in Bristol. In about 1625 he came back home and persuaded Gloucester Corporation to lend him £200 and find him 30 boys to set up a pin-making operation in his home city. Tilsley undertook to 'give unto every of the said boyes 12d by the weeke during the firste yeare, and 15d by the weeke duringe the second yeare and 18d by the weeke duringe the third yeare … and to pay them every satterdaie night'.

GLOUCESTER MUSEUMS SERVICE

By the 1630s Tilsley was employing over 80 boys and girls, and he had become a rich man. The industry grew until by the mid 18th century it was the most important industry in Gloucester; in the early 19th century there were 9 factories employing about 1500 people, as well as outworkers working from home, and Gloucester was exporting pins all over the world. But the Napoleonic Wars intervened. Gloucester could no longer sell her pins abroad, and the trade declined. This decline was hastened by technological innovation – pins were soon being made by machine. Gloucester's heyday as a pin-making centre was over.

So how used pins to be made? Because they were made by hand, and because various separate processes were involved, they did not necessarily require special buildings – outhouses or even the upper floors or living rooms of domestic buildings could be used for the various stages of making pins.

GLOUCESTER MUSEUMS SERVICE

The pins were made from brass wire. The long coils of wire were straightened, cut into short lengths, and sharpened to form the shanks. The pin heads were made from very fine wire, again cut into short lengths, and softened in a furnace; they were struck with a heavy hammering machine to fix them to the shanks. Then the pins were boiled to clean them, tin plated, and finally stuck into cards so that they could be sold in a haberdasher's. Most of these separate processes could be done by women or children, who worked long hours for a pittance. Small wonder that the children ran riot on Sundays, their one free day.

ABOVE: HAND-MADE PINS, THE HEADS MADE FROM A SPIRAL OF WIRE AND 'CRIMPED' TO THE PIN SHANK

LEFT: A PIN HEADING RAM WITH TREADLE-OPERATED DROP WEIGHT. IT WAS USED TO SECURE PIN HEADS TO THE PIN SHAFT

# John hears about Robert Raikes's legacy

JOHN TALKS TO
LOCAL JOURNALIST
HUGH WORSNIP

HARE LANE AND THE
COACH AND HORSES
AS THEY ARE TODAY

SIGN DEPICTING ROBERT RAIKES ON
HIS HOUSE IN SOUTHGATE STREET

Hugh Worsnip, a local journalist, met me at what I hoped was the place the Frith photograph on pages 192-193 had been taken – I showed him the picture to make sure. 'This pub is still the Coach and Horses', said Hugh, 'but clearly the building on the opposite corner is different today (see photograph, centre). The cottage in the Frith photograph is one of the four original Sunday schools which eventually evolved into a national and then international movement. By 1880, in Frith's time, seven and a half million children in Britain alone received their only education in Sunday school.'

Hugh went on to tell me about Robert Raikes, editor of the local paper in the 18th century, who was appalled to see local children running wild on a Sunday. 'With Thomas Stock, the local vicar, he drew up a list of the 90 poorest and most neglected children so that they could go to the four Sunday schools that he set up'. I wondered what the children did for the rest of the week. 'They worked making pins', said Hugh, 'six days a week, from seven o'clock in the morning to six o'clock in the evening, with Sunday their only free time. Both boys and girls went to Raikes's Sunday schools, and their ages ranged from seven to fourteen.'

Hugh took me to see a large gabled timber-framed house (see the Frith photograph on page 194). 'This is one of Raikes's houses', Hugh told me. 'He lived here for 37 years, and it was also his printing office.' 'One of his houses?' I said. 'How many did he have?' 'Five altogether, and three of them still survive', said Hugh. Raikes must have been a bit of a media magnate, I thought! The sign hanging on the house was a portrait of him – he looked benign (see photograph, left). 'He may look kind', said Hugh, 'but he wasn't above wielding a stick himself when he was doing one of his inspections of his schools. On one celebrated occasion he put a child's hand on a hot stove, because, he said, liars were worse than thieves.' 'Well,' I said to Hugh, 'that's still true today – as journalists, you and I should know that!'

While we were talking, the headmistress of a Gloucester school, Tamara Brito, arrived at the house with some of her pupils. She was wanting to tell them about the man who had influenced the lives of so many children. The boys were reluctant to pose for the cameras. I remembered that Raikes had once chained down a child to stop him from running away – I felt it was a method I might need myself!

I asked the teacher if children were easy to discipline today, or difficult. 'Sometimes they're easy!' she said. 'In Raikes's day, discipline was very strict. It's different now. I believe it's better today, because we are more positive. We focus on what the child does well.' But did she think that Raikes was a great man? 'Of course! Thanks to him, all children have access to education. He's a hero.'

THE HEADMISTRESS AND CHILDREN FROM
THE RAIKES CENTRE OUTSIDE
ROBERT RAIKES'S HOUSE

## JOHN'S PHOTOGRAPH OF GLOUCESTER

### ROBERT RAIKES'S HOUSE, 2011

*I like the way the lines of this photograph all go off into the background – they give depth and a sense of perspective, and I hope they make it more classy than a mere snap. Although Robert Raikes's house is now a pub, the outside at least hasn't changed much since Frith's time. You might think it odd that his home should be turned into a pub, but just think of the journalists who'd like to see that happen to their homes! Also, we must remember that Raikes wasn't a killjoy.*

*What's more, he was what we'd call now a campaigning journalist. Not only did he take the views of his readers very seriously, but he also wanted to improve their lot.*

LIVERPOOL, THE EXCHANGE 1887 FRITH 20001

# A Great Port and Cotton Trading Centre

*'The great maritime and mercantile city of Liverpool is where Francis Frith became a wealthy businessman, and it's here that he first became interested in photography. Liverpool was a rich seedbed for all kinds of enterprises. So who are the people in the photograph on the previous pages? What do they have to do with Liverpool's wealth? They are standing outside Liverpool's Exchange, and they are the people who enabled Liverpool's vastly profitable trade.'*

LIVERPOOL,
GEORGE'S DOCK c1881
FRITH 14149

Liverpool in the 19th century was the trading city *par excellence*, with ships plying up and down the River Mersey bringing huge quantities of goods in and out. Her prosperity, like so many of Britain's ports, was founded on the slave trade; it was as early as 1699 that her first slave ship, the 'Liverpool Merchant', left for the African coast. By the end of the 18th century Liverpool controlled about 80% of Britain's trade in slaves.

Many other commodities were traded in Liverpool, however. Professor John Belchem of Liverpool University points out that the reason Liverpool was so prosperous was that it was a general cargo port. It handled raw materials, foodstuffs, and manufactured goods as well as people – all these things were traded through Liverpool. The most important articles imported into Liverpool were cotton, grain and flour, sugar, tobacco, wool, tea, hemp, and timber. In the 19th century nearly half of the world's trade was conducted here, and at times during this period Liverpool's wealth was greater than London's. In 1851 the city was described as 'the New York of Europe', and later as 'gateway to the British Empire'

and 'door to the New World'. Its civic buildings, vast, grand and extravagant, reflected the city's sense of its own importance.

Liverpool's docks were central to its development. The Old Dock, the world's first wet dock, was built in 1715. Perhaps the best known is the Albert Dock, built in 1846, the most advanced dock of its time. George's Dock (see the photograph on the opposite page) was built out from the original shoreline and opened in 1771. At the time it was Liverpool's third and largest dock, covering 26,793 square yards; it could hold, as we can see, a considerable amount of shipping. It had to be built because the Old Dock was prone to silting, while Salthouse Dock (opened in 1753) was now too small for the larger ships then being built. It was linked to the two older docks and the graving dock, allowing vessels to move between them without having to enter the Mersey. The dock was closed in 1900, and was filled in to form George's Parade, now occupied by three iconic waterfront buildings, the Mersey Docks & Harbour Board, the Cunard Building, and the Royal Liver Insurance Building.

At the time of Frith's photographs, Liverpool would have had upwards of two hundred ships leaving each week for every corner of the British Empire, and indeed the world. Ships went to Canada for corn, and carried iron goods to South America and Africa, and railway carriages to Brazil and South Africa. People still arrived and left – not slaves, but immigrants from Ireland and

*In the 19th century nearly half of the world's trade was conducted here*

LIVERPOOL,
ST GEORGE'S PLATEAU
c1881 FRITH 14071T

VICTORIAN
ENGRAVING OF
MILL WORKERS

BELOW LEFT:
LIVERPOOL,
THE EXCHANGE 1890
FRITH 26663

BELOW RIGHT:
LIVERPOOL,
EXCHANGE FLAGS
TODAY

emigrants to the New World. It is significant that Elgar's 'Pomp and Circumstance March No 1', which could be regarded as the national anthem of the British Empire, was dedicated to the Liverpool Orchestral Society and was first performed in Liverpool.

One of the most important commodities imported into Liverpool was cotton, which was to feed the innumerable mills of the North of England and fuel the Industrial Revolution. In 1770 the port landed its first cargo of cotton from the West Indies and the American colonies. It comprised 6037 bags, three barrels and three bales of cotton; by the 1850s the trade had grown to over 2 million packages a year, of which at least 1.7 million were from the United States.

With all this cotton coming through the port, Liverpool itself might be expected to have become a major centre for cotton spinning. In 1796 a mill was opened in Cheapside, but it burnt down. Kirkham & Co opened a mill for spinning cotton twist and Edward Pemberton established a spinning mill in Bolton Street, yet both of these businesses closed. The last fling came in 1839 when a mill opened at Canal Bank, but it too burnt down in 1853. The bulk of the cotton landed at Liverpool went to Manchester and beyond; a railway between the two cities had opened as early as 1830, and it transported more cotton than the canals and roads put together.

Instead of spinning cotton, Liverpool's energies were spent on trading in it; cotton futures were first traded on the Liverpool Cotton Exchange in the late 1700s. Cotton traders, and traders in the myriad other commodities that were landed at Liverpool, first met on a patch of open ground. It was very muddy in rainy weather, so the area was paved, and the brokers' business became

TOP:
JOHN TALKS TO
JOHN BELCHEM
AND ROBERT LEE

ABOVE:
LIVERPOOL'S
ALBERT DOCK TODAY

known as 'trading on the flags'. An exchange building was later erected – the one in the Frith photographs on pages 200-201 and on the opposite page was the third on the site, designed by T H Wyatt and opened in 1863 – and the square was, and is, known as Exchange Flags.

Professor John Belchem explains that the large crowd in the Frith photograph on pages 200-201 were the traders during Liverpool's heyday as a maritime and mercantile city. The people depicted here ranged from merchant princes to humble clerks, with brokers and traders prominent in the mix. These were the middlemen, responsible for working out the value of cotton, for instance, when it was landed on the docks, and for fixing a good price for the buyers. Much of the shipping, insurance and commodity trading business of the port was done on this square behind the Town Hall, usually in the open air, despite the typical Liverpool weather. Only if it was very cold or wet would deals be closed in the newsrooms and counting houses of the Exchange building.

The crowd in the photograph seems especially large. Professor Robert Lee of Liverpool University feels that this must be because the traders had been told that the photograph was to be taken that day. This gave them the opportunity to demonstrate the importance of the merchant community to the Frith photographer and thus to the wider public. They were happy to emphasise the centrality of Liverpool as one of the world's leading commercial centres. And, of course, the Frith company was keen to take this particular photograph: it was highly probable that everyone in it would buy a copy.

In the middle of the Flags stands a monument to Nelson; it was erected in 1813, Liverpool's first public monument. The statue, designed by Matthew Cotes Wyatt and carved by Richard Westmacott, depicts a naked Nelson crowned in victory yet threatened by death, surrounded by figures in chains representing prisoners of war taken in his battles. Admiral Lord Nelson was a hero to the merchants of Liverpool, for his victories meant that they could ply their trade throughout the world with complete freedom. Thanks to Nelson, their city would remain the greatest trading city of the empire.

# John Sets a Challenge to Frith's Successors

IRENE DRUMMOND

TONY MYERS

TED BAKER

COLIN THWAITE

MARTIN REECE

Here in Liverpool the two sides of Francis Frith's character came together: his skill as a business entrepreneur and his genius as a photographer. It was in Liverpool that Frith not only built up his wholesale grocery business but became interested in photography.

We know little about the birth of the talent that would make him famous, but we do know that by 1853 he was one of the first members of the Liverpool Photographic Society. I was excited to be meeting members of the South Liverpool Photographic Society, because they are direct links with Frith himself – their society incorporated the Liverpool Photographic Society a few years ago.

The members of this society operate in a very different technological world from their Victorian predecessor. I wondered what they thought of his work. Did it give them a sense of fellow feeling?

'I've got immense admiration for the Frith photographers,' one member replied. 'The wooden cameras they carried around were large, the same size as the finished print. This was because the final print was a contact print, the same size as the glass plate on which the scene was recorded as a negative image. So they had to carry big unwieldy cameras and glass plates that were both heavy and fragile. Photography then was hard work.'

Another member spoke up. 'What I get from Frith's work is the fact that it's a social document. It's a means of looking at the past, and looking at it in a direct and vivid way.'

'What we have to appreciate', said another member, 'is that today we have infinitely more possibilities than Frith had. We can catch anything, any time. We can catch a vehicle going fast, for instance – but he had to wait for the scene to be empty of anything other than what he wanted in it, otherwise there could have been an unsightly blur right in the middle of the picture. He had to take a lot more time just to take one photograph.'

Well, time was one thing the society didn't have that morning. About 120 years after the Frith photographer had captured the many faces of the Exchange, I wanted to see how modern Liverpool photographers would choose to record their city. 'Go outside and take a photograph of Liverpool', I told them. 'That shouldn't be too difficult – but you've got to do it in 15 minutes.'

It struck me that one thing hadn't changed since Frith's day – there's no shortage of material in Liverpool. Street scenes, shopping, buildings, people, ships in the docks: these are all the kind of thing that would catch a Victorian photographer's eye. Would it be the same for these modern photographers? The results were quite revealing. Architecture was dominant in the society members' photographs, as well as a sizeable dollop of modern Liverpool culture, shops and shoppers.

'And the winner is … Irene!' I exclaimed. Her picture was terrific – two happy shoppers in the rain. It'll always remind me of Liverpool.

## JOHN'S PHOTOGRAPH OF LIVERPOOL

THE PHOTOGRAPHIC SOCIETY, LIVERPOOL, 2011

*I asked the members of the South Liverpool Photographic Society to be part of my small moment of Liverpool's history. My picture shows that here in Liverpool the art of photography is not short of modern devotees, but since Frith's day photography has changed almost as much as local industry. I wanted to snap these modern-day Friths on the Exchange Flags that the Victorian photographer once caught bustling with trade; behind them is the balcony from which the Frith photographer took his picture.*

# An Imposing Symbol of Commercial Prosperity and Civic Pride

BOLTON, MARKET HALL 1895   FRITH 35852

'*This is a picture of a building that was startlingly modern to Victorian eyes. It opened in 1855, an innovative structure of cast iron and glass, taking its cue from the ground-breaking Crystal Palace. We are in Bolton, in Frith's time a thriving cotton-spinning industrial town, and this is Bolton's Market Hall.*'

## Bolton was where Samuel Crompton had developed his spinning mule in 1779. This machine revolutionised the industry

VICTORIAN ENGRAVING OF
A COTTON MILL

BOLTON, DEANSGATE 1903
FRITH 50155

C otton was a vital element in Bolton's prosperity, just as it was in Liverpool; but whereas in Liverpool it was the trading of cotton that was important, in Bolton it was the spinning and weaving of it.

Bolton was where Samuel Crompton had developed his spinning mule in 1779. This machine revolutionised the industry; there was less thread-breakage than with the spinning jenny, and it was also capable of producing very fine yarn. Bolton was also where Richard Arkwright had worked as a barber before going on to invent the cotton spinning frame and the carding engine. The first power mill in Bolton had opened in the 1780s, and by the mid 19th century Bolton was a major player in the manufacture of cotton.

Like so many urban centres in the industrial North of England, Bolton was originally a small market town; it grew almost out of recognition thanks to the Industrial Revolution, with more and more people crammed into more and more crowded houses and narrow streets, with little respite from the hard, monotonous work in the factories. The 19th century brought what we now think of as Victorian values. Philanthropists and civic leaders realised the need for decent living and working conditions, fresh air and public open spaces, and higher standards of hygiene – and morals.

BOLTON,
THE MARKET HALL
1895
FRITH 35851

The market that had originated in the Middle Ages, held in the open air, was where dirt and rough behaviour met. Sheep and cattle were not only sold but slaughtered at the market, making the area not only smelly but insanitary. Bear baiting and dog fights attracted rogues, thieves and pickpockets. Strong liquor was sold there, and rowdy men and women roamed the streets. The newly awakened Victorian moral sensibility demanded that order be created out of this chaos: the idea of the indoor market hall was born.

Bolton created its innovative environment for buying and selling relatively early, around 1855. Its Market Hall, designed by the architect G T Robinson, was huge, measuring 218ft by 300ft, far larger than other civic buildings or railway stations of this period. The exterior was suitably dignified, built in the classical style with a massive pillared portico 50ft high. The interior was cathedral-like in its arrangement of wide aisles crossing in the centre. The construction of large spaces like this was now possible thanks to the new technology of cast iron and glass that had been perfected at the Crystal Palace.

This imposing building had a dual purpose. Firstly, the light, airy interior improved the health of Bolton's citizens by removing the sale of foodstuffs from the insanitary open market; the hall was also a much more convenient place for the town's growing population to shop. Secondly, the Market Hall was a status symbol, emphasising Bolton's wealth and importance with its grand architectural display.

BELOW LEFT:
BURY,
THE MARKET 1902
FRITH 48562T

BELOW RIGHT:
ACCRINGTON,
THE MARKET HALL
1897 FRITH 40117

BOLTON, THE MARKET HALL TODAY

BOLTON, BRADSHAWGATE 1903
FRITH 50157T

The northwest was booming, and Bolton was not alone in having its own market hall. The Frith photographers travelled to Blackburn, Accrington, Halifax, and Bury, and photographed their market halls too.

Flags waving above the streets, church bells ringing, a public holiday – 19 December 1855 was a special occasion. Over 20,000 people, with 3,000 women seated in the galleries, watched the opening ceremony of Bolton's new Market Hall. This was also the opening of a new era. The innovative building was not only to bring cleanliness, convenience, and visual delight to the town; it was also a symbol of civic pride, social cohesion and moral uplift. Very Victorian – and very modern too in its anticipation of the shopping malls of today.

# John experiences a unique blend of old and new

JOHN TALKS TO LOCAL HISTORIAN
BOB SNAPE

THE INTERIOR OF
BOLTON'S MARKET
HALL TODAY

I rode up the modern escalator inside the Victorian Market Hall to meet local historian Bob Snape. I showed him the Frith photograph as we walked along the gallery, and he was able to identify the spot from which the photograph was taken.

It struck me that the hall was very cheerful and bright, and I wondered how it used to be lit in Victorian times. 'By gas', Bob told me. 'There were 900 gas jets. It was very exciting for people used to rooms lit by a candle or two. The gas meant that the hall could be open when it was dark, in the evenings and on winter afternoons. People would have felt that this place was something quite spectacular.'

I thought that it must have been quite an undertaking to build this hall. 'It was one of the biggest urban developments of 19th-century Britain', agreed Bob. 'The dirty open-air market wasn't acceptable any more. This was an industrial town; people weren't living off the land as they used to, and they needed a clean, well-stocked centre where they could buy everything they needed.'

So what did the shops and stalls sell? 'Fruit and vegetables,' said Bob, 'and meat – there were a lot of butchers here. Fishmongers, too. In the gallery, there was livestock: pigeons and rabbits, and pets. This was the forerunner of the modern shopping mall in many ways; you could shop here in pleasant surroundings whatever the weather.'

To prove the significance of this revolutionary new way to shop, Bolton Museum preserves a copy of the original plans of the Market Hall. Bob took me there to meet historian Matthew Constantine, who showed me the beautiful coloured drawings of the Market Hall's classical exterior.

I asked Matthew what was so different and exciting about the building. 'Consider what Bolton was like in the 1850s', he said. 'There weren't many large buildings here apart from the cotton mills. The civic buildings were still quite small – the Town Hall, which dominates the town centre, hadn't yet been built; it arrived in the 1870s. So this was the largest building in the town; it was a demonstration of civic pride. It put Bolton on the map. It said: "We're rich, we're up-and-coming". When it opened, the newspaper reports compared it

JOHN WITH MATTHEW CONSTANTINE

favourably with Liverpool's market hall. Ours was bigger, better, and posher!'

'Well, of course!' I said. 'Anyone from Bolton would say the same!'

Matthew pointed out that places like Bolton were the first modern industrial cities. 'They were pioneers', he said. 'People here had to find a way to live together in crowded conditions. How do you feed yourself? How do you organise yourself? A building like this represents their story. Our Market Hall is a powerful building with a history of rapid social change that's worth remembering today.'

## JOHN'S PHOTOGRAPH AT BOLTON

MARKET HALL, 2011

*Bolton is rightly proud of its historic shopping centre. Few market halls have survived so well to the present day. That's why I felt it was only right that I should follow directly in Frith's footsteps for my own photographic record of Bolton. Taking an architectural shot was tricky, but I think I've managed to capture an element of the Victorian past and plenty of the modern world too. We can see the straight lines of the present-day balcony, along with the Victorian glass and cast iron arches above. The picture shows the mixture of old and new that I wanted.*

BLACKPOOL,
THE TOWER
1894  FRITH  34798A

# Sun, Sands, Sea and Down-to-Earth Fun

*'We've come 30 miles north of Liverpool to the biggest tourist attraction in northern England: Blackpool. The Frith team were lucky to come here just at the time when the town was booming. The most famous landmark on the northwest coast was brand new. It was, of course, Blackpool Tower.'*

BLACKPOOL, THE SOUTH JETTY FROM THE WELLINGTON HOTEL 1890  FRITH 22881T

I t is hard to visualise Blackpool as anything other than a hugely popular seaside resort with miles of neon lights and gaudy attractions, but like so many resorts, it began as a tiny coastal hamlet which became popular in the mid 18th century when its beaches attracted those people eager to participate in the new fashion for sea bathing.

The first bathing machines had been imported by an enterprising innkeeper as early as 1730, though whether or not they were available for hire on Sundays (as the two machines at nearby Lytham were) so that the frail could be trundled straight to the sea from church is unknown. Baileys Hotel, later the Metropole, opened in 1776. In 1781 a new road giving access to the sands was built, and stagecoaches began running to Blackpool from Manchester and Halifax in the 1780s. By 1801 the population had grown to an impressive 500.

During the 1830s Blackpool was developing along genteel lines, though it must be said that for several decades the tradition of Lancashire working people and their families visiting the town had already begun, albeit on a small scale. Many would make the journey by cart, some would even walk, just to spend a few hours away from the dust, grit, grime and monotony of mill and factory life.

When the railway arrived in Blackpool in 1846 it was already

BLACKPOOL,
THE WINTER
GARDENS 1890
FRITH 22892

PARIS,
THE EIFFEL TOWER
c1890
FRITH P706301

a resort attracting several thousand visitors a year. With the coming of the railway, investment in Blackpool's infrastructure and attractions gathered momentum. The North Pier opened in 1863 and was followed by a second, the South Jetty, in 1868 (see photograph on previous page). When the Victoria Pier (now the South Pier) was opened in 1893, the South Jetty was renamed Central Pier. In 1879 electric lighting was introduced along the promenade, and the first electric tramcars ran along Blackpool's seafront as early as 1885.

By the 1870s many Lancashire cotton workers were enjoying the luxury of three unpaid days' holiday a year, which when tacked onto a weekend gave a handy five-day break. Another important development for Blackpool's holiday industry was the passing of the Bank Holidays Act in 1871. With specific days allocated for holidays, the railway companies could schedule special excursion trains, knowing that they would be filled. In the 1890s the population of Blackpool soared to around 35,000, and the town could accommodate a quarter of a million holidaymakers.

While Scarborough, along with Southport and Morecambe, provided for the genteel classes, Blackpool was developed along more down-to-earth lines. When it was opened in 1878 the Winter Gardens was probably the town's last throw at catering for a sophisticated audience. It housed a library, a reading room, an art gallery and a concert hall (see photograph above). Alas, the acoustics were very poor. When the great actress Sarah Bernhardt was engaged to play the female lead there in 'The Lady of the Camellias' in 1882, she had so much difficulty in making herself heard that she walked out at the end of the first act and never went back, offended by the cries of 'Speak up, lass!' from the audience, who had paid good money to see her and wanted their money's worth. The writing was on the wall for cultural pursuits as early as Whit weekend 1879, when the Gardens' principal attraction was a young woman being fired from a cannon.

Blackpool's world-famous Blackpool Tower was built in the 1890s and completed in 1894, the year the Frith photograph on page 214 was taken. It was inspired by Gustave Eiffel's great tower in Paris, which had opened five years earlier, but at 518ft Blackpool's Tower is only a little over half the height of the Eiffel

BLACKPOOL,
FROM NORTH PIER
1906  FRITH 53853T

Tower. It boasted a ballroom, a permanent circus, a menagerie and an aquarium, all incorporated within the building at its base. The Tower Ballroom was famed for its Wurlitzer organ, which would feature in countless BBC broadcasts and make the organist Reginald Dixon a household name from 1930 until the late 1960s.

It would be hard to find a more opulent spot in Britain than the Tower Ballroom at Blackpool, commissioned by John Bickerstaff in 1899 and decorated in the French Renaissance style, modelled on the Paris Opera House. On a busy night in, say, the 1930s, as many as 6,000 couples might have been dancing on the parquet floor composed of 75,000 blocks of mahogany, oak, maple and walnut. Laurel and Hardy entertained here, as did Duke Ellington and Arthur Askey. At one time, the Spinsters' Ball was a popular occasion, where thousands of rose petals were showered on to the dancers.

Other resorts tried to copy Blackpool's fame and pulling power by building their own towers, but none of them has endured. Norfolk's biggest and most popular holiday resort, Great Yarmouth, was known for its Revolving Tower, built in 1897. It was 120ft high with a cage capable of holding 150 people that rotated as it went up and down. The tower was demolished in 1941 and the metal sent for wartime salvage. The tower at Cleethorpes also revolved. It

BLACKPOOL,
THE TOP OF THE
TOWER AND THE
GLASS FLOOR

opened in 1902, 150ft high, with a lift that rotated as it carried passengers up to the top. Later, flying machines were hung from it. The New Brighton Tower (see below) was completed between 1896 and 1900 at a cost of £120,000, and officially opened in 1898. Its height was 567ft 6in to the top of the flagstaff, and it was the tallest structure in England at the time. During the First World War New Brighton's tower was allowed to rust and rot, and in 1918 it was declared unsafe. By Easter 1921 it had been dismantled.

But Blackpool Tower still stands, as popular as ever. In the 120 years since the Frith photographer took his photograph, the tower has woven itself into the fabric of Blackpool life. In 1994, to commemorate its centenary, abseiling painters highlighted the sides of the Blackpool Tower with gold, and today myriad holidaymakers shudder with pleasurable vertigo as they stand on the glass floor at the top of the most iconic seaside building in the world.

NEW BRIGHTON,
THE TOWER AND SANDS 1900
FRITH 45163

# John enjoys the view from the top of the tower

JOHN WITH
ARCHIVIST
TONY SHARKEY

THE TOP OF
BLACKPOOL TOWER
TODAY

I walked along Blackpool's beach with archivist Tony Sharkey to find the spot where the Frith photograph of Blackpool Tower had been taken.

Tony was impressed by the picture. 'What skilful photographers they were back in the 1890s. This photo really emphasises the height and grandeur of the tower. It was taken just after the tower opened to the public. The cost of the tower was £250,000, which seems very little in today's money, but it was a considerable investment at the time, and a considerable risk, too.'

I wondered how much the tower had cost in today's money. 'The equivalent of £40 million', Tony told me. 'It was an effort to emulate the Eiffel Tower in Paris. It was the vision of one man, John Bickerstaff, mayor of Blackpool, local hotelier and entrepreneur. He believed that an outstanding landmark would put a seal on Blackpool's growing reputation.'

'But where did all that money come from?' I asked. 'From the cotton wealth of north-west Lancashire', said Tony. 'Bickerstaff called on all the cotton barons of Burnley, Blackburn and Preston, and persuaded them to invest in the project. He convinced them that to provide Blackpool with an emblem that was unmissable and unforgettable would make the enterprise highly profitable.'

'So the plan to build the tower was founded on the cotton industry?' I asked. 'It's often been said', Tony replied, 'that Blackpool Tower is built on bales of cotton. Of course, figuratively speaking, that's actually true.'

I wondered how many people had been attracted to Blackpool for their holidays. Tens of thousands? 'Millions of people!' said Tony. 'All the millions of workers in Lancashire and beyond who wanted a break from the drudgery of the cotton mills and the factories. In Frith's time there were other resorts in the market, and so Blackpool was trying to do things bigger and better

than anyone else. Blackpool built attractions at a level that neighbouring resorts didn't reach. That's why it was so successful, and that's why it still draws millions of holidaymakers every year.'

I enjoyed the view from the top of the tower, and it was good to chat to all the people who are still choosing Blackpool as their mecca for holiday fun.

## JOHN'S PHOTOGRAPH OF BLACKPOOL

BLACKPOOL AMUSEMENTS, 2011

*Blackpool Tower is a symbol of everything that the town stands for, so I was tempted to make it the subject of my photograph. But the Frith photograph of it is so much better than anything I could achieve that I decided to find another subject. I wanted to capture the past heritage of Frith's time, but also the fun, even daftness, of today. I think I've found it all at North Pier. I've caught two people – they're slightly blurred, I hope in the Frith manner. The key thing is that word 'amusements' in brightly coloured letters. People have been amused here for more than 100 years, and I'm sure that in more than 100 years' time they'll still be amused in Blackpool.*

BLACKPOOL,
THE BIG WHEEL
1896   FRITH 38865

# Ping-pong, Tea and Cakes at 200 Feet Up

*'We are still in Blackpool, and the Frith photographer has timed his visit to arrive precisely when another huge tourist attraction has just opened - Blackpool's Big Wheel, seen in the photograph on the previous page, and opposite. Its life was a short one, just over 30 years. Today it's almost forgotten, and it's hard to find where it stood. But I did discover another attraction, one that has been going strong since the time the wheel was built.'*

A VICTORIAN
ENGRAVING OF
A BIG WHEEL

**B**ig wheels have been popular as long as fairs have, but it was not until the 19th century that more advanced engineering methods made it possible to construct the huge big wheels of the kind we love so much today. Also, the growing number of international exhibitions, of which Britain's Great Exhibition of 1851 was the pioneer, led to the realization that special attractions were needed to draw the public. During the late 1860s American engineers were the leaders in patenting big wheel designs. The most famous of them was George Washington Gale Ferris, who gave his name to the Ferris Wheel. His first sizeable project was a big wheel for the Columbian Exposition in the 1890s.

Blackpool hoped that its very own Great Wheel would be a huge attraction, one that would be almost as popular as the Blackpool Tower. It was erected beside the Winter Gardens on the corner of Adelaide Street and Coronation Street, and opened in 1896, the year the Frith photographs on page 221 and opposite were taken.

The man responsible for Blackpool's wheel was a British engineer, Walter Basset, the managing director of a marine engineering company. He had the foresight to see that there was money to be made from 'catering to the public craving for new sensations', as he put it in a newspaper interview in 1895. 'If a man wants to make a pile, he has to get hold of some novelty.'

He had in 1894 constructed a pioneering great wheel at Earl's Court which was both popular and profitable, and together with his draughtsman,

BLACKPOOL,
THE BIG WHEEL 1896
FRITH 38867

*The Wheel turned out to be a financial disaster ...*

a Mr Booth, he had just designed the wheel for Blackpool. The interviewer asked for some details. 'The wheel, you must know,' Mr Basset replied, 'is constructed on the principle of the bicycle wheel. It will be 200 feet high, carrying 30 carriages, each of which will hold 40 passengers. That gives a total capacity of 1,200, and as the wheel will make four double revolutions per hour, we calculate to handle nearly 5,000 persons during that time. The entire weight of the machine will be about 1,100 tons, and the people will probably weigh another 100 tons.'

Mr Basset went on to tell the interviewer that the axle would be forged out of solid steel, and would weigh 25 tons. 'The spokes', he said, 'will be steel wire ropes, and the wheel will be driven by two wire hawsers, which will help to ensure the silent running we desire. The driving power will be given from two steam engines, each of about twelve horse power.'

Mr Basset expected the cost of the wheel to be in the region of £45,000, but he felt it was bound to be profitable since the running costs would be 'absurdly trifling', about £100 a week. 'Oh yes,' he continued, 'the Wheel will be perfectly safe. We have escaped without accident, so far, although before we got properly running at Earl's Court some of the passengers got stuck up in the air for a little time!'

However, Mr Basset's optimism was unfounded. The wheel turned out to be a financial disaster, unpopular with visitors because every time one of the carriages reached the bottom, the wheel had to be stopped while passengers embarked and disembarked. Despite attempts to attract people by serving tea inside the carriages and by allowing passengers to play ping-pong while they revolved, the wheel had to be dismantled in 1928, and the carriages were sold off as garden sheds.

# John enjoys a 'pleasurable kind of fright'

JOHN WITH
DAVID CAM
FROM BLACKPOOL'S
PLEASURE BEACH

I wandered around the streets of Blackpool trying to work out where the Big Wheel had stood. Despite the help of two charming Blackpool ladies, we all had to agree that the area had changed so much that is was impossible to imagine how it had looked when the wheel was soaring above in all its glory.

Like many other thrill-seeking trippers I headed instead for the southern end of Blackpool, where another tourist attraction besides the wheel had opened in 1896. It made a big impact then, and it still does today. Blackpool's Pleasure Beach hosts one of the world's great collections of roller coasters. It's not my natural habitat, but its Director, David Cam, kindly agreed to look after me.

I asked him which was the first ride at the Pleasure Beach. 'The oldest surviving ride is the Flying Machines', David told me. 'They were designed by Hiram Maxim in 1904. The idea then was that the visitors might never go on a real aeroplane, but they could go on one here!' You can read about Hiram Maxim on page 226.

'What is the most important thing about the Pleasure Beach?' I asked. 'Our mission statement dates from 1896', said David, 'when William George Bean, our founder, said that the aim was to create "an American-style amusement park, the fundamental principle of which is to make adults feel like children again and to inspire gaiety of a primarily innocent character." So from the start it was to be a family attraction through and through – and that's what we still aim at.'

'But some of the rides are surely meant to be frightening!' I said. 'Oh, yes!' David laughed. 'Families can be frightened together – it's a pleasurable kind of fright. And there are rides for everybody – scary rides for teenagers, gentle rides, and rides for little children.'

A massive structure was towering over our heads, and I asked David what it was. 'This is The Big One', he told me. 'This is one of the fastest roller coasters in the world – it goes at 85 miles an hour, and it's got the steepest drop ever. It's the most magnificent ride we've ever built.' I told David that I wanted to go on something a little bit more quiet and gentle than that,

COLOUR AND THRILLS AT THE PLEASURE BEACH

SIR HIRAM MAXIM'S FLYING MACHINE RIDE IS
STILL A FAVOURITE WITH VISITORS TODAY

maybe even something historic. He led me to
an elevated railway, in which we skimmed above
the Pleasure Beach at a suitably sedate pace.

I asked David if he ever looked back to the
Victorian era, and if he had a fellow feeling with
the people who founded this attraction. 'Yes,'
said David, 'I don't think people have changed
that much since then. That's why our rides, some
of which were built many years ago, like the Big
Dipper, for instance, are still so popular these
days. People have always wanted to let their hair
down. They love to be thrilled, to be excited, to
put their everyday lives on hold. They want to
forget the mortgage, the car payments, and all
their worries. The pace of life may be a bit faster
now than it was in Victorian times, but people
still want to leave all their troubles behind and
have fun. Kids will always be kids!'

# Sir Hiram Maxim's Captive Flying Machines

BLACKPOOL, THE FLYING MACHINE 1906   FRITH 53857

In 1896 Alderman William George Bean founded Pleasure Beach, Blackpool. The 42-acre site was in the perfect spot, opposite the tram terminus, and Blackpool hoped that this new amusement park would be a big success. One of the early rides at Pleasure Beach was Sir Hiram Maxim's Captive Flying Machines. The ride was built in 1904, and hurtled round at an exhilarating 40mph; it is still in operation today, and remains as popular as when it was first built.

Sir Hiram Stevens Maxim (1840-1916) seems at first glance to be an unlikely person to have given his name to an amusement park ride, for he was a distinguished inventor. Born in America, he emigrated to England in 1881 and became a British subject in 1900. His most famous invention was the Maxim gun, the first portable fully automatic machine gun. He claimed that it was he, not Edison, who had first invented the incandescent light bulb, and he patented many other inventions, including the mousetrap.

Maxim's inventive spirit led him to look at the possibility of flight. He had first experimented in the 1870s, when he had tried to design a helicopter. He began work on a flying machine in 1889; it was 145ft long, with a wingspan of 110ft, and was powered by two 360hp steam engines. In trials his machine, running on a railed track, theoretically achieved enough lift to take off, but was so unstable that the test was aborted.

Maxim needed funds to continue his research and to popularise the idea of flying machines. Therefore to raise money and public interest he designed and built an amusement ride for the Earl's Court exhibition of 1904: captive cars revolved and swung outwards, simulating flight. He couldn't help feeling a certain amount of disdain for the project, but the ride was so successful that in 1904 his company built more versions for the Crystal Palace and seaside resorts including Blackpool, which were equally well received.

The Blackpool Flying Machines ride, virtually unchanged from Maxim's original design, is still careering around and thrilling visitors today; it is the oldest operating amusement ride in Europe.

BLACKPOOL, FROM VICTORIA PIER 1896   FRITH 38859

## JOHN'S PHOTOGRAPH AT BLACKPOOL

THE BIG DIPPER, BLACKPOOL PLEASURE BEACH, 2011

*When the Frith photographer took his photograph of the Big Wheel, the Pleasure Beach was about to be opened. That's why I felt I had to take my photograph here, at an attraction that perfectly spans Blackpool's history between Frith's time and today. David Cam stands in front of the Big Dipper, one of the oldest roller coasters in the world. David has spent 40 years at the heart of Blackpool tourism, and he knows more than most how hard Blackpool works to rejuvenate itself with every passing season. It's amazing how the town's purpose has barely altered in over a century.*

LOCH KATRINE, TROSSACHS PIER 1899 FRITH 44590

# Romantic Setting for Scott's 'Lady of the Lake'

*'The photograph on the previous pages was taken in the glorious scenery of the Trossachs National Park in the Highlands of Scotland. In Frith's day the railway brought tourists here in droves, and the Frith photographers came to create souvenir pictures for the tourists to take home. This is an example: a steam-powered boat, the 'Rob Roy', waits for passengers on one of the most picturesque of Scottish lochs, Loch Katrine. I was to learn a lot about the loch, its boats, and its bard, Sir Walter Scott.'*

*'Loch Katrine bursts upon the view, presenting a vast sheet of water basking in solitude amidst the hills …'*

This is how 'Robertson's Tourist Guide' (1857) describes the visitor's first sight of this beautiful loch set at the heart of the Trossachs.

Being situated so close to the city of Glasgow, the Trossachs were immensely popular with visitors as a day out in wild mountain country. They enjoyed excursions to Loch Lomond, and Lock Katrine was only a little further on, reachable by steamer and carriage. Serpentine in shape and encircled by lofty mountains, the loch offered scenery that made a strong appeal to the Romantic sensibility of the Victorians. In the early years of the 19th century Sir Walter Scott had visited the Trossachs and wandered the wild country at Loch Katrine. He found the locality rich in lore and legend, and it inspired him to write 'The Lady of the Lake', his epic poem of love and clan rivalry in medieval times. He described its beauty in typically romantic poetic diction:

LOCH KATRINE TODAY

SIR WALTER SCOTT
FRITH 39198A

*One
burnished
sheet of
living gold,
Loch Katrine
lay beneath
him rolled …*

LOCH KATRINE 1899
FRITH 44593

'Where, gleaming with the setting sun,
One burnished sheet of living gold,
Loch Katrine lay beneath him rolled,
In all her length far winding lay,
With promontory, creek, and bay,
And islands that, empurpled bright,
Floated amid the livelier light,
And mountains, that like giants stand,
To sentinel enchanted land.'

Scott was equally lyrical when he gave the reader a first glimpse of Ellen Douglas, the Lady of the Lake:

'A damsel guider of its way,
A little skiff shot to the bay,
That round the promontory steep
Led its deep line in graceful sweep,
Eddying, in almost viewless wave,
The weeping-willow twig to lave,
And kiss, with whispering sound and slow
The beach of pebbles bright as snow.
The boat had touched this silver strand,
Just as the hunter left his stand,
And stood concealed amid the brake,
To view this lady of the lake.'

It is not surprising that the poem proved immensely popular. After the railway made the region more accessible, the Trossachs and Loch Katrine, home of the Lady of the Lake, had became favourite tourist destinations.

As early as the 1840s a trip out on the still waters was an especial favourite. The first vessel to ply the loch was a galley called the 'Water Witch'. She had eight rowers, all decked out in traditional kilts, which must have added to the intense Highland atmosphere. In 1843 the steamer 'Gypsy' took over much of the rowers' business, and there was vigorous competition between the two.

LOCH KATRINE,
ELLEN'S ISLE 1899
FRITH 44599

> *❛Loch Kateran, which being interpreted, signifieth The Loch of the Robbers❜*

However, the 'Gypsy' operated for a very short time indeed, for during the night of 18 July 1843 she disappeared mysteriously and was never seen again – rumour had it that the angry oarsmen, deprived of their living, had scuttled her.

In 1845 a luxurious new steamer, the 'Rob Roy', was introduced to the loch. Soon afterwards a second 'Rob Roy' was introduced, and she carried visitors up until 1899. Sailings were regular throughout the summer months, with two trips a day from each end of the loch, the timings coinciding with the arrival of the steamer from Loch Lomond. As the 'Rob Roy' steered its course down the lake there were picturesque views on each side of 'silent mountains reposing in solitary grandeur', as a Victorian tourist put it, 'with only here and there a lonely cot, and perhaps a shepherd on the mountain side to tell that man has an existence there'. It was a landscape that fully met the Victorian concept of the untamed setting of 'The Lady of the Lake', and a risk-free way for the ordinary working man to experience some grandeur and wild scenery without any serious exertion or effort. However, it was not all plain sailing – the outing along the lake was just a part of the tourist visit. Many visitors needed accommodation, and they found themselves at the mercy of the locals. Black's Guide of 1851 gives a graphic account of their trials:

'The crowds of tourists visiting the Trossachs, during the summer months, make it a matter of great uncertainty whether accommodation can be obtained at the inn …The boats upon Loch Katrine belong to the inn, and after paying the regular fare (2s 6d) the boatmen proceed to extort gratuities from the passengers, which they state (with what truth we know not) to be the only remuneration they receive for their services. The charge of these Highland gillies, for conveying luggage from the inn to the loch, is also most extravagant. The distance is about a mile, and three shillings have been occasionally extorted for carrying a small parcel this trifling distance. These practices, it must be admitted, are calculated, in a high degree, to uphold the ancient reputation of Loch Katrine, or, with more correctness of etymology, Loch Kateran, which being interpreted, signifieth The Loch of the Robbers.'

In 1899 the 'Rob Roy' was replaced by the SS 'Sir Walter Scott', named after the poet who had made the region so famous. She was built by the shipbuilders Denny Bros at Dumbarton, and it was not an easy job to transport her to the loch. The parts were carried by barge along the river Leven, towed to Inversnaid, and then hauled in wagons by horses up hill and down dale before being reassembled at Stronachlachar on Loch Katrine. She has never sailed on any other water than the beautiful loch where she still operates today.

# Sir Walter Scott, the Bard of Loch Katrine

ABBOTSFORD, FROM THE TWEED 1890 FRITH A92001

Sir Walter Scott's poems and novels are perhaps not read as widely today as they once were. In his time he was a highly popular author and hugely influential in Britain and on the Continent. He virtually invented the concept of the historical novel, and his depiction of Scotland (and especially the Highlands) as a land of nobility and virtue as opposed to the home of dangerous rogues and rebels was an important stabilising political influence.

Born in Edinburgh in 1771, Scott grew to love the Scottish Borders when as a boy he was sent to his grandfather's farm in Tweedale to recuperate after the attack of polio which lamed him for life. Indeed, his first major work was 'The Minstrelsy of the Scottish Border' (1802-03), Border ballads collected (and sometimes 'improved') by Scott. He began to build his house, Abbotsford, in the Borders in 1811, and worked seemingly tirelessly here and in Edinburgh on his poems and novels, including 'The Lady of the Lake' and 'Rob Roy'.

In 1825 a financial crisis erupted in London and Edinburgh. The printing business of Scott's friends the Ballantyne brothers, in which he had invested heavily, went bankrupt, and he was ruined. Scott decided that rather than go bankrupt himself, he would write his way out of debt. From this time until his death he kept up a phenomenal output. He was still in debt when he died in 1832, but as his works remained best-sellers, his estate was able to repay what he had owed. Scott was buried beside his ancestors in Dryburgh Abbey, close to Abbotsford.

# John goes on board the SS 'Sir Walter Scott'

Sheltered by an umbrella, I strolled along the path beside Loch Katrine with Louise Corrieri, one of the crew of the SS 'Sir Walter Scott' and an expert on this area and the loch in particular. I was hoping that she could help me identify exactly where the Frith photographer had taken his picture.

'I think this must be it', said Louise. 'The Frith photograph was taken from a high viewpoint, and just above us is a rock face where the photographer could have scrambled up. Hard work to get there with his big heavy camera, though.' The boat in the Frith photograph is the 'Rob Roy', so I asked Louise when the 'Sir Walter Scott' had come here. 'Her first official season was in 1900,' said Louise, 'only a year or two after the Frith photograph was taken.'

JOHN WITH
LOUISE CORRIERI

Louise took me on board, and I really enjoyed this gentle way of enjoying the beautiful loch. 'Here we are on a boat named after the famous poet and novelist', I said. 'Do you tell the passengers much about him?' 'Yes – you see this island coming up, for instance?' answered Louise. 'That's where Scott used to sit to write "The Lady of the Lake". And, of course, we point out the spectacular scenery, because that's what inspired him. Even on a wet, misty day like today, it's all so romantic and mysterious. It doesn't matter what the weather's like; the loch always looks stunning.'

THE SS 'SIR WALTER
SCOTT' TODAY

When the 'Sir Walter Scott' was built, her steam engine would have been state-of-the-art; only a steam engine could power a large passenger

vessel like this. I went down to the engine room to find out more. There I was delighted to meet the chief engineer, Malcolm Stylec, who showed me his gleaming engine working busily, its pistons rapidly gliding up and down.

I asked what fuelled the engine originally. 'Coal', Malcolm told me. 'There used to be coal-fired boilers there beside us in the same place as these oil-fired boilers are now.' He pointed to two big blue cylinders with labels proudly proclaiming that they were named 'Cochran Wee Chieftain'. Not so wee, I thought! 'Now we run on biofuel', Malcolm told me.

JOHN WITH CHIEF ENGINEER
MALCOLM STYLEC

'These boilers are fuelled by vegetable oil, basically. Then the steam comes down this pipe over our heads into the regulator here beside us, and that's where we control the speed of the engine. The steam is used three times. That's why this engine is called a triple expansion steam engine.'

Malcolm went on to tell me that the engine was 112 years old. 'It was built in 1899. Over the years the bearings have had to be replaced, obviously; they're moving parts, and so they wear. But fundamentally this engine is just as it was in 1899.'

'Does it ever go wrong?' I asked. Malcolm's answer came quick as a flash. 'Not on my watch!'

# Rob Roy, Scotland's Robin Hood

Rob Roy (Robert MacGregor, 1671-1734), later romanticised as a noble Jacobite hero and a Scottish Robin Hood, in fact led a life that was tougher and more mundane than his legend suggests. He was born at Glengyle at the head of Loch Katrine, and lived in the Trossachs all his life; his grave is in the churchyard of St Angus, Balquhidder, in his native glen.

At the age of 18 Rob Roy ('Roy' means 'redhead') joined the Jacobite rising led by Viscount Dundee, immortalised by Scott: 'So let each cavalier who loves honour and me Come follow the bonnet of Bonny Dundee'. The rebellion was crushed in 1689.

Rob Roy made his living as a cattleman. At this time cattle rustling and selling protection against the theft of cattle was normal, and even bordered on the legal. He was doing well, and borrowed a lot of money to increase his herd, but his herdsman ran off with the money. Rob could not repay the debt and was branded an outlaw – he and his wife and family were evicted from their house and lands at Inversnaid by the Duke of Montrose, whom Rob regarded thereafter as his life-long enemy. Eventually the Earl of Breadalbane, who had no love for Montrose, gave Rob some land in Glen Dochart, where Rob returned to his life as a cattleman. It was during this time that he gained his 'Robin Hood' reputation by helping those poor people who were downtrodden by Montrose.

Rob was captured twice by Montrose, but both times managed to escape. He took part in the Jacobite rising of 1715, and was later wounded at the battle of Glen Shiel in 1719, another Jacobite attempt to restore the Stuart kings. In 1720 he moved to Balquhidder, and resumed his normal way of life there. After a short illness he died in December 1734 just as a piper was playing 'I shall return no more'.

In 1817 Walter Scott immortalized Rob in his novel 'Rob Roy'. Scott depicts Scotland just before the 1715 Jacobite rising, with Rob as a mysterious, dashing figure who crosses the path of the hero: 'Speak out, sir, and do not Maister or Campbell me – my foot is on my native heath, and my name is MacGregor!'

# The Wordsworths visit Loch Katrine

'After long waiting, and many clumsy preparations, we got ourselves seated in the boat; but we had not floated five yards before we perceived that if any of the party – and there was a little Highland woman who was going over the water with us, the boatman, his helper, and ourselves – should stir but a few inches, leaning to one side or the other, the boat would be full in an instant, and we at the bottom; besides, it was very leaky, and the woman was employed to lade out the water continually.'

FROM DOROTHY WORDSWORTH'S JOURNAL, 1803

## JOHN'S PHOTOGRAPH OF LOCH KATRINE

LOCH KATRINE STEAMER, 2011

*Here among this glorious scenery I felt at one with the Frith photographer of over 100 years ago. I wanted to take a similarly romantic picture, and I think the rain and the mist added to the evocative atmosphere – and, of course, modern cameras mean that the autumn colours came through really well. So here she is: a lovely boat, 112 years old. She is the true Lady of the Lake.*

# An Enchanting Town at the Meeting of the Waters

CALLANDER, MAIN STREET 1899 FRITH 44634

*At the time this photograph was taken, large numbers of excursionists were coming to the Highlands, and stopping off at small towns en route. Here we are at one of them: Callander, 10 miles east of Loch Katrine. Here in its busy High Street Victorian tourists would find shops, restaurants and hotels where they could rest and refuel before continuing their tour of the beautiful Trossachs.'*

CALLANDER,
MEETING OF THE
WATERS 1899
FRITH 44631

Callander, a charming small town 14 miles north-west of Stirling, is the eastern gateway to Loch Lomond and the Trossachs National Park; its position is a delightful one, where the River Teith and the River Leny meet, and near three lochs – Loch Vennachar, Loch Achray and Loch Lubnaig. Lofty Ben Ledi and the Callander Crags tower over the town, and the scenery is simply enchanting. For many visitors the 'real' Scotland of romance and myth starts here.

Callander's story goes back a long way. Prehistoric archeological sites nearby include Scotland's largest chambered cairn (a Neolithic burial mound), and a Roman military camp built during Agricola's campaigns in the 1st century. Perhaps the history of the town itself can be said to have begun in the 6th century, when St Kessog, a disciple of St Columba, came here to teach and preach from a mound still known as Tom-na-Chessaig (the hill of Kessog) near St Kessog's Church, now the Rob Roy Centre.

Life here in the Highlands was dominated for centuries by the close-knit loyalty of the clan system. Apart from cattle rustling and the odd bout of clan warfare, nothing of great moment occurred in this area until the huge upheaval of the Jacobite Rising in the early 18th century. It was during this period that a military road was driven through to aid the English in their 'pacification' of the Highlands.

The Jacobites were finally defeated at Culloden in 1746, and the Highland Clearances meant that a displaced population had to be housed in the towns. The Duke of Perth instigated the building of the 'new town' of Callander in the 1770s, making it the first planned town in rural Scotland. Spacious streets and squares, along with a new parish church, were built, and veteran soldiers and Highland families settled here and set up small businesses and shops.

CALLANDER 1899
FRITH 44625

TOP:
CALLANDER,
THE BRIDGE AND BEN
LEDI 1899
FRITH 44621

ABOVE:
VICTORIAN ENGRAVING
SHOWING THE BATTLE
OF CULLODEN

It was now that the era of the Highlands as a tourist destination began. The Rev Dr James Robertson, minister of St Kessog's in the 1790s, wrote one of Scotland's first tourist guides, 'A Pamphlet Descriptive of the Neighbourhood of Callander'. Dorothy and William Wordsworth came here in the early years of the 19th century, and were followed by Sir Walter Scott. His 'The Lady of the Lake' and 'Rob Roy' attracted hundreds of visitors, and their numbers increased vastly with the arrival of the railway in 1858, bringing prosperity to Callander.

New hotels and houses were built, and Callander railway station opened in 1870. What with improved roads, and steamers on the lochs, Callander had become the ideal touring centre for the Trossachs and Loch Lomond. Its popularity increased over the years along with the rise of motor transport, and it had a burst of fame in the 1960s when it was the location for the fictional Tannochbrae in the popular 'Dr Finlay's Casebook' television series. Today the railway is no more, but the former Callander and Oban Railway line is now part of the National Cycle Network and the Rob Roy Way. Thousands of visitors still come to Callander on their way to Sir Walter Scott's 'enchanted land' of the Trossachs.

# John learns to make traditional oatcakes

JOHN TALKS TO
LOCAL HISTORIAN
AND BAKER ROB KERR

Local historian and businessman Rob Kerr works in Callander's High Street, and he was pretty sure that he could show me where the Frith photograph on page 237 was taken from. As we strolled along, he looked carefully at the picture. 'Probably the most prominent feature is the corner turret of the Dreadnought Hotel to the right. The building still stands – it's recently had a facelift.'

I thought everything around us looked surprisingly similar to the Frith picture. 'It does', said Rob. 'Recently they've spent a lot of Lottery money on keeping the fascias looking the same as they always did. The buildings have been restored, and the view has changed little from Frith's time.'

Rob identified the spot where the Frith photographer would have stood. 'The only obvious difference is the clothes people are wearing and the tarmac on the roads. The main content of the photograph has remained the same – and some buildings, like the hotels and guest houses, are still used for the same purpose as they were in Victorian times.'

THE MHOR BAKERY

Rob's business, Mhor Bread, is another example – it's been here for over 100 years, and would have been selling bread, cakes and pies when the Frith photographer was here. Rob's bread is made traditionally by hand, using flour milled in Scotland. The bakery makes award-winning traditional pies, and old Scottish classics like the oatcake. Rob set me a challenge - I had to bake some oatcakes.

He took me into his immaculate tiled bakery where racks for bread and cakes and huge mixing machines lined the walls. I felt a little bit intimidated as we stood in front of a gleaming stainless steel table. 'I thought oatcakes were supposed to be an easy thing to make', I said. 'So they are', answered Rob. 'Easy to make, nourishing, and cheap – the perfect everyday family food.'

My first job was to weigh out the ingredients, and from a big metal scoop I carefully poured oats into a bowl. I felt that you shouldn't have too much whisky before doing this task. Then we added an ingredient that I'm sure can't be traditional. 'I've measured this out for you', said Rob. 'This is 250 grams of olive oil.' 'Scottish olive oil?' I asked. 'It comes from the Highlands!' joked Rob. After the oats and oil were mixed together, it was time to get kneading.

JOHN REMOVING
HIS OATCAKES
FROM THE OVEN
USING A
TRADITIONAL
BAKER'S PEEL

First Rob threw some flour on the table: one effortless throw, and the working surface was evenly covered.

'Now,' said Rob, 'tip out your oat mix, gather it together, give it a good knead, and then roll it out.' I really had to put my back into this part of the job, so Rob helped with the rolling. With a cutter we formed round oatcakes, and set them in neat rows on a baking tray. Then Rob had one final test for me. 'You don't want your oatcakes to fall off the tray, and you don't want your tray to knock into people. That's why we bakers carry our baking trays above our heads.' I followed his example. 'You look like a real baker now!' said Rob.

We put the tray in the oven, and 15 short minutes later we pulled the tray out using a tool that looked like a big wooden paddle – this is the traditional baker's peel. I thought my oatcakes looked terrific, but there had to be a final test: the tasting. I tried them out on the customers of Rob's shop, and the general verdict was that they were crumbly and delicious. The Scottish baking tradition is well and truly alive here, just as it was in Frith's time.

# The Magnificent Bracklinn Falls

BRACKLINN, UPPER FALLS 1899
FRITH 44639

'Above a chasm where the Keltie Burn precipitates itself from a height of at least fifty feet, there is thrown a rustic foot-bridge, of about three feet in breadth, which is scarcely to be crossed by a stranger without awe and apprehension.'

Thus 'Black's Picturesque Tourist of Scotland', a Victorian guidebook, described Bracklinn Falls, near Callander, defining them as the essentially spectacular and romantic scenery that 19th-century excursionists craved.

The huge vertical slabs of sandstone are part of the Highland boundary fault formed about 410 million years ago when the land masses of Scotland and England collided. The water has eroded the rocks to form the gorge; the water falls in five sparkling cataracts, the biggest about 25ft high.

The 'rustic foot-bridge' mentioned in Black's guide was replaced by a new cast iron one in about 1870, when Queen Victoria came to see the falls. It had to be repaired over the years, for the last time in 2000. Then came a catastrophe. In August 2004 a storm caused a flash flood. The Keltie rose 50ft and washed away not only the bridge, but also a 100-ton boulder. The rocks of the gorge were scoured and parts of the footpath had gone, and sightseers had no means of exploring across the burn. At last in 2010 Callander Community Development Trust found the funds to build an exciting new bridge and make Bracklinn Falls the outstanding tourist destination it always used to be.

FROM DOROTHY WORDSWORTH'S DIARY,
11 SEPTEMBER 1803

Immediately after breakfast, the morning being fine, we set off with cheerful spirits towards the Trossachs … The country near Callander is very pleasing; but, as almost everywhere else, imperfectly cultivated. We went up a broad vale, through which runs the stream from Loch Ketterine, and came to Loch Vennachar, a larger lake than Loch Achray … The Trossachs, overtopped by Benledi and other high mountains, enclose the lake at the head; and those houses which we had seen before, with their corn fields sloping towards the water, stood very prettily under low woods …

After some time we went into the pass from the Trossachs, and were delighted to behold the forms of objects fully revealed, and even surpassing in loveliness and variety what we had conceived. The mountains, I think, appeared not so high; but on the whole we had not the smallest disappointment; the heather was fading, though still beautiful …

We have never had a more delightful walk than this evening. Ben Lomond and the three pointed-topped mountains of Loch Lomond were very majestic under the clear sky, the lake perfectly calm, the air sweet and mild … The sun had been set for some time, when, being within a quarter of a mile of the ferryman's hut, our path having led us close to the shore of the calm lake, we met two neatly dressed women, without hats, who had probably been taking their Sunday evening's walk. One of them said to us in a friendly, soft tone of voice, 'What! you are stepping westward?' I cannot describe how affecting this simple expression was in that remote place, with the western sky in front, yet glowing with the departed sun. William wrote the following poem long after, in remembrance of his feelings and mine:

'What! you are stepping westward?' Yea,
'Twould be a wildish destiny
If we, who thus together roam
In a strange land, and far from home,
Were in this place the guests of chance:
Yet who would stop, or fear to advance,
Though home or shelter he had none,
With such a sky to lead him on?

The dewy ground was dark and cold,
Behind all gloomy to behold,
And stepping westward seem'd to be
A kind of heavenly destiny;
I liked the greeting, 'twas a sound
Of something without place or bound;
And seem'd to give me spiritual right
To travel through that region bright.

The voice was soft; and she who spake
Was walking by her native Lake;
The salutation was to me
The very sound of courtesy;
Its power was felt, and while my eye
Was fix'd upon the glowing sky,
The echo of the voice enwrought
A human sweetness with the thought
Of travelling through the world that lay
Before me in my endless way.

CALLANDER, FROM THE RIVER 1899  FRITH 44629

## JOHN'S PHOTOGRAPH AT CALLANDER

THE OLD BAKERY, CALLANDER, 2011

*I didn't want to copy the Frith photographer and take a picture of the High Street – little has changed there since his time. It was the mouth-watering pies of the Mhor Bakery that I wanted to be the star of my photograph, so here's Rob, posing proudly with a big plate of pies in front of him. Were the pies they sold here in Frith's day as good as they are now? Rob doesn't think so. Bridies, haggis pies, steak and black pudding pies – you really want to get munching. Let's hope they carry on making pies here for at least another 100 years.*

# The Spectacular Castle where Wallace Battled for Scotland's Independence

STIRLING, OLD PARLIAMENT HOUSE 1899 FRITH 44697

*'This building is part of one of Scotland's most important military fortifications, Stirling Castle, which sits in a commanding and strategic position on top of a crag with cliffs on three sides. We are looking at the Great Hall, one of the first examples of Renaissance architecture in the country. But at the time of the Frith photograph, it was a shadow of its former self. I was keen to find out why.'*

After tranquil Loch Katrine and the peaceful little Highland town of Callander, Stirling Castle comes as a striking contrast, both in scenery and in history. It stands on the core of an extinct volcano that juts fiercely and steeply upwards above a strategic crossing of the River Forth, and this position has meant that its story is one of warfare and slaughter – and of royal grandeur, too. It was the favourite residence of many of the Stuart monarchs, and Mary Queen of Scots was crowned in its Chapel Royal.

STIRLING,
THE CASTLE FROM
KING'S KNOT 1899
FRITH 44693

One of Scotland's greatest royal fortresses, Stirling Castle was begun in the 11th century. It changed hands a number of times during the Wars of Independence between Scotland and England, which raged for 60 years after Edward I invaded Scotland in 1296, and it witnessed the bold exploits of William Wallace ('Braveheart') and Robert the Bruce.

It was in 1320, not long after the Scots were victorious at nearby Bannockburn, that in the Declaration of Arbroath the Scots appealed to the Pope to recognise that Scotland was not a possession of the English: 'As long as but a hundred of us remain alive, never will we on any conditions be brought under English rule. It is in truth not for glory, nor riches, nor honours that we fight, but for freedom – for that alone, which no honest man gives up but with life itself.' The Pope was persuaded to acknowledge Robert Bruce's kingship, and this was eventually to culminate in Scottish independence.

Nearly all the buildings in the castle that we see today were built between 1490 and 1600 at the time when it was an important residence of the Stewart kings James IV, James V and James VI. The architectural style derives from that of England and the continent – the Stewarts wanted their palace to reflect Scotland's international importance. Several of James V's masons, for instance, came from France, and two were Dutch.

Today the Great Hall, or Parliament Hall, looks very different to the way it does in the Frith photograph (see photograph opposite and page 249). Gary D'Arcy has been Senior Steward here for 13 years, and he explains that the striking

STIRLING,
BRUCE STATUE 1899
FRITH 44680

JOHN WITH SENIOR STEWARD
GARY D'ARCY

STIRLING,
THE CASTLE FROM
LADIES' TOWER 1899
FRITH 44691

yellow surface is harling, a thick layer of lime plaster. This was applied to the outsides of buildings in medieval times as waterproofing, but it also had the purpose of making important buildings like this one stand out. The Great Hall was built by James IV, and was completed in 1503; Gary D'Arcy tells how over the next 100 years it bore witness to feasts, banquets and two sessions of the Scottish Parliament – in the 1570s supporters of the young James VI met here. It has been described as 'the grandest secular building erected in Scotland in the late Middle Ages', and contains some pioneering Renaissance features. At 138ft by 46.5ft, it is the largest great hall in Scotland.

Charles II was the last monarch to stay at the castle. During the turmoil of the Jacobite Rising in the 18th century the castle was held by the English, and was unsuccessfully besieged by Bonny Prince Charlie. The Napoleonic Wars led to a severe shortage of army accommodation in Scotland, and Stirling Castle became a military barracks – this is why it looks so different in the Frith picture, Gary D'Arcy explains. In 1800 the Great Hall was remodelled to create a four-storey building; the original hammer beam roof and the crenellated parapet were removed, and additional floors, cross walls, staircases, windows and doorways were inserted. At the time of the Frith photograph the castle was owned by the War Office. Since 1881 it had been the home of the Argyll and Sutherland Highlanders, and run as the regiment's depot and recruiting centre.

The army left Stirling Castle in 1964 (although the Argylls still use part of it as their Regimental Museum). The vast Great Hall has been restored to its medieval glory and was formally opened by the Queen on St Andrews Day, 1999. It now has a new oak hammer beam roof, restored wall walks, leaded windows, and interior galleries, and the exterior has been harled, as it used to be. The new appearance of the hall was the subject of some fierce controversy. Many believed that the building looked too new and bright. It was eventually accepted that this is in fact how the building would have looked originally, and it is now widely admired (see John's photograph on page 249).

But if the Great Hall was in a sad and sorry state at the time of the photograph, why did the Frith photographer take it? Gary D'Arcy believes that he wanted to record a building that despite its use as a barracks was vitally connected with Scotland's history and governance.

# John views Stirling's Great Hall upside down

When the Frith photographer came here, photography was a much more laborious process than it is today. Alex Boyd is a photographer interested in historical processes, and he came to Stirling Castle to show me just what Victorian photography entailed.

'It was difficult', he told me, as he set up his huge wooden camera on a tripod. 'These big cameras were very heavy, and they were cumbersome too. This camera I've brought today is quite a basic one, much the same as the one Frith would have used. It's a bellows extension camera: it's fixed at the front, and if you want to focus, the bellows let you slide the camera back along the frame. This lens is a 19th-century one from the 1870s or 80s, just like the ones Frith used. The rest of the camera is an accurate replica.'

I wondered how it worked, and what Alex would have to do to take a picture. 'It's a much less complex mechanism than a modern camera. The lens is covered with a cap. You take off the cap to expose your plate, and close it up again when you've finished.' Alex was wearing a not very elegant pair of rubber gloves, and I asked him why. 'The Victorian photographic process involved lots of chemicals, some of them quite hazardous. One example is silver bromide. If you get it on your skin, it stains your hands black.'

'What would a Victorian photographer see?' I asked. Alex helped me cover my head and the camera with a thick lined cloth, and on the screen at the back I could see the great hall. 'It's clear and bright,' I said. 'Another thing that you can see', said Alex, 'is that Victorian cameras turn the image upside down'. (See photograph below). As he spoke he moved in front of the

BELOW LEFT:
JOHN WITH
PHOTOGRAPHER
ALEX BOYD

BELOW RIGHT:
THE REVERSED IMAGE
AS SEEN IN THE
VICTORIAN CAMERA

ALEX BOYD SHOWING HOW TO EXPOSE THE GLASS
PLATE IN THE VICTORIAN CAMERA

DEVELOPING THE IMAGE

A VICTORIAN ENGRAVING SHOWING A
PHOTOGRAPHER AT WORK

camera. He was quite right – looking through the lens I saw him upside down.

It was all very confusing, I thought. Alex was going to have to work under tremendous difficulties to take a good photograph with his old-style camera. We headed up to where Alex had worked out that the Frith photograph had been taken, a rather awkward spot on the battlements. We had decided to go head to head and time how long it took each of us. 'It'll take 30 seconds for me to expose the plate', said Alex. It seemed an age before he put the cap back on the lens.

Then Alex developed the glass plate in his makeshift darkroom: an array of trays and bottles on the castle flagstones. He fixed the image using potassium cyanide, swishing the liquid over the plate in a plastic tray. To get a print, the negative would have had to be laid in contact with a sheet of specially coated photographic paper – that would have been done back in the Victorian photographer's studio.

From setting up his camera to developing and fixing the glass plate had taken Alex the best part of an hour. It had taken me less than a second to press the button on my modern camera – and it took me less than a second to press the button on my printer and another second or two for my photograph to emerge. Frith would have found the modern process pleasantly easy, I thought.

*From setting up his camera to developing and fixing the glass plate had taken Alex the best part of an hour*

STIRLING,
THE CASTLE
1899
FRITH 44696

# JOHN'S PHOTOGRAPH OF STIRLING CASTLE

STIRLING CASTLE, THE GREAT HALL, 2011

*The advantage of my taking the same picture here as the Frith photographer did is that we can see how much work went into building the Great Hall in the first place, and how much expertise went into its restoration. It was fascinating for me to see exactly how Frith and his photographers took their pictures, and it's made me appreciate their patience and skill. I think I prefer the modern method, though – the Victorian photographer had to work really hard, but all I had to do was press a button!*

# Two Masterpieces of Scottish Bridge Engineering

STIRLING, BRIDGE OF FORTH c1890    FRITH S194304

'This impressive structure, Stirling Old Bridge, probably built in the late 15th century, stands at what has been a key crossing point over the river Forth for many hundreds of years. I was to learn that one of the most important battles in Scotland's history was fought here, and I was to discover another impressive structure – a much more modern one.'

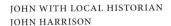

A VICTORIAN ENGRAVING OF
STIRLING BRIDGE

JOHN WITH LOCAL HISTORIAN
JOHN HARRISON

For centuries all of Scotland north of Stirling would have been relatively inaccessible; indeed, some very early maps show the north of Scotland as an island. The River Forth blocks the way. Stirling Old Bridge, shown in the Frith photograph on the opposite page, is known well by local historian John Harrison. He explains that this has long been a crossing point because this is the lowest possible place to bridge it – the River Forth is tidal, with ferocious currents.

John Harrison tells how anyone coming from or to the Highlands would almost certainly cross here – there were alternatives, but they were more difficult, and this spot would always be the favoured option, especially in the troubled times of the Middle Ages when Scotland was in turmoil. To get a medieval army across this river, you needed a bridge.

Near this spot, John Harrison says, there used to be an even older bridge, the site of one of the most important battles in Scotland's history. It was in 1296 that Edward I, 'the hammer of the Scots', had invaded to assert English control of Scotland, sparking off the Scots' long battle for freedom. A confident English force led by John de Warenne, Earl of Surrey, and Hugh de Cressingham, Edward I's treasurer, marched north in 1297 to find themselves on the south bank of the Forth, facing the Scots, led by William Wallace and Andrew de Moray, on the northern side of the river.

It was from a commanding position on the slopes of Abbey Craig that Wallace launched his attack against de Warenne's troops as they attempted to cross the narrow wooden bridge over the Forth – it was only broad enough to let two horsemen cross at a time. Cressingham had stopped Surrey using a ford that would have allowed him to bring his cavalry, mounted on heavy horses, across the river and hit Wallace in the flank. Instead the horsed troops struggled to get over the bridge and deploy in line on the marshy ground on the other side.

Wallace held back until about half the English force, cavalry and infantry as well, had crossed. Then he sent his spearmen rapidly down to hold the bridgehead and separate the two halves of the English force. The heavy cavalry were bogged down and cut to pieces, and then the Scots fell on the English infantry. English losses were high, and many of the foot-soldiers threw off their armour and swam back over the river – or drowned. Cressingham knew how to die and fought on until he was cut down. It is said that he was flayed. The Lanercost Chronicle (a 14th-century history of events in northern England and Scotland) records that Wallace had 'a broad strip [of skin] taken from the head to the heel, to make therewith a baldrick for his sword'.

STIRLING BRIDGE
TODAY

De Warenne had stayed south of the river, and he still had command of a large force of archers; he could have held a strong position here, and denied the Scots access to their territory across the Forth. But his confidence was shattered, and he retreated south, leaving the triumphant Scots to regain possession of Stirling Castle. The Battle of Stirling Bridge was their first decisive victory in their long struggle for independence.

Stirling Old Bridge, the one we see in the Frith photograph on page 250, was built long after the battle, probably in the late 15th century. It is a handsome sandstone structure with four round arches, the two centre ones larger than the other ones. The three supporting piers stand on built-up foundations that look like islands. Between the two centre arches, a small refuge is set into each parapet; it was here that in the Middle Ages customs men sat in a booth to receive the duties that were levied on goods entering the town. During the Jacobite Rising of 1745 the southernmost arch was blown up by the English to stop the Highland forces from coming south; it was not to be repaired until 1749.

John Harrison speculates that the Frith photographer took a picture of this bridge not just because it was beautiful and impressive, but also because it was such an important historical structure. Thousands of Victorian tourists came to Stirling attracted by its long and significant history, of which this bridge is a vital part. Today the bridge is a Scheduled Monument cared for by Historic Scotland, and vehicular access is denied; traffic crosses today via Stirling New Bridge, built in 1831 and designed by one of Scotland's many talented engineers, Robert Stevenson.

# John gets brought down by Archimedes' Principal

JOHN WITH PHIL
MARTIN, BUSINESS
IMPROVEMENT
MANAGER

THE WHEEL AND THE
VISITOR CENTRE 2005
FRITH F248711K

The 19th century was a boom time for Scottish engineers, but nowadays there are not so many opportunities for them to display their talents. However, I was off to see a terrific example of modern Scottish engineering design skill – the Falkirk Wheel, just 10 miles south of Stirling Old Bridge.

This amazing, unique structure is a rotating boat lift that connects the Union Canal with the Forth & Clyde Canal. I was hoping that the Business Improvement Manager Phil Martin would explain its simple yet elegant design to me. We walked beside a canal basin under what looked to me like a very modern bridge that stops abruptly in the middle of nowhere. I asked him how it all worked.

'That structure above us is an aqueduct', he told me. 'The boats go along it until they seemingly come to a dead end. We have to bring them down – they're 30 metres above us at the moment – to this basin here.' I wondered how that could possibly be done. 'At the end of the aqueduct is a huge wheel', said Phil. 'It has one gondola at the top, and another at the bottom. A boat moves into the gondola – each gondola can carry up to eight boats at a time – and then the wheel rotates 180 degrees so that the boat is transferred from the aqueduct above us down into the basin here beside us, and from there it can go on via the other canal. The water in the top gondola and in the bottom one is at the same level, so both gondolas weigh the same. They each hold about 300 tonnes of water.'

'How much power do you need to rotate the wheel?' I asked. 'Very little, in fact', Phil told me. 'It's the same amount of power as boiling 8 kettles of water, about 1.5 kilowatts of electricity.' I wondered where the boats came from and where they were going. 'The Union Canal starts in Edinburgh', said Phil. 'The

THE AQUEDUCT

boats come on the Union all the way from Edinburgh to Falkirk, then the wheel carries them down to the Forth & Clyde Canal, and they can go on to Glasgow.'

I learned that the Forth & Clyde Canal had been designed by the engineer John Smeaton between 1767 and 1790, the greatest construction project Scotland had ever seen. In 1822 the Union Canal linking it to Edinburgh joined it at a large basin called Port Downie; the levels of the two canals were very different, so a flight of 11 locks had to be constructed – and the Union Inn was built to keep the travellers happy during the long wait (see photograph on opposite page).

The coming of the railways, and then better roads and the internal combustion engine, spelt the end for the canals. In 1962, the Forth & Clyde Canal was closed to navigation, although fishermen and yachtsmen were still using it. But with the millennium came the Millennium Link project to restore and re-open the Union and the Forth & Clyde Canals.

EMERGING FROM THE GONDOLA WITH THE WATER LEVELS EQUALLED

The Falkirk Wheel's simple design is based on the perfect poise of the two gondolas. 'The wheel uses Archimedes' principle of water displacement', said Phil. 'Each boat displaces its own weight of water, so the wheels always balance. The wheel transports the boats from one canal to the other in 15 minutes – a lot quicker than the whole day it used to take to negotiate the flight of 11 locks that was here before.'

I felt it was important to experience the wheel for myself, so Phil took me on board a tourist boat for a closer look. I asked him how many visitors came to see the wheel every year. 'About half a million', he said. 'We didn't expect it to be a tourist attraction when we built it. Initially it was built simply as a replacement for the locks. Then when we realised that lots of people loved coming here, we built the Visitor

Centre so that the wheel could be an attraction as well, with boat rides like this one so that visitors could take a journey on it.'

Scottish engineers have never been afraid to innovate, and this is no exception – and on a striking scale, too. I'm sure that if Francis Frith could travel in time he'd be as impressed as I am with this magnificent structure.

UNION INN, PORT DOWNIE 2005
FRITH F248704K

## JOHN'S PHOTOGRAPH OF THE FALKIRK WHEEL

THE FALKIRK WHEEL, 2011

*My picture is a sharp contrast to the Frith photograph on page 250. That photograph shows a bridge that takes you back 500 years, whereas mine takes you back just 11 years. Both pictures, though, show the fascination we all have for big engineered structures. I wanted to get a bit of age – the canal boat – into my picture of this wonderful modern wheel. The old needs the new to move it up and down.*

# An Elephant Rock and a Monkey Spy

HARTLEPOOL, ELEPHANT ROCK 1886 FRITH 18845

*'We are on the northeast coast in what is an industrial town today, but what once was a popular seaside resort in Victorian times: Hartlepool. The Frith photographer has headed straight for the shore to take a picture of a most unusual tourist attraction, known for obvious reasons as Elephant Rock. I was looking forward to meeting the elephant myself – but I was to be disappointed.'*

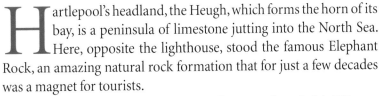artlepool's headland, the Heugh, which forms the horn of its bay, is a peninsula of limestone jutting into the North Sea. Here, opposite the lighthouse, stood the famous Elephant Rock, an amazing natural rock formation that for just a few decades was a magnet for tourists.

The rock was not indestructible. William Fordyce, in his 'History and Antiquities of the County Palatine of Durham' (1857), reported: 'A large portion of the Elephant Rock, after weathering the storms of past centuries, and being frequently an object of interest to the artist, was, after a storm, broken away by the high surf on the 22nd October, 1841 … It is thought by many as a somewhat singular coincidence, that two elephants should have been brought into the town, in the menagerie of Mr Wombwell, within a few hours before the fall of their huge rocky effigy on the neighbouring shore; and that this was probably the first occasion in which an elephant had ever been seen in Hartlepool.'

Nevertheless, as we can see from the photograph, the elephant strode on through the years still looking remarkably like his menagerie brothers despite his injuries. Alas, he had not much longer to live after the photograph was taken. The seas eroded the rock away, and the elephant finally collapsed in May 1891. The only parts of him that remain today are his feet and the tip of his trunk, which can sometimes be seen at low tide.

During the Victorian era, Hartlepool was a popular seaside resort, and like so many resorts, had originated as a fishing town. Because of its natural harbour, Hartlepool was a thriving port during the Middle Ages, one of the busiest on the east coast. For many years the townspeople relied almost wholly on fishing for their livelihood. The fishermen would go out to sea in their cobles, while the women and children would collect shellfish, mend nets and clean and sell the fish. But by the beginning of the 18th century, the port had gone into decline and the harbour had fallen into ruin. Luckily, at the beginning of the 19th century a petition was made to restore the harbour, and it was reopened.

Then the railway brought the tourists, who swelled the town in the summer and brought more prosperity. Commercial docks were built, too, and along with industry came a huge influx of workers. The peaceful fishing town suddenly

*This was probably the first occasion in which an elephant had ever been seen in Hartlepool*

HARTLEPOOL,
THE PROMENADE
1903 FRITH 49995

became a hive of activity. In 1801 the population had been less than 1,000, but by 1841 it was over 5,000.

In the 1851 supplement to Cuthbert's 'History of Hartlepool', he writes that the young cockle women and shrimpers made a colourful sight with their red kerchiefs on their heads and their scanty petticoats tucked up showing bare legs and feet. When industry and the navvies appeared, their costume changed to smart caps, sometimes with wreaths of flowers as adornment, and shoes and white stockings on Sundays.

HARTLEPOOL 1886
FRITH 18839

In 1854 a ferry was established by the corporation for the hundreds of workers that travelled to the shipyards and engine works at Middleton. The photograph (above left) looks across to the town wall from Middleton Sands, and the ferry landing is visible to the extreme left. But as we can see from the cobles and fishing boats in this photograph, plenty of people still made a living from the sea.

Hartlepool in the 19th century had become both a thriving modern commercial town and a highly popular seaside resort with a promenade and bandstand. It is very possible that many of the older people in the crowd on the promenade (see photograph on previous page) had made a visit to Elephant Rock, an essential part of their holidays here in past years.

## The town's dastardly Napoleonic spy

Hartlepool is famous for another animal besides its elephant. You will sometimes hear Hartlepudlians being teased for being 'monkey hangers'. How did they get this strange nickname?

Back in the time of the Napoleonic Wars, there was much apprehension about the possibility of French spies infiltrating Britain. The story goes that a French ship was wrecked off the coast of Hartlepool, and the fishermen kept their eyes peeled in case a dastardly invader appeared. However, the only survivor was a pathetic half-drowned pet monkey dressed in uniform. The fishermen questioned the monkey, and thought that his chatter was a foreign language. They held a trial on the beach, and concluded that the monkey had to be a French spy. There and then they condemned him to death, and hanged him from the mast of one of their fishing cobles.

Could the hanging story be true? During the Napoleonic Wars, the French were portrayed by British propaganda cartoonists as grotesque monkey-like creatures, so to uneducated fishermen in the time before photography the unfortunate ship's pet could well have seemed to them to be a hated enemy. Maybe they did indeed hang the monkey.

# John searches out the elephant's feet and trunk

JOHN WITH
ARCHAEOLOGIST
MARK SIMMONS

THE REMAINS OF
THE ELEPHANT'S
FEET

I walked along beside the shore to meet archaeologist Mark Simmons. I always expect things to have changed a bit from the way they looked in Frith's day, but on this occasion I had a major disappointment in store.

'The bad news', said Mark, 'is that you can't take a photograph of Elephant Rock, because it was washed away in a storm in 1891. You're just a little bit too late! But we can still go down to the foreshore and see where the Frith photographer took his photograph.' We clambered down a ladder to the rocks along the shore.

I learned that Elephant Rock had existed for no more than a few decades, a blink of an eye in geological terms, so the Frith team were lucky to be in the right place at the right time. 'The coastline has altered a lot in the last 150 years or so', Mark told me. 'It used to be about 100 yards further out than it is now. All this broken area where we are standing used to be a cliff of solid rock.'

Mark went on to explain that it wasn't just natural forces that had first created and then destroyed Elephant Rock. He showed me a drawing of the coastline made in 1847: 'This drawing shows that the limestone cliffs were quarried for building stone. We can see that the quarrying is pushing the coastline inwards, leaving rock stacks standing on the headland – Elephant Rock was one of those stacks. So it was partly quarrying and partly the action of the waves that formed the elephant.' I wondered where the elephant had stood. Mark pointed outwards: 'You can just see where the sea has left the feet and the tip of the trunk behind.'

'Why did the Frith photographer take this picture?' I asked. 'He knew it would sell well', answered Mark. 'There were big profits to be made from souvenir photographs, and this one was also turned into picture postcards that were sold in their thousands here on the promenade from the ice cream shop and the bandstand.'

It wasn't just Elephant Rock that vanished. As Hartlepool became more industrialised in the 20th

HARTLEPOOL'S
RESTORED
DOCKYARD

STUART FIRING THE
CANNON

century, visitors stopped coming here for their seaside holidays. For a while, Hartlepool's tourist industry all but died out. Recently, however, there's been a resurgence with the opening of the award-winning Maritime Experience at the historic dockyard. Here you can wander along the cobbled quays, see restored sailing ships and experience the seaport as it was at the time of the Napoleonic wars.

Re-enactments pull in the visitors, and on one of the quays I met Stuart Burke and Nina Cole in their authentic-looking Georgian costumes. Stuart explained to me how to fire a cannon. 'Cannons are rated by the size of the ball they fire', he told me. 'This is a three-pounder. You can also fire chain shot from a cannon like this – chain shot is two balls chained together. You'd use that to take down the rigging of a ship to disable it, but not sink it, especially if you were going to take it as a prize.'

First Stuart riddled the barrel of the cannon to make sure there was no smouldering residue inside that might set off the cannon prematurely. 'When you feel nothing in the barrel, you know it's safe', he said. 'Then in the old days you'd put in the charge and the ball – I'm putting in a cartridge. Next, I put a little powder in the touch hole at the other end of the barrel, and we're ready to fire.'

'Will it be loud?' I asked. 'You might want to step back a little further!' said Stuart. It was indeed a big explosion. A flock of seagulls few up in alarm, and Nina and I fanned the smoke away from our faces. It was exciting to be transported back in time.

## JOHN'S PHOTOGRAPH AT HARTLEPOOL

### HISTORIC HARTLEPOOL 2011

*The Frith photograph was of Hartlepool's star attraction in Victorian times. Now, 125 years later, mine shows the star attraction today. Stuart and Nina are the inspiration for my photograph. The re-enactments they do and this wonderful recreation of the past get plenty of tourism awards. For a long time it looked as if Hartlepool would never again be a magnet for tourists, but now it really does attract visitors once more.*

# A Smooth Glide Down to the Sands by Water Power

*'The lovely seaside resort on the Cleveland coast of Saltburn-by-the-Sea has got sandy beaches, spectacular views, a pier – and a water-powered funicular railway to take visitors to and from the beach. I arrived here 120 years after the Frith photograph on the previous pages was taken, but I found that this perfect Victorian way to get to the beach was keeping the past alive.'*

ONE OF THE CLIFF LIFT CARRIAGES

The *raison d'être* of a seaside resort is, of course, the sea and the beach. It is vital that visitors and holidaymakers can get to the shore easily so that they can enjoy all the amusements the place has to offer. At Saltburn-by-the-Sea, the obstacle was cliffs 120 feet high. Steps up and down weren't the answer – the very young, the old and the frail would find them hard to negotiate. So how were the visitors to get up and down to the long sandy beach?

A local engineer, John Anderson, found the answer in 1884. His ingenious solution was a water-powered cliff lift. The two carriages (very smart ones with comfortable seats and stained glass windows) are connected by cables running round pulley wheels, and each carriage has a water tank beneath it. When water is run into the tank of the top carriage, the carriage moves down thanks to the weight of the water, and the carriage at the bottom is pulled up. When the first carriage reaches the bottom, it releases the water from its tank so that the process can begin again. To this very day the lift, the oldest working water balance cliff lift in Britain, carries around 70,000 visitors up and down its 207ft track every year.

The charming resort of Saltburn-by-the-Sea was the dream of Henry Pease, a director of the Stockton & Darlington Railway, who decided in the 1860s that this breezy cliff-top would make an ideal resort. The railway was extended to Saltburn

(originally a tiny fishing village), and 'New' Saltburn was born. The town still holds on to its 19th-century roots, recalled in the Saltburn Victorian Celebrations that are held every year.

Elegant hotels, boarding houses and terraces were built in the distinctive white 'Pease' brick. The impressive façade of the Queen Hotel is angled – it was originally envisaged as a section of a 'circus' of buildings, close to the approach road to the town's railway station (see photograph, left). In the event, only one side of this circus was ever completed.

That vital component of any self-respecting Victorian resort, the pier (see photographs below and overleaf), was also designed by

ABOVE LEFT: SALTBURN-BY-THE-SEA, PIER ENTRANCE 1913 FRITH 66354

LEFT: SALTBURN-BY-THE-SEA, THE QUEEN HOTEL 1891 FRITH 29197

BELOW: SALTBURN-BY-THE-SEA, HUNTCLIFF 1901 FRITH 46926

SALTBURN-BY-THE-SEA, THE PIER 1913
FRITH 66358

SALTBURN-BY-THE-SEA, HALFPENNY BRIDGE
c1885   FRITH 18109

John Anderson and opened in 1869; when first built, it was an impressive 1500ft long. Like the cliff lift, it was innovative – it was the first iron pier to be built on the north-east coast. Despite facing due north into the cruel North Sea, it has survived repeated storm damage; after major refurbishment in the 1990s, in 2009 it received the National Pier Society's Pier of the Year award.

Another Victorian attraction was the Halfpenny Bridge (see photograph below), built in 1869 to span Hazelgrove, a valley between the cliffs, where a picturesque walk from the shore to the western side of the town was laid out. A spectacular 140ft high, Halfpenny Bridge proved a handy observation platform for those holidaymakers eager to look at the views. The toll to cross was a halfpenny for pedestrians when it opened – hence its name. Its condition gradually deteriorated, and it was demolished by explosives in spectacular fashion in 1974.

# Speed Trials and Races on Saltburn Sands

SERIES MAURIE HILL, DREAMSTIME.COM

1906 DARRACQ RACE CAR COMPETING IN A HISTORIC REVIVAL
AT THE FESTIVAL OF MOTORSPORT 2010

The firm, flat beaches of Cleveland have been used for other things besides sand castles and paddling. In the early part of the 20th century, the sands at Saltburn attracted motor racing enthusiasts. In July 1906 a crowd of 60,000 watched Warrick Wright set a Yorkshire record of 96.5mph.

The main attraction for the next few years was Algernon Lee 'Algy' Guinness, a member of the wealthy brewing family, with his 200hp Darracq, said to be the world's fastest car. In 1907 he raced the Maharajah Tikara on Saltburn sands and reached 111.84mph, despite bad weather – the local paper reported that 'the heavy rain had made the sands wet and heavy but with a whirr and a flash the cars went by appearing to almost rival the streaks of forked lightning which a few minutes before had flashed across the sky.'

Algy returned to Saltburn with his Darracq in 1908 and 1909, both times reaching speeds of over 120mph. Incidentally, the Darracq's engine, having passed from owner to owner, was recently restored, and visited Saltburn again in 2009.

In 1911 Pietro Bordino drove a 300hp Fiat S76 all the way from Brooklands to Saltburn (sometimes at over 120mph) for a sprint event, where he won the flying mile record. It wasn't until after the First World War that the excitement began again, this time thanks to the world-famous driver Malcolm Campbell. On 17 June 1922 he set the first Land Speed Record of 138.08 in a 350hp Sunbeam V12 (the previous month Algy Guinness had driven the car at Brooklands to reach 133.75mph).

In the 1930s the sands at Saltburn became increasingly unsuitable for motor racing, and the Second World War brought an end to it entirely. Between 1948 and the early 1960s the sands saw some motorcycle racing, but the glory days of heart-stopping speeds on the sand were over.

WITH ACKNOWLEDGEMENTS TO REBECCA HILTON AND WWW.SALTBURNBYSEA.COM

# John experiences 'a delightful contraption'

Saltburn didn't evolve, it was a planned seaside resort. I headed to the beach to find out more from industrial historian Stephen Sherlock. 'Yes, Saltburn was the vision of one man', Steve told me. 'Henry Pease of Darlington was a Quaker, and he had a very clear picture of how the town should grow. For instance, as a Quaker he was teetotal, so he didn't want any pubs to be built – he wanted to see more improving things here, such as reading rooms.' I wondered when the first pub had been built. 'Not until 1986!' said Steve.

I learnt that the entrepreneur and politician Henry Pease may have been a visionary, but primarily he was a businessman. Two things preoccupied him above all others: iron mining and railways. His family had been directors of the famous Stockton & Darlington Railway, the world's first passenger line, and in 1861 he built an extension round the coast all the way to Saltburn.

'So did Pease build the railway extension to bring more visitors here?' I asked. 'No,' replied Steve, 'at first he was thinking of it purely in business terms. At that stage it was a mineral railway. The use of it by tourists was a secondary consideration, a spin-off. He wanted to secure the mineral deposits near the railway, so he arranged to pay the landowners royalties, and tramways carried the minerals to the railway which in turn conveyed them to the furnaces of Teesside.'

But also, I thought, Pease had wanted to build a town to be proud of. 'Certainly', said Steve. 'He left us a legacy here. Perhaps the most important part of it is the funicular tramway.'

I thought it was time I experienced this delightful contraption, and I sat myself down in the carriage opposite a young mum and her son. As the tramway took us upwards, I asked her why she thought people enjoyed it so. 'Well, look at the fantastic views!' she said. 'Also, it's lovely to actually experience some real Victoriana. And being powered by water makes it natural, not polluting.'

We arrived at the top, and I went to speak to Bob Cook, the cliff tramway operator, in his booth. 'Everybody likes it, don't they?' I said. 'Yes, I've never heard anyone complaining!'

said Bob. 'This is one form of transport that's quite rightly appreciated by everyone.' I wondered if it was difficult to work it. 'No, it's typically Victorian – ingenious, but really simple', said Bob. 'Come inside and I'll show you'.

I went into his booth, which was dominated by a big spoked wheel like a ship's wheel. 'First I press the bell', said Bob. 'Then I reset the safety brakes – they're modern, the only thing here that is – by pressing this button on the control panel. Next I start to put water in the tank of the car at the top. As the tank fills I ease the big wheel a little and wait for the car to start to move down. All I have to do now is to control the speed with the big wheel. The other car's coming up – I slow it down, and now it's coming in to land at the top. I disengage the wheel, put the safety brake on, and open the door.'

As the happy customers disembarked, Bob gave them a big smile. 'There we go, folks – thanks very much now!'

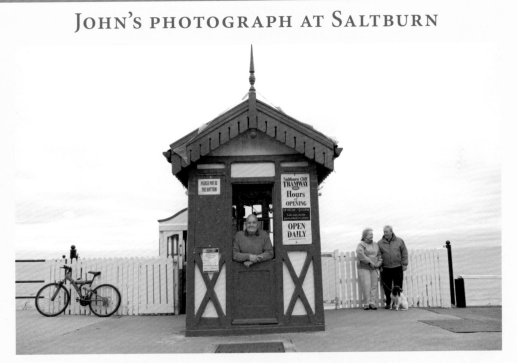

## JOHN'S PHOTOGRAPH AT SALTBURN

SALTBURN CLIFF LIFT, BOB COOK IN HIS BOOTH, 2011

*When the Frith photograph on pages 262-263 was taken, the tramway was an innovation, and key to Saltburn's success as a seaside resort. Today, it's not just a means of transport, but an attraction in its own right. So here's Bob in his booth, and beside him a bike and two smiling dog walkers. Happiness is the theme here. This tramway is the kind of thing that cheers people up; and as for Bob – well, he admits he's got one of the best jobs in the world.*

# A Prosperous Resort Built on Miners' Toil

SALTBURN-BY-THE-SEA, CAT NAB c1885   FRITH 18103

*'This photograph shows the clash between the old village way of life and the new sophisticated resort town of Saltburn. You can still see the old farm buildings in the centre and, on the horizon, the recently built houses for visitors. Just visible at the top left is a bridge. The miners walked across it every day to reach the mines, for Saltburn's growing prosperity in the Victorian era was based firmly on mineral rights. The rapid programme of change was once again the vision of the Pease family.'*

JOHN COMPARING THE
FRITH VIEW WITH THE
SCENE AS IT IS TODAY

Part of the coastline on this the north-east coast of England is harsh and rugged, with towering cliffs and rocky coves. In sharp contrast there are long stretches of sandy beaches, and secret inlets and sheltered bays where the waves lap gently at the shore. Whatever the mood of the coast, the scenery is glorious. The coast is varied, and so are the towns and villages that sit upon the cliffs and shores. Most of them, including Saltburn, were once no more than tiny hamlets depending on fishing for their livelihood. It was the vision, energy, and innovative spirit of the Pease family that were to dramatically alter the community's fortunes.

In the 18th century, rich sources of iron ore were discovered in Cleveland, and it was this mineral wealth that was to bring change and prosperity to the region. As early as 1811 attempts were made to smelt this iron ore, but it was so intractable as to be considered valueless. It was the introduction of the hot-blast furnace in the 1830s that turned Cleveland into a rich centre of mineral wealth. Its mines grew in importance as a rich source of ore, and by the 1860s the total yield of ironstone mined from the area each year amounted to a million tons.

A VICTORIAN
ENGRAVING OF A
BLAST FURNACE

SALTBURN-BY-THE-
SEA, CAT NAB, c1885
FRITH 18102

The Pease family were at the forefront of the industry. In the early years they dug their ore from open workings in the hillside above the village of Skinningrove near Saltburn. However, they were great innovators and were soon digging shafts to work the ore deep underground. A railway line carried the ore from the mines down an incline to a jetty where it was transferred into ships.

There was a huge demand for iron in Victorian times. It was used for building railways, bridges, gates and

BELOW LEFT:
WARRINGTON,
TOWN HALL, NEW
GATES 1895
FRITH 36688

BELOW RIGHT:
MACHYNLLETH,
THE CORRIS RAILWAY
1899
FRITH 44555

street furniture (see the photographs of a locomotive and decorative iron gates below) as well as grand iron and glass buildings such as the Crystal Palace in London, home of the Great Exhibition of 1851. As a result, the Skinningrove mines prospered and the Pease family swiftly developed Saltburn into a favourite destination for Victorian tourists.

The Pease family had several other successful business interests. For instance, at Darlington they operated extensive woollen mills, employing 800 men, women, and children. Some of the wool they sold as yarn, and some they wove. Their company was famous for its cloth, winning awards at the 1851 Great Exhibition (see below).

# H Pease & Co Awarded Prestigious Prizes

❝At the Great Industrial Exhibition in London in 1851, a prize medal was awarded to Messrs H Pease & Co for Cobourg cloths, single and double, twill worsted weft and cotton warp. The lower and middle qualities were much stouter than the majority of such goods, and were remarkably even and regular. The fine qualities were equally commendable. The firm exhibited 144 samples of worsted merino yarns. In descanting on the wonders of the exhibition, F Mewburn Esq observed, on a public occasion, 'In the midst of all this marvellous show, have not Darlington and its neighbourhood borne their part? The material of which the flags which decorated the exterior of the building and fluttered a welcome to all, was made here by Messrs Henry Pease & Co; the very iron was smelted by Pease's coke; Mr Pease's fire-bricks gained a prize; patent fuel made at Middlesbro', a council medal; and the exquisite fabric exhibited by Henry Pease & Co known as Cobourg cloth, and manufactured here, carried away a prize'.❞

FROM 'THE HISTORY AND ANTIQUITIES OF THE COUNTY PALATINE OF DURHAM' BY WILLIAM FORDYCE 1857

# John learns about the hard life of Saltburn's miners

JOHN WITH ALAN RICHARDSON IN THE ENTRANCE
TO THE SKINNINGROVE DRIFT MINE TUNNEL

THE TUNNEL LINED WITH PEASE BRICKS

I paid a visit to the Skinningrove iron mine, just four miles south-east down the coast from Saltburn. It was established in 1848 by – yes, you've guessed it – the Pease family. It's now a museum, and I was shown around by retired miner Alan Richardson.

Alan told me that Skinningrove was one of the largest mines in the area, employing around 860 people. The Pease family, who owned and ran it, were very moral, being Quakers. 'Safety standards weren't very high', said Alan, 'but then they weren't anywhere in those days. The excuse for workers dying was that it was probably an act of God rather than anything to do with conditions in the mine. But the Pease family did try to look after their employees.'

IMAGE COURTESY OF THE CLEVELAND IRONSTONE MINING MUSEUM

LOFTUS IRONSTONE
MINE: ENTRANCE TO
TRAVELLING WAY

Despite the dangers of mining in the mid 1800s, thousands came to work in the county of Cleveland at over eighty mines. The area became one of the global hotspots of the iron industry – Britain was producing more iron than the rest of the world put together.

Alan told me that conditions in the Skinningrove mines in those early days were not very good. 'It was very wet, and there was always water dripping. They used to say that if it rained on the surface on a Monday it would rain underground on a Tuesday, as it took a day for the water to percolate through.' We entered the old drift mine, walking along a sloping tunnel that runs hundreds of metres to the iron face. When it was being operated at its peak the tunnels in the mine were extended by at least metre a day. Alan showed me how the Pease family protected their tunnels by using three layers of bricks in the arched ceilings. I asked him where the bricks came from. 'From a brick works owned by the Pease family. They owned everything, didn't they?'

They could be tough employers. 'For instance', said Alan, 'in those days people had large families. If a miner got killed at work the mine clerk would go to the house as soon as it was known, not only to inform the widow that her husband had been killed, but to give her fourteen days notice.' I asked him if this was notice to quit the house. 'Yes, to vacate it, because there was no longer a miner living there.' Well, I thought, you can't get tougher than that. We'd regard it as inhuman.

THE MINER'S FRIEND

Today the original Skinningrove iron faces are flooded with water, but to get a feel for life in the mines the museum has recreated the scene in impressive detail. Alan handed me a heavy iron chisel with a sharp point called a jumper. He showed me how it was used to punch a hole in the rock a yard deep. When this was done the miner inserted gunpowder, stood well back, and then exploded it. This would release the iron ore which would then be loaded into trucks and carried to the surface.

I found myself looking at a rat – luckily, an

imitation one. 'He's the miner's friend', said Alan. 'There were rats everywhere down here. In fact they were a help, because they're very sensitive to foul air and gas, and they seem to have a sixth sense about the instability of the rock.' 'So when you were a miner,' I asked, 'how often would you come across a rat?' 'Every day', replied Alan, 'they really were the miner's friend.'

Having talked to Alan, I felt that life underground must have been rather grim. However, if it wasn't for the mines bringing jobs to the area the grand new houses in Frith's photograph would never have been built. Saltburn would not have been transformed from a sleepy backwater into the thriving seaside resort it is today. But if it was the Pease family that had the vision, it was Alan and his predecessors down the mines that made it all possible.

## JOHN'S PHOTOGRAPH AT SKINNINGROVE

IRON MINER ALAN, 2011

*It was Alan's work as a miner that I wanted to photograph. I was keen to tell the story of what happened below ground level. So my photograph shows Alan Richardson, a real miner, in what is now just a mining museum. I hope it helps us to remember that Saltburn was built on the backs of the miners and their hard labour.*

WHITBY, THE PEART CHILDREN 1891  FRITH 28866

# A Whaling Port and a Family of Fisherfolk

*'The photograph on the previous pages was taken on Yorkshire's east coast in Whitby, a port with a long and fascinating history. This is a highly unusual example from the archive – people were not usually the main subject of a Frith picture. Also, I was to find out that this is one of the rare occasions when it is possible to identify the photographer who took it.'*

For centuries Whitby families have earned their living from the sea. The town was once a whaling port, and when whaling declined, the herring fishery took over. These wonderful photographs of the children of a Whitby fishing family are not only full of charm, but exemplify the toughness and resilience that seafaring folk needed in the face of hard times and even tragedy.

The main photograph on the previous pages is a study of the Peart children. Their parents were Jane (née Leadley) and David Peart, and the family lived on Tate Hill (the photograph on the next page shows the view from near where they lived). The Pearts' eldest daughter Amelia, aged about 17 at this time, holds her baby brother George; Amelia later married Tom Eglon. The twin boys (Matthew and Robert) are beside her on the seaweedy rock, and Jane (nicknamed Ginny) and Tom watch the photographer put them all in the frame for posterity. There were also two other brothers, David and William, in the Peart family – they are not shown in this photograph. Ginny married Ernest Swales, a ship's carpenter, in 1909. She died in 1977 at the grand old age of 92. She bore three daughters and four boys, and also stillborn twins, giving birth to her youngest child when she was 44. Several descendants of the Peart children still live in the Whitby area.

It's hard to believe that the twins in their hats and

WHITBY, MATTHEW
AND ROBERT PEART
1891 FRITH 28862

dresses are boys, but it was very common in the past for boys to wear dresses when they were very young, especially in poor families where the elder girls' dresses could be passed down. Boys they certainly are! Matthew (to the left in the photograph on the opposite page, below) and Robert Peart were three years old when the photographs were taken. In later years Robert's life was tragically cut short when he drowned after being swept overboard near St Petersburg on 19 July 1908, aged 20. Their younger brother George (the baby being held by his sister Amelia in the main photograph) also died by drowning; he was only 23 when the HMS 'Hogue' was sunk during the First World War on 22 September 1914.

When Whitby was an important whaling town, ships sailed from here to Greenland and the Arctic in search of a catch. Whale oil used to be a vital commodity; it was used for lamp oil, lubrication, and in the manufacture of soap, textiles, varnish, paint and explosives. A reminder of Whitby's whaling heritage is the arch on West Cliff made from a pair of whale jawbones. During the whaling

STAITHES, NEAR WHITBY, TYPICAL FISHERMEN'S
COBLES c1885 FRITH 18210

*Whitby fishermen fished for
herring and salmon from
clinker-built cobles*

years, when a ship was returning to Whitby's harbour from a whaling trip it was the custom to trice up a pair of whale jawbones to the mast, decorated with ribbons, as a sign that the voyage had been successful.

In later years, Whitby fishermen fished for herring and salmon from cobles (pronounced 'cobbles'), the traditional fishing boats of the northeast coast (see photograph, left). Open sailing boats, they are designed to be launched and landed bow first on the beach, often in rough seas, so they are sturdy vessels, clinker-built to give maximum strength with minimum weight. The shallow aft section and flat, raked stern help the waves to lift the boat off or up onto the shore. A conventional keel would dig into the sand or pebbles of the beach, so from amidships to the stern, cobles have two 'drafts', which act like sledge runners. This is why cobles need an extra long rudder to keep the boat stable in the absence of a full-length keel. Fishing still plays in important part in Whitby life, and the Fish Quay is still busy today.

WHITBY, THE HARBOUR 1885  FRITH 18168

WHITBY, EAST CLIFF 1913 FRITH 66263

# Whitby's famous son, Captain Cook

Captain James Cook, the famous navigator, surveyor and explorer, was a North Yorkshire man; he was born in the village of Marton in North Yorkshire, now a suburb of Middlesbrough, in 1728. In 1736 his family moved to Great Ayton, where young James was educated. He started work as a grocer's apprentice in Staithes, but he moved to Whitby at the age of seventeen, where he was apprenticed to John and Henry Walker, local ship-owners. Cook embarked on his first sea voyage from Whitby in 1747, on a coal carrier. He spent some years in the coasting and Baltic trade, and then joined the Navy, where he rose through the ranks, becoming master in 1759. He displayed exceptional ability as a navigator and surveyor, and in 1768 he commanded the 'Endeavour' for the Royal Society's expedition of discovery to the Pacific, Australia and New Zealand. This was the first of his three major expeditions, in each of which he sailed in boats built in Whitby, including the 'Endeavour' and the 'Resolution'. A statue of Captain Cook now overlooks Whitby harbour from West Cliff. With a map in one hand and dividers in the other, Cook looks out to sea, his eyes on the distant horizon.

# John finds out about Frank Meadow Sutcliffe and the Peart family descendants

JOHN WITH MIKE SHAW

WHITBY, THE ABBEY 1897   FRITH 39482

Francis Frith's photographic business became so successful country-wide that Frith alone couldn't possibly have kept up with the workload and the travelling, so he employed a team of photographers located all over Britain. Most of their names are long forgotten, but I was about to find out who took the photograph on pages 276-277 from Sutcliffe Gallery owner Mike Shaw. We sat down together on the quay.

'Francis Frith's agent in Whitby was the great photographer Frank Meadow Sutcliffe', Mike told me. 'One of the first commissions Frith gave him was to photograph Whitby Abbey and other subjects round about, and one of his pictures was this one of children on the shore.' I wondered how Mike knew it was a Sutcliffe photograph. 'From the style,' said Mike, 'and from the subject matter. Frith photographs are usually topographical, with any people in them purely incidental. Frank Meadow Sutcliffe's subjects weren't the streets of Whitby, but its fisherfolk.'

'Where was the picture taken? I asked. 'By the look of the rocks in the photograph, I'd say on the shore opposite us', said Mike, 'at the foot of the cliff the church stands on. Quite a few of Sutcliffe's photographs show people beside those rocks. We know that the picture shows a well-known local family, the Pearts. Peart is a good old Whitby name.'

Mike told me that his father had bought all Sutcliffe's photographs. 'He bought them at the time when I was born, and now I'm the owner of the Sutcliffe Collection. It's about 1600 glass

ABOVE: JOHN WITH
SUSAN STORR

LEFT: WHITBY, GINNY
PEART 1891 FRITH 28863

BELOW: GINNY PEART
CELEBRATING HER
DIAMOND WEDDING

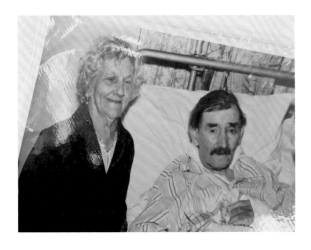

negatives, a small amount in comparison with the Frith Collection, but there's superb quality there.'

Here in Whitby there's still a direct connection to the family seen in the Frith photograph. We'd tracked down a descendant of the Pearts, Susan Storr, who is still very much part of the Whitby community 120 years after her family was photographed for the Frith archive. She welcomed me into her house, and we sat down at a table scattered with photographs.

'Ginny – she's the one second from right in the main Frith photograph – was my grandmother. She was the youngest girl of the family. Here's another photo of her.' We looked at a picture of a thin little girl posing beside a big rock. I thought she didn't look very happy. 'Maybe it was because she had a hard life from the start. Fisherfolk have always had to suffer tough times, just as we still do in my family!'

I asked what happened to Ginny in later life. 'She had three daughters', said Susan, 'and she outlived all of them. See this photo? Here she is celebrating her diamond wedding, sitting beside her husband in his hospital bed. She was 85 at the time, and she lived until she was 92.'

'So,' I said, 'although in the photograph of her as a child she looks as if she could do with a square meal, she must have been strong.' 'She was only 4ft 10in!' said Susan. 'But she was a hard worker – she worked until she was 76 years old. It must have been all that sheep's head soup she used to cook.' 'Sheep's head?' I exclaimed in horror. 'Yes, she was always making sheep's head soup. I can't remember it, but my brothers can. They used to run a mile when she said dinner was ready!'

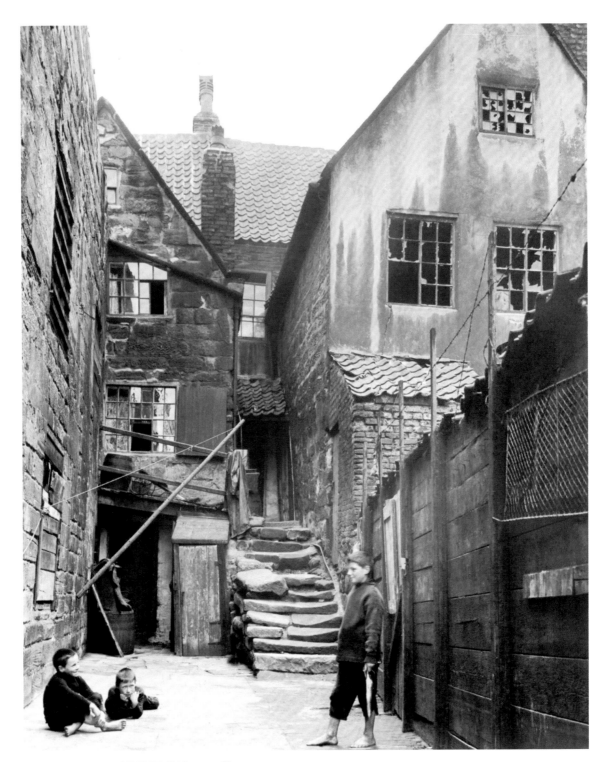

WHITBY, ARGUMENTS YARD 1923 FRITH 66290P

## Bram Stoker on Whitby

❝The houses of the old town … are all red-roofed, and seem piled up one over the other anyhow … Right over the town is the ruin of Whitby Abbey, which was sacked by the Danes and which is a scene of part of 'Marmion', where the girl is built up in the wall. It is a most noble ruin, of immense size, and full of beautiful and romantic bits; there is a legend that a white lady is seen in one of the windows. Between it and the town there is another church, the parish one, round which is a big graveyard, all full of tombstones. This is to my mind the nicest spot in Whitby, for it lies right over the town, and has a full view of the harbour and all up the bay, to where the headland called Kettleness stretches out into the sea.❞

FROM 'DRACULA', 1897

## JOHN'S PHOTOGRAPH AT WHITBY

THE PEART FAMILY, WHITBY HARBOUR, 2011

*The Peart family has continued to thrive in Whitby. With Susan Storr's help I assembled a family line-up for my photograph, which I took in about the same spot that Frith's agent Frank Meadow Sutcliffe took his. At the back are Susan's second cousins Lesley and Robert, and in front from left to right are Susan's daughter Lisa, grandson Travis, Susan herself, brother David, and first cousin once removed Dave. So here they are again, the Pearts of Whitby, but this time the 21st-century Pearts.*

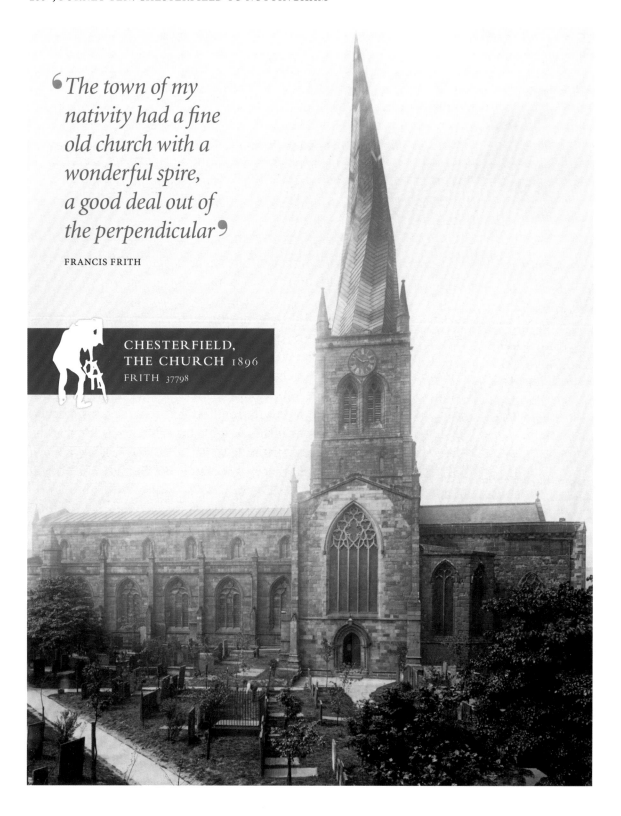

*'The town of my
nativity had a fine
old church with a
wonderful spire,
a good deal out of
the perpendicular'*

FRANCIS FRITH

CHESTERFIELD,
THE CHURCH 1896
FRITH 37798

# A Tale with a Twist

*'The magnificent church seen in the photograph on the opposite page, the Church of St Mary in Chesterfield, Derbyshire, meant a lot to Francis Frith. He was born here, and his family had deep roots here. It was fascinating to walk round Frith's home town and to visit this church to hear its story – a story with a twist in the tail!'*

FRANCIS FRITH

CHESTERFIELD'S
COLOURFUL MARKET
TODAY

Chesterfield's famous crooked spire was part of Francis Frith's boyhood. He was born here in 1822, and in his autobiography, 'A True Story of My Life', he wrote: 'The town of my nativity had a fine old church with a wonderful spire, a good deal out of the perpendicular. I have no doubt that spire has twisted itself vigorously into my mental frame, for I was generally sent by my mother, for a run before breakfast, to see if it had fallen …'

Perhaps Frith's mother had heard that the lean of the spire had recently been measured (in January 1818), and that 'the ball on which the weathercock is fixed, was found to lean towards the south six feet from the perpendicular of its base; and four feet four inches towards the west'. It was felt that the time would inevitably come when the deviation of the spire 'will be so much increased, that [the spire] must inevitably drop to the ground.' Well, it's still standing today!

Francis Frith was born into a prosperous Quaker family who had lived and worked in this bustling Derbyshire market town for many generations. His father was a cooper, or barrel maker, and it was from him that the young Francis inherited a skill in business and a love of the arts. Chesterfield has been a market town since the early 13th century, and today its flourishing open-air market is one of the largest in Britain. Frith had vivid memories of how it was in his boyhood:

'There was a great open market-place which attracted on Fair-

CHESTERFIELD,
MARKET HALL 1896
FRITH 37802

days the elite of showmen and tumblers and cheap-Johnnies. There were miles, as it seemed to me, of gingerbread-stalls, and toys and cheap crockery ornaments. There I saw too a pig-faced lady whose face and form are far more vivid in my memory than are those of thousands of beautiful women whom I have since beheld. The peculiar wild-beast smell of Wombwell's Menagerie is fresh in my nostrils, the mangy hyena still occasionally shows me his teeth, and a huge bald-headed stork that walked about the menagerie loose, gingerly picking up his sticks of legs and winking knowingly at the public, has always been associated in my mind with certain dried-up and wise-looking men whom I have occasionally met in my "walks through life".'

As well as being a market town, Chesterfield has long been a centre for industry. From Roman times onwards leatherworking and mining for lead, coal and iron ore have been carried on here, and by the 17th century there was iron making as well – there were five blast furnaces hereabouts at that time. The Chesterfield Canal is one of the earliest in England, and helped to further the Industrial Revolution. The railways came early, too – Stephenson routed his North Midland Railway through Chesterfield. Francis Frith, then, was growing up here when the town was buzzing with all kinds of business and industry. It must have been an inspiring background for the future millionaire and entrepreneur.

CHESTERFIELD,
MIDLAND STATION
1896
FRITH 37795A

CHESTERFIELD, HIGH STREET 1902   FRITH 48884

# Old Nick Visits Chesterfield

Perhaps Francis Frith had heard the local Derbyshire legends that explain why the spire of the parish church twists so markedly out of true. One story says that a magician managed to persuade a blacksmith in Bolsover to shoe the Devil's cloven hooves. After he drove the first nail into the Devil's foot, the Devil howled in pain and took flight, and lashed out in agony as he flew over Chesterfield, catching the spire with his foot and causing it to twist round. Another version of this story says that the tower buckled under the Devil's weight when he sat on it.

There are also two other traditions, neither of which is very complimentary to Chesterfield's inhabitants! One tells how the Devil visited Chesterfield one day and sat on the top of the church spire so that he could have a good look at the place. As it was windy, Old Nick twisted his tail around the spire to prevent himself from falling. When he heard a local person speaking the truth he was so surprised and shocked that he flew off in a hurry without unwinding his tail, causing the spire to twist. The other tells how the spire itself was so amazed to hear that a virgin was being married in the church that it twisted round in an effort to see this wonder for itself. According to this tale, the spire will straighten itself up should such a rare event ever occur again!

*The Devil howled in pain and took flight, and lashed out in agony as he flew over Chesterfield, catching the spire with his foot …*

# John hangs on to his hat and feels giddy

It seems clear to me that Chesterfield's twisted spire captured Frith's imagination. It had captured mine, too. I was longing to know all about the spire, and why it was twisted, so I met the verger of St Mary's, Paul Wilson, outside the church. I showed him the Frith photograph, and we worked out where it had been taken from. But was that the best place from which to see how twisted the spire is? We moved to a better spot. 'The spire looks more twisted from here than it does in the Frith picture', I said.

'It certainly looks that way', said Paul. 'There's very strong evidence to say that it has moved quite considerably since that photograph was taken. The spire was given a new backbone in 1898, but it's still twisting very slightly, by a fraction of an inch every time it's been measured since.' I wondered if this was the most famous twisted spire in Britain. 'Absolutely', said Paul, 'and possibly in the world!'

We went inside – it's an impressive sight. St Mary's is the largest church in Derbyshire; a church here was documented in 1100, but the oldest parts of the present structure were built in the 13th century. The church was restored in 1843, and it was at this time that the fate of the spire was decided: thank goodness that the church decided to keep it.

Paul led me up a narrow medieval stone spiral staircase so that we could see the inside of the spire. From the top of the stair we were looking up at a complex structure of wooden beams, the spire's skeleton. 'How much does it all weigh?' I asked. 'About 200 tons', Paul told me. 'The general opinion is that it was made of unseasoned timber. A lot of people think that it was common practice to use green wood. To shape and fashion a big structure like this, you needed a certain amount of flexibility. It's thought that the original medieval craftsmen possibly weren't as knowledgeable as they might have been as to what extent the wood was going to warp.'

It seemed incredible to me that the beams were still slowly twisting, but Paul assured me that it was so. He told me that to really see what the spire was like, we needed to look at it from outside. We emerged high up on a narrow ledge at the base of the spire. The view from up here was spectacular, but I must admit it was a daunting experience for me – I haven't got a good head for heights.

The spire is covered with a herringbone arrangement of metal plating. 'It's all lead', Paul told me, 'and it's continuously being patched up over the years. The original lead was far too thick and heavy for the wooden frame to cope with.' I was holding my hat down in the wind with one hand, and clinging to the spire with the other. 'So the lead was one of the major causes of the twist?' I managed to ask. 'Certainly,' said Paul. 'Also, there are problems with the lead when the sun comes out. The sun warms the lead, it expands, the sun goes in again, the lead contracts as it cools down, and the wood beneath moves with the lead to some extent.'

Paul told me to look up. Because of the twist, the tip of the spire was leaning right over our heads. It was a dizzying and somewhat nerve-wracking experience, and I was glad to get back to solid ground.

> *'It was a daunting experience for me – I haven't got a good head for heights'*

THE LABYRINTH OF THE SPIRE'S TIMBERS

THE TWISTED SPIRE

'*I have no doubt that spire has twisted itself vigorously into my mental frame*'

FRANCIS FRITH

CHESTERFIELD, ST MARY AND ALL SAINTS CHURCH 1902   FRITH 48888P

CHESTERFIELD, VIEW FROM QUEEN'S PARK 1902    FRITH 48896

# JOHN'S PHOTOGRAPH AT CHESTERFIELD

### THE CROOKED SPIRE, CHESTERFIELD, 2011

*Chesterfield's church spire has defined the town for centuries, and it was very special to Francis Frith too, I imagine. So it was obvious to me that it was St Mary's and her unusual crowning glory that I had to capture in my photograph. I wanted to make this picture a dramatic story, so I took it from where the spire looks at its most crooked. It's a picture of a magnificent church – and one with the quirkiest spire you could possibly imagine.*

# Tragedy and Heroism in a Remote Derbyshire Village

EYAM, THE PLAGUE COTTAGES 1896   FRITH 37811

'This photograph was taken in the Derbyshire village of Eyam. Its title is 'The Plague Cottages' because it was here in 1665 that the dreaded bubonic plague broke out in the village. I was fascinated to hear the story of this picture, a story that tells of Eyam's bravery and Eyam's tragedy, and I was encouraged when I heard that the story ends on a note of hope.'

Eyam is an attractive village set high in the hills in the Derbyshire Peak District. Francis Frith was born not far away in Chesterfield, and in his autobiography he says that 'in and near this little, sleepy, midlands-counties town my father's ancestors had lived for many generations.' Some of those ancestors lived in Eyam and are buried here; it seems that either Frith's father or his grandfather moved from Eyam to Sheffield. Frith himself was apprenticed to a cutler in Sheffield, possibly his uncle.

JOHN OUTSIDE THE
PLAGUE COTTAGES

But the village of Eyam is most famous for the sacrifice made by its inhabitants during an outbreak of bubonic plague in 1665-66. The plague came to Eyam in a parcel of lengths of cloth sent to a tailor, George Vicars, who was living in one of the cottages in the photograph on the opposite page. The parcel came from plague-ravaged London; the cloth was infested with fleas carrying the deadly disease. The great novelist Charles Dickens tells the story vividly in his magazine 'All the Year Round' (1869): 'George Vicars at once observed a peculiar smell; for, exclaiming "How very damp they are!" he hung them before the fire to dry. Even while attending to them a violent sickness seized him, and, other serious symptoms following, the family and neighbours were greatly alarmed. Next day he was much worse, and became delirious. Large swellings rose on his neck and groin; on the third day the fatal plague spot appeared on his breast, and on the following night, September 6th, he died in horrible agony.'

The villagers were naturally terrified, and many wanted to flee the village. But the heroic vicar, William Mompesson, persuaded them otherwise. 'He showed them', Dickens wrote, 'the frightful consequences their flight would bring on the surrounding villages. He told them how surely disease was already at work with many among them, lying invisible in their bodies and clothes; he warned them against the guilt of carrying the plague far and wide; and he prevailed with them to lessen their own hope of safety in consideration for the lives of others. On his part, Mompesson promised to remain with them, and do all in his power to help and guide them. Associated with him in his labours, we find another clergyman named Stanley, then living at Eyam, who shared the danger and the toil of the time.'

Under the encouragement of their vicar, the villagers bravely decided to put themselves into voluntarily quarantine and isolate Eyam from the outside world to contain the outbreak and prevent it spreading further afield. 'Mompesson wrote a letter to the Duke of Devonshire,' says Dickens, 'who was then at Chatsworth (five miles from Eyam), telling him that if they could depend on adequate supplies of necessaries, he had little doubt of prevailing with the people to remain in the village. The prompt reply was an expression of deep sympathy, and a promise that supplies should be provided.'

Mompesson and Stanley then decided that food and medical supplies for the villagers should be left at the outskirts of the village to the north and south, at either the Boundary Stone or Mompesson's Well. The villagers left

MOMPESSON'S WELL
1919   FRITH 69215

coins for payment, either cleansed in the bubbling water from the well spring, or left in holes in the Boundary Stone filled with vinegar, to prevent infection spreading to those who were helping them. 'Here, very early in the morning, supplies were left, which were fetched by persons whom Mompesson and Stanley appointed for the purpose. And here would be left the record of deaths, with other information for the world outside Eyam. A line was drawn around the village, marked by well-known stones and fences; and it was agreed upon by all within it that the boundary should not be overstepped. No need to caution those beyond it! The fear of entering Eyam was general, and its inhabitants were left to meet their enemy alone.'

There is one note of comedy in this tale of tragedy and heroism. One foolhardy man is said to have entered Eyam. Let Dickens tell his story: 'His employment was carrying wood from the Chatsworth woods to the neighbouring villages. Against advice and entreaty, he insisted upon going, as usual, through Eyam. The day was wet and boisterous; he caught a severe cold; and shortly after returning was attacked with fever. So great was the alarm, that a man was set to watch his house, and the neighbours declared they would shoot him if he attempted to leave it. The Duke of Devonshire interfered; he sent his doctor to make due inquiry, but the doctor would not go near the man. He took his station on one side of the River Derwent, and spoke across the river to his patient on the other bank. The man had simply caught a cold, and was by this time better.'

By the time that the outbreak of plague had abated at least two thirds of the courageous villagers had died. Their brave stand undoubtedly saved the lives of thousands of people.

EYAM, THE VILLAGE 1896   FRITH 37812

# Bubonic Plague and Delta 32

High temperature, vomiting, diarrhoea, pain, black boils (or bubos – hence the name of the disease), and almost certain death within a few days: no wonder bubonic plague was feared and dreaded the world over. In its guise as the Black Death it killed a third of the population of Europe in the 14th century, and a lesser outbreak, the Great Plague of London in 1665, was the source of the plague in Eyam. It is caused by a bacterium, Yersinia pestis, carried by rodents and spread to humans by bites from infected fleas.

Bubonic plague was deadly, and it still kills today. So how did some people survive? In Eyam's outbreak, for instance, tradition says that Elizabeth Hancock's six children and her husband died within one week, but she stayed well. The gravedigger was in close contact with plague-ridden bodies, but he survived too.

A researcher in genetics from the USA, Dr Stephen O'Brien, suggests that their immunity came from the mutated form of the gene CCR5, called 'delta 32'. His work with HIV had shown that delta 32 prevents HIV from entering human cells by blocking the gateway the disease organism needs. He thought that delta 32 could block plague, too, so he tested the DNA of the descendants of Eyam villagers who had survived the plague. Sure enough, he found that a significant proportion of them had delta 32. It's highly interesting that a mutation can save lives, and another indication that genetic research is an invaluable weapon against disease.

# John hears a sad tale of two young lovers

JOHN WITH
JOAN PLANT INSIDE
EYAM CHURCH

Joan Plant is one of the descendants of the families that survived the plague. We met at Eyam's church, where, she told me, the villagers made an almost unbelievably brave decision. 'The minister, and the previous minister, Stanley, thought that there was something dreadful happening in the village. They formed a plan to close the church, the churchyard, and the village itself, and then called the villagers together to ask them to consent to their plan.'

Why did the villagers accept the plan, I wondered? 'At that time, I think,' said Joan, 'people had great faith in God, and obviously the minister meant a lot to them. When he asked them to consent, they believed that it was what God wanted them to do. They decided to try to stop the plague spreading over Derbyshire and the rest of the country.'

Joan showed me a framed list of names hanging on the wall of the church. It was the roll call of those villagers who died of the plague. 'Here's George Vicars at the top of the list,' Joan told me. 'He was the first to die, on 7 September 1665. The last person on the list is Abraham Morten, who died on 1 November 1666.

THE ROLL CALL OF
THE DEAD WITH
GEORGE VICARS'S
NAME AT THE TOP
OF THE LIST

That's 14 months that the plague raged through the village, and 260 people died. There were 83 survivors.' I was aghast. 'So only one third of the village survived!' 'Yes, it's a terrible, devastating story', said Joan.

I wanted to understand how the villagers coped when they were completely closed off from the outside world. Joan led me to a well in a walled enclosure. 'This is Mompesson's Well. This was the north boundary of the village when they closed it off, and this is where the villagers came to collect the food that the Duke of Devonshire would have left. The money to pay for the food would have been put in the water to disinfectant it.' I could hardly believe that the villagers had to pay for the food that would help them survive. 'Yes, it's incredible', agreed Joan. 'Even at a time like that they wanted to carry on in a normal way and pay for what they were given.'

'There must have been some people,' I said, 'whose personal relationships must have been affected by the plague.' Joan told me this touching story: 'Emmott Sydall, a girl who lived opposite the plague cottage, had a sweetheart, Rowland Torre, who lived in the next village. When Eyam shut itself off, they couldn't meet. She would come to the top of Cucklett Delf, at the edge of the

*If you had delta 32 on both sides of your family, then you could survive the plague*

village, and he'd come to the bottom, just so that they could see each other. One day, when Rowland came, Emmott wasn't there. He kept coming back for the next few days, and still she wasn't there. He feared the worst. Rowland was one of the first people to come into Eyam after the plague was over, only to find that poor Emmott had died the April before.'

The villagers who did not contract the plague, such as Joan's ancestors, were buried in the churchyard, whilst the plague victims were buried in graves on their own land. Why did some villagers survive? Joan told me that recent medical research had shed new light on the matter. 'It's all down to my ancestors' genes. They must have had this gene called delta 32, and I've got it too. If you had delta 32 on both sides of your family, then you could survive the plague. That must have been the case with my ancestors – here I am to prove it!'

## JOHN'S PHOTOGRAPH OF EYAM

PORTRAIT OF THE SURVIVORS, EYAM CHURCH, 2011

*It's extraordinary to think that the ability to survive the plague was probably down to genetics, and I wanted to capture the story of Joan and her ancestors in my picture. What I wanted was a happy picture of a survivor standing next to the gravestone of some of her family. It's amazing that centuries after the plague Joan was able to find out why they were so lucky. Thanks to their genes, Joan and her ancestors are great survivors. I'm glad that my photograph of Eyam is a picture of hope and cheerfulness.*

HADDON HALL, FROM ABOVE THE BRIDGE c1862   FRITH 1432

# Ancient Stones, Romantic Trysts

*'The beautiful photograph on the previous pages shows Haddon Hall in Derbyshire, a fortified medieval manor house. I think Frith worked very hard to make this picture look just right. I love the harmonious composition, and the way the light falls across the picture in such an atmospheric way. It's the perfect romantic photograph – and the house has a romantic story to tell.'*

The beautiful, atmospheric photograph of Haddon Hall is an almost perfect match for a Victorian tourist's description of it in 1852: 'The sun was fast declining in the "far west" when we attained the eminence near Haddon. This relic of a by-gone age, with its weather-beaten towers and battlements, we observed peering from amidst the thick foliage, its numerous turrets and windows gleaming in the sun-light' ('Description of Buxton, Chatsworth, Bakewell, Haddon Hall, and Castleton', W Adam).

Described as 'the most romantic and complete medieval manor house in England', Haddon Hall, the Derbyshire home of the Manners family, the Dukes of Rutland, stands three miles south of Bakewell on a limestone bluff overlooking the valley of the River Wye and surrounded by woods and trees.

For over 30 years Jo Walker has been the steward here, and she explains that the present building mainly dates from the rebuilding of the 12th century Norman castle by Sir Richard Vernon in the 14th century, with some additions from the 15th and 16th centuries. Haddon Hall remains today much as it was then; no changes were made to the house in later centuries, because after

JOHN AND STEWARD JO WALKER AT THE SPOT WHERE FRANCIS FRITH TOOK HIS PHOTOGRAPH IN THE 1860s

HADDON HALL,
THE COURTYARD c1870
FRITH 5232

*Ancient approaches, ample courts, moss-grey balustrades, a venerable chapel …*

the dukedom of Rutland was conferred on the family in 1703, they moved to Belvoir Castle, and Haddon lay untouched for over 200 years.

Haddon's picturesque qualities were much appreciated by Victorian tourists. 'Ho! for a long summer-day', wrote Spencer Timothy Hall in his 'Days in Derbyshire' (1863), 'to ramble at will about and through all the ancient approaches, the ample courts, the magnificent terrace and shaded garden-walks; to lean over the moss-grey balustrades, and imagine the scene as it thence appears in the light of days far past; to wander through the interior,—the venerable Chapel; the old quaintly furnished and galleried Banqueting Hall; and to linger in the Long Gallery [see photograph overleaf], at oriel windows, or climb the Eagle Tower and the Watch Tower, taking calm and perfect metagraphs of the glowing landscape—of river and woodland, mead and mansion, and distant spire!'

Jo Walker explains that from the early 17th century Haddon was maintained by staff, but no alterations were made. An example is the Banqueting Hall, which was built in the 14th century and has remained much the same ever since. One ancient medieval table still stands in the room; there would originally have been many other trestle tables, which could be taken down at night to make room for the household to sleep on the floor.

Haddon's romantic looks are matched by the romantic story of Dorothy

ABOVE:
JOHN WITH
JO WALKER IN THE
BANQUETING HALL

Vernon, the daughter of the house in the 16th century. Sir John Manners, the second son of the Earl of Rutland, fell in love with her, and persuaded her to elope with him. Being the last in line of the Vernon family, she inherited the Hall, which then became part of the Manners estate. In All Saints' Parish Church in Bakewell you can see the monument to Sir John Manners and Dorothy Vernon, which represents them and their four children (see photograph, left).

It was not until the early 20th century that Haddon Hall woke from its long sleep. The 9th Duke and Duchess of Rutland restored the beautiful house and gardens, and once again made it habitable; today it is a perfectly preserved example of a medieval country manor.

LEFT: BAKEWELL, ALL SAINTS CHURCH, DOROTHY VERNON'S TOMB 1890
FRITH 24630

BELOW: HADDON HALL, THE LONG GALLERY c1870  FRITH 5236

# A Ghostly Monk, White Ladies, Cold Spots on the Stairs ...

Victorian visitors to Haddon Hall would be shown round by a caretaker, who would have plenty of stories to tell to enhance the romantic atmosphere of times gone by. Ghost stories, of course, would be part of the caretaker's repertoire, and Haddon has plenty of those. Cold spots on the stone staircases, a white lady in the Banqueting Hall, a dog whose yapping can be heard in the garden, a monk, a mysterious blue woman, even Dorothy Vernon herself – tales of ghostly apparitions have sent shivers down the spine of many a tourist.

VICTORIAN ENGRAVING OF THE HALL AT NIGHT

But the favourite story seems to have been the tradition of the manacle. Attached to the panelled screen in the Banqueting Hall is an iron manacle and lock. It was placed there to confine people as a punishment for trivial offences, and to enforce the rules imposed on the servants. A wrongdoer, or a servant who had neglected his duties, had his hand locked to the wainscot higher than his head, and cold water was poured down the sleeve of his doublet.

There is also a tradition that guests could suffer the punishment of the manacle. If a guest 'did not drink fair' – in other words, if he refused a horn of ale, or if he drank too much – his wrist would be locked in the manacle and the other guests, or the host, would pour his drink down his sleeve!

# Sullivan – but not Gilbert

Gilbert and Sullivan, the geniuses of light opera, librettist and composer of 'The Mikado', 'HMS Pinafore', and so many other immortal works, fell out in 1889. The impresario Richard D'Oyly Carte was desperate to find a substitute for W S Gilbert so that the profitable stream of popular light operas could continue to flow at the Savoy Theatre.

He recruited the librettist Sydney Grundy, who had adapted many French light operas for the English stage. In 1892, the Grundy and Sullivan opera 'Haddon Hall' was produced. Set at Haddon, it tells the story of Dorothy Vernon's elopement.

Grundy moved the story forward to about 1660, so that the Civil War between the Cavaliers and the Roundheads formed the background to the plot. The whole tone of the piece is perhaps more serious than the other Savoy operas. However, comic relief is provided by a Scottish character, The McCrankie. The Times review in 1892 said that he is 'a figure wholly unnecessary to the development of the plot' and that his 'surprising mixture of Scottish characteristics' is 'scarcely credible'!

The first production had a modestly successful run, and 'Haddon Hall' remained quite popular, especially with amateur operatic societies, up to the 1920s, but it has not often been performed since then. A recording of the opera was made in 2000.

# John investigates traces of Haddon's origins

JOHN WITH LORD EDWARD MANNERS IN
THE COURTYARD AT HADDON HALL

*Sir John would ride over
from Belvoir for secret trysts
with Dorothy in the woods*

VICTORIAN ENGRAVING SHOWING LADY
VERNON SLIPPING OUT OF THE HALL TO
MEET SIR JOHN MANNERS

I met Lord Edward Manners, who lives in Haddon Hall today, in the handsome courtyard. He told me that Haddon was originally a Norman fortress built in the early 12th century. 'At that time it belonged to the Vernon family. When my family married into the Vernons in the 1560s, it passed to the Manners family.'

I had heard that there was a romantic story about that marriage. 'Yes, indeed,' said Lord Edward. 'Dorothy Vernon, the heiress, eloped with Sir John Manners. It's not certain how much of the story is Victorian embellishment and how much actual fact, but it's said that Sir John would ride over from Belvoir for secret trysts with Dorothy in the woods. At last she managed to escape the eagle eye of her father and ran down the garden and across the packhorse bridge. There Sir John was waiting for her. She jumped on his horse and off they rode and got married. When her father died, she inherited Haddon Hall, so that's how it came into the Manners family.'

At the time when the Frith photograph on pages 300-301 was taken, Haddon was in a state of picturesque disrepair. But great changes came about at the beginning of the 20th century, as Lord Edward told me. 'One of the most remarkable parts of Haddon's history is its restoration. It began in 1912, and the bulk of it took place in the 1920s. If my grandfather hadn't taken it on, Haddon would be a ruin by now.'

Lord Edward took me into the chapel, where we looked at the beautiful wall paintings. The walls are covered in ornate, colourful patterns, and depictions of a boat in a rough sea, skeletons, people, foliage and flowers. 'During the restoration,' Lord Edward told me, 'all sorts of discoveries were made – these murals, for example. They are frescoes, painted in the 1420s using the secco technique – that means they were

painted on dry plaster. My grandfather discovered them in the 1930s. They were hidden under white plaster, and he painstakingly picked it off using dental tools.' I wondered why the paintings had been covered up. Lord Edward told me that it had happened during the Reformation. 'Then, these sorts of paintings were either destroyed, or painted or plastered over. We were lucky here that they were plastered over, because that preserved them.'

I felt that these frescoes were an outstanding example of how Haddon Hall has emerged almost unchanged from the distant past.

FRESCOES ON THE WALLS OF THE CHAPEL

## JOHN'S PHOTOGRAPH OF HADDON HALL

### DOROTHY'S BRIDGE, HADDON HALL, 2011

*Beautiful, picturesque Haddon Hall really inspired the Frith photographer, and I wanted to do the place justice too in my photograph, and to capture its romance. But I found that I couldn't do it by photographing the house – the trees have grown too big, and they're all in the wrong places today. So I decided to take a picture of the packhorse bridge, which tells the intriguing story of how Dorothy Vernon eloped in 1567. This bridge was a high point on the tour of Haddon for Victorian excursionists, and it still is today. This is the most romantic bridge in Derbyshire!*

# Sport and Fun for Everyone on the Forest Racecourse

NOTTINGHAM, THE FOREST RACECOURSE 1893   FRITH 33255

*'We are in the ancient city of Nottingham, looking down on Nottingham Forest Racecourse. This area is now a recreation ground, used by the community for sport and all sorts of activities. The famous Nottingham Goose Fair, which probably dates from the 13th century, has been held on this site since the 1920s. In Frith's day, competitive sports like football and cricket were highly popular, and were being given formal rules for the first time. One sport in particular flourished: the royal sport of horse racing. I was hoping to learn all about it on my visit to Nottingham.'*

*The town was the cradle of many inventors and industrialists*

NOTTINGHAM,
THE MARKET 1890
FRITH 22808

VICTORIAN
ENGRAVING SHOWING
A WOMAN CYCLIST

As a successful businessman and entrepreneur, Francis Frith would have found Nottingham's later history highly interesting, for the town was the cradle of many inventors and industrialists. In the 18th century, for instance, weaving, framework-knitting and bobbin lace were Nottingham's main occupations. James Hargreaves introduced his Spinning Jenny machine into a small spinning mill in Nottingham in 1767, making him one of the founding fathers of the Industrial Revolution. His invention mechanised the spinning of yarn, speeding up the production process. In 1771 Richard Arkwright also set up his first spinning mill in Nottingham. These were both defining moments in the Industrial Revolution.

In later centuries Nottingham became famous for leather, textiles, engineering, tobacco, and bicycles. The Raleigh Cycle Company was founded in Nottingham by Frank Bowden, who in 1887 invested in a small bicycle works and within a few years had created the world's largest bicycle factory. James Samuel Archer, the co-inventor of the famous Sturmey-Archer three-speed bicycle gear, lived in Nottingham and worked at the Raleigh Cycle Company.

Two of Nottingham's most successful entrepreneurs of the 19th century were Jesse Boot and John Player; the former developed a health empire, and the latter did his best to counter it by manufacturing billions of cigarettes! Jesse Boot, the founder of the chain of Boots the Chemist shops, started life in his widowed mother's herbalist shop

VICTORIAN
ENGRAVING
OF A BATSMAN
FROM
THE 1840S

HORSE RACING,
c1888
FRITH H390501

on Goose Gate in Nottingham, and went on to found the Boots Pure Drug Company in 1888. The first Boots the Chemist's shop opened in Pelham Street in Nottingham in 1892. There had been a small tobacco factory in Nottingham for over 50 years when John Player took it over in 1877, but it was in the late 1890s when the great expansion in the business took place which led in 1901 to the foundation of the Imperial Tobacco Company.

Nottingham's hardworking citizens had been relaxing at sporting events for a long time. They had been enjoying horse racing at Nottingham Forest since the 17th century at least, and football, cricket and other sports had long been played here too.

Two football clubs have their grounds in or near Nottingham: Notts County, the oldest Football League club in the country, and Nottingham Forest. Nottingham Forest FC was born out of a group of players of a game called 'shinney', a popular 19th-century game similar to hockey. In 1865 the shinney players decided to form a football club, and Forest came into being. They called themselves Nottingham Forest because they played on the Forest Recreation Ground. Their early years were marked by a number of 'firsts'. They were the first English team to wear shinguards. They also played in the first game where a referee's whistle was used. Most importantly, they are credited with inventing, under the leadership of Sam Widdowson, the classic football combination of three fullbacks, three halfbacks, and five forwards, the formation which was almost universal for more than 50 years.

# History of the Nottingham Forest Racecourse

❝On the 21st of October 1776, at a meeting of noblemen and gentlemen, held at the White Lion Inn, a subscription was entered into for the erection of a stand on the race-course; no person being allowed to subscribe less than twenty guineas, which would entitle each subscriber to two silver tickets, to be transferable; each ticket to admit a lady or gentleman, during the races. The principal subscribers were the Dukes of Newcastle, Norfolk, and Portland, with Lord Edward Bentinck, 200 guineas each [and many other aristocrats and racing enthusiasts contributed]. The total sum subscribed amounted to £2,460. The structure was erected in the following year …

Nottingham race-course, in its first formation, was four miles round: early in the eighteenth century it was reduced to two miles. The course, as then formed, continued without alteration till the year 1797, when, on the enclosure of that portion of the forest which appertained to Lenton and Radford, it was all but utterly destroyed. In 1798 another course was made, which, from the circumscribed extent of the ground, was laid out in the form of a figure of eight. In consequence, however, of the universal complaint of the bad view of the sport thus obtained, it was destroyed, and another, of an oval shape, a mile and a quarter in extent, formed in its stead. This, since its first formation, has undergone various improvements; so that when the alterations, at present in progress, are completed, it will be one of the best and most commodious courses, both for horses and spectators, in the kingdom.❞

'ANNALS OF NOTTINGHAMSHIRE', THOMAS BAILEY, 1852

## The flight of a stag interrupts the racing

❝The noble family of Newstead, from the proximity of their residence to Nottingham, have always been associated in a certain measure with the borough. On the 26th of November, 1764, we find that the Lord Byron of that period, who was master of His Majesty's staghounds, won popularity by turning out a fine stag on the Nottingham racecourse, amidst thousands of spectators. The noble animal, it is related, ran thirty miles in less than three hours, over a rough country, crossing the Leen, the Erewash, and the Trent, and being taken while attempting to cross the Soar.❞

'OLD AND NEW NOTTINGHAM', WILLIAM HOWIE WYLIE, 1853

# John places a bet and loses his money

JOHN TALKS TO
JOHN BECKETT

*It was frequented by rough people, the kind of people you wouldn't want your daughter to know!*

ENGRAVING SHOWING
RACING IN VICTORIAN
TIMES

Professor John Beckett, a social historian from Nottingham University, met me at the spot where the Frith picture on page 308 was taken. We looked at the photograph together, and I asked him how important this place was for horse racing.

'It was famous for horse racing, and for football, cricket, and other sporting activities. Racing took place here because in the early days of organised horse racing the courses were much longer than they are now, so you needed a lot of space to lay out your course. We know that there was racing here in the 1680s. It was almost certainly a major course early on, because one of the trophies to be won here was the King's Plate. If you're running for the King's Plate, that implies that you've got royal approval.'

I thought that the Frith photograph looked rather empty. 'Perhaps the Frith photographer is celebrating the fact that football is being played,' said John, pointing out the game in progress in the middle ground of the photograph. 'Many football teams would play here on Saturdays and Sundays, the most famous one being Nottingham Forest, of course.'

Going back to horse racing, I mentioned that I'd heard it was a bit rough in the old days. 'Yes, it was', said John. 'It was frequented by rough people, the kind of people you wouldn't want your daughter to know! There were prostitutes there, betting, gambling, cock fighting, and occasionally boxing matches. But strangely enough it did bring the social classes together, because wealthier people loved coming to the races. They would sit in the grandstand – we can see it to the left of the Frith photograph. It was built in 1777 to the design of John Carr of York, one of the most eminent architects of his day.'

I asked how many people would come to the races. 'Thousands of people used to assemble here,' said John, 'and in the old days there was no charge to get in. That's why in the late 19th century the racing moved to the other side of the city. At that time almost all the open courses became enclosed, or moved to enclosed premises, so that it was possible to charge for entry.'

JOHN TALKS TO
PIP KIRKBY,
MANAGING DIRECTOR
OF NOTTINGHAM
RACECOURSE

It was hard to imagine what racing used to be like at Nottingham Forest, so to get the authentic flavour I went to the new Nottingham racecourse at Colwick Park to soak up the atmosphere and maybe have a flutter. There I met Pip Kirkby, the Managing Director of the racecourse. 'There has been racing here since 1892,' she told me, 'so this is a racecourse steeped in history, character and local colour.'

I pulled out my race card. 'I've got £20 to spend, so what's your tip?' I asked her. 'I think you should go for Monopolise and Sunday Bess,' said Pip. I wondered if I was going to win. 'Best of luck,' she said, 'but I'm a rotten tipster!' Feeling hopeful, nonetheless, I found a bookie and put £10 to win on each horse. 'What are my chances?' I asked him. 'Good! Very good!' 'So are you worried?' 'No, not really!' he laughed. Well, my horses lost. I tore up my betting slips in disgust – but it had been an exciting race, and a wonderful day.

## JOHN'S PHOTOGRAPH OF NOTTINGHAM RACECOURSE

A DAY AT THE RACES, COLWICK RACECOURSE, NOTTINGHAM, 2011

*The thing about horse racing, and I'm sure that it was as true when the Frith photograph was taken as it is today, is that you'll find characters there. The Frith picture on page 308 is a bit short on character, so I've gone for character in a big way in my picture. Here are my bookie, the bookie next door to him, and a punter, and they're all smiling and happy. They all admitted that they hadn't done very well that day, so my picture shows that win or lose, everyone has fun at the races. My horses lost too – but my photograph is a winner!*

# Afterword

The good news is that the business Frith founded did not die with him, but is still very much alive today. The Francis Frith Collection is considered by historians to be of prime national importance, and it is the only archive of its kind remaining in private ownership. Its future is both bright and exciting.

After Francis Frith died in 1898, Frith & Co continued to be managed by his sons and grandsons, and teams of Frith photographers continued to travel round Britain taking pictures of cities, towns and villages. There were changes, though. In 1902 the popular 'divided back' picture postcard came into being, with space for address and message on one side and a picture on the other, and by 1910 Frith products also included the much cheaper postcard. For many years Frith & Co were the leading postcard publisher, and their name became synonymous with holiday postcards – many people alive today will have sent at least one!

By 1939 there was no one in the Frith family in a position to run what had become a very competitive business, so Frith & Co was sold. The business continued to prosper under new owners up to the 1960s, but at that point it failed to keep pace with the change to colour postcards. In 1970 one of Britain's first historians of photography, Bill Jay, heard that the company was being closed down and their premises demolished. Bill recognized the importance of the company's archive in the history of photography and as a record of social change. He persuaded Rothmans, the cigarette company, to save the archive. They were just in time: a week later the bulldozers arrived. Rothmans moved the archive – hundreds of thousands of precious glass negatives and prints, ledgers and company records – and saved it for the nation.

Five years later, a Rothmans executive, John Buck, persuaded the company to allow him to create a new business based on the Frith archive. The original business had offered photographic prints or postcards as holiday souvenirs, but John Buck realized that every photograph in the archive was potentially fascinating to people who had not just been on holiday in that location, but who also had a personal connection to the scene depicted in the photograph – it might show where they had been born, or grew up, or been to school, or been married. In other words, the Frith archive documented thousands of places that have helped create and shape our lives, and each photograph potentially represented an invaluable record of someone's life.

In August 1977, following a change of policy at Rothmans, John Buck bought the archive and embryonic business from the company, and he has run it as an independent business ever since. In the pre-digital days of the 1970s it was very difficult and expensive to communicate to potential customers the vast range of images in the archive, but the company survived and prospered. By the 1990s The Francis Frith Collection was able to take advantage of digital technology.

Today The Francis Frith Collection can offer approximately 360,000 photographs, with over 120,000 of them available on its website, all in a wide variety of formats. It has published over 1,100 books, all based on photographs in the Frith archive. The Frith photographs can be seen in thousands of pubs, hotels, offices and commercial buildings around Britain, where they bring a touch of nostalgia and an appreciation of how much life has changed – or stayed the same – in the last 150 years. The company's website has been ranked in the top ten UK gift websites for over five years, and continues to make the Frith photographs more accessible today than at any time since Frith founded the business in 1860. The Frith archive is now valued at over £2 million, and is recognized as the only nationally important photographic archive in private hands.

Frith's legacy to us today is of immense significance and value, for the magnificent archive of evocative photographs he created provides a unique record of change in the cities, towns and villages throughout Britain over 150 years. Frith and his company's teams of photographers revisited locations many times down the years to update their views, compiling for us an enthralling pageant of British life and character. It is this sheer wealth of visual data, the painstaking chronicle of change in dress, transport, streets, public buildings, housing and landscape, that captivates us so much today. His images offer us a powerful link with the past and with the lives of our forebears.

Francis Frith, with his steadfast belief in making photographs available to the greatest number of people, would undoubtedly approve of the computer technology that allows his work to be rapidly transmitted to people all over the world by way of the internet. His photographs depicting our shared past are still bringing pleasure to millions of people.

# Francis Frith Products & Services

Francis Frith would doubtless be pleased to know that the pioneering publishing venture he started in 1860 still continues today. Over a hundred and forty years later, The Francis Frith Collection continues in the same innovative tradition and is now the foremost publisher of vintage photographs in the world. Some of the current products and activities include:

### FRITH PRINTS

All Frith photographs are available in a range of print sizes and formats, including mounted, framed and on canvas. Customers may choose from over 120,000 images on the Frith web site.

Mounted Prints

### FRITH BOOKS

The Francis Frith Collection has published over 1,100 books, including many local histories of towns, counties and regions. See the web site for a complete list of those currently available.

### GIFT PRODUCTS

Other products published by Frith include local Calendars, Postcards, Personalised Jigsaws and Historical Maps centred on any address in the UK.

### INTERIOR DECOR

Today Frith's photographs can be seen framed and as giant wall murals in thousands of pubs, restaurants, hotels, banks, retail stores and other public buildings throughout the country. In every case they enhance the unique local atmosphere of the places they depict and provide reminders of gentler days in an increasingly busy and frenetic world.

Framed Prints

### GENEALOGY AND FAMILY HISTORY

As the interest in family history and roots grows world-wide, more people are turning to Frith for images of the towns, villages and streets where their ancestors lived. Photographs of the churches and chapels where ancestors were christened, married and buried are an essential part of every genealogy tree and family album.

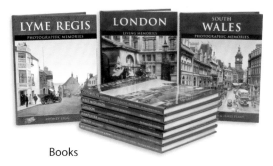
Books

### REMINISCENCE THERAPY

Historical photographs are recognized to be beneficial in stimulating the memory of the elderly and those with dementia. Frith photographs are used as décor in care and residential homes and in reminiscence therapy software.

### PHOTO LIBRARY

Frith images are regularly licensed to other publishers & manufacturers for use in their own products.

### PRODUCT PROMOTIONS

Frith products have been used by many major companies to promote the sales of their own products or to reinforce their own history and heritage.

Historical Maps

## SHARE YOUR FAMILY MEMORIES

We hope this book will have sparked memories of your own. Why not take a moment to remember the places that have been important in your life - where your family comes from, where you were born, went to school or married; the towns and villages where you've lived and worked since. Recapture and rekindle those precious memories by visiting our web site and enjoy browsing over 120,000 historical photographs of British towns and villages. Simply visit our web site and search for your favourite places. While you are there why not read some of the thousands of memories contributed by other visitors and then share your own.

Prints on Canvas

Jigsaws

Calendars

### THE FRITH WEBSITE

You can see the complete range of Frith prints, books and gifts on our web site and enjoy browsing historical photographs, maps and memories of over 11,000 cities, towns and villages throughout Britain. Visit:

## www.francisfrith.com

This web site is regularly updated with the latest publications and additional photographs from The Francis Frith Collection, so it is worth visiting regularly.

## READER VOUCHER

If you have enjoyed this book you may wish to purchase other products from The Francis Frith Collection. As a returning customer you will enjoy a 15% discount off your next order when you use this Voucher Code:

### Voucher Code: BFPA15

To redeem your voucher:

- Visit our website: www.francisfrith.com and enter the Voucher Code at the Checkout.
- By Mail: Write with details of your order quoting the Voucher Code and deducting 15% from your payment (excluding the P&P charge).
- By Phone: Call 01722 716 376 to talk to our knowledgeable staff and quote your Voucher Code.

Small Print: The 15% discount will be applied to your order value (excluding Post & Packing charges) but may be redeemed at any time – there is no end date. This offer only applies to orders placed directly with The Francis Frith Collection and is subject to the limitations detailed above. This offer does not apply to trade customers. Please note this offer is limited to one order only (per customer/delivery address) and may not be combined with any other offer.

## THE FRANCIS FRITH COLLECTION

Oakley Business Park, Wylye Road, Dinton, Wiltshire SP3 5EU, England.
Telephone: **01722 716 376** Fax: **01722 716 881**
email: **sales@francisfrith.co.uk**

BBH Publishing Limited, T/a The Francis Frith Collection. Registered office: Westbury House, 14 Bellevue Road, Southampton SQ15 2AV England. Registered No.2801469. Vat No. 619 885781. © The Francis Frith Collection. Photographs © Heritage Photographic Resources Ltd. The Frith logo and name is a registered trademark of Heritage Photographic Resources Ltd.